CONTEMPORARY
Black
Biography

ISSN-1058-1316

CONTEMPORARY

Black

Biography

Profiles from the International Black Community

Volume 57

THOMSON

GALE ™

Detroit • New York • San Francisco • San Diego • New Haven, Conn. • Waterville, Maine • London • Munich

Contemporary Black Biography, Volume 57

Sara and Tom Pendergast

Project Editor
Pamela M. Kalte

Image Research and Acquisitions
Leitha Etheridge-Sims

Editorial Support Services
Nataliya Mikheyeva

Rights and Permissions
Lisa Kincade, Tim Sisler, Andrew Specht

Manufacturing
Dorothy Maki, Cynde Bishop

Composition and Prepress
Mary Beth Trimper, Gary Leach

Imaging
Lezlie Light, Mike Logusz

ISBN 13: 978-0-7876-7929-3
ISBN 10: 0-7876-7929-1
ISSN 1058-1316

This title is also available as an e-book.
ISBN 13: 978-1-4144-1115-6
ISBN-10: 1-4144-1115-4
Please contact your Thomson Gale sales representative for ordering information.

Printed in the United States of America
10 9 8 7 6 5 4 3 2 1

Advisory Board

Contents

Introduction

Contemporary Black Biography provides informative biographical profiles of the important and influential persons of African heritage who form the international black community: men and women who have changed today's world and are shaping tomorrow's. *Contemporary Black Biography* covers persons of various nationalities in a wide variety of fields, including architecture, art, business, dance, education, fashion, film, industry, journalism, law, literature, medicine, music, politics and government, publishing, religion, science and technology, social issues, sports, television, theater, and others. In addition to in-depth coverage of names found in today's headlines, *Contemporary Black Biography* provides coverage of selected individuals from earlier in this century whose influence continues to impact on contemporary life. *Contemporary Black Biography* also provides coverage of important and influential persons who are not yet household names and are therefore likely to be ignored by other biographical reference series. Each volume also includes listee updates on names previously appearing in *CBB*.

Designed for Quick Research and Interesting Reading

- **Attractive page design** incorporates textual subheads, making it easy to find the information you're looking for.
- **Easy-to-locate data sections** provide quick access to vital personal statistics, career information, major awards, and mailing addresses, when available.
- **Informative biographical essays** trace the subject's personal and professional life with the kind of in-depth analysis you need.
- **To further enhance your appreciation** of the subject, most entries include photographic portraits.
- **Sources for additional information** direct the user to selected books, magazines, and newspapers where more information on the individuals can be obtained.

Helpful Indexes Make It Easy to Find the Information You Need

Contemporary Black Biography includes cumulative Nationality, Occupation, Subject, and Name indexes that make it easy to locate entries in a variety of useful ways.

Available in Electronic Formats

Diskette/Magnetic Tape. Contemporary Black Biography is available for licensing on magnetic tape or diskette in a fielded format. Either the complete database or a custom selection of entries may be ordered. The database is available for internal data processing and nonpublishing purposes only. For more information, call (800) 877-GALE.

On-line. Contemporary Black Biography is available on-line through Mead Data Central's NEXIS Service in the NEXIS, PEOPLE and SPORTS Libraries in the GALBIO file and Gale's Biography Resource Center.

Disclaimer

Contemporary Black Biography uses and lists websites as sources and these websites may become obsolete.

We Welcome Your Suggestions

The editors welcome your comments and suggestions for enhancing and improving *Contemporary Black Biography*. If you would like to suggest persons for inclusion in the series, please submit these names to the editors. Mail comments or suggestions to:

The Editor

Contemporary Black Biography

Thomson Gale

27500 Drake Rd.

Farmington Hills, MI 48331-3535

Phone: (800) 347-4253

William Gilchrist Anderson

1927—

Physician, educator

Anderson, William Gilchrist, photograph. Photo courtesy of Dr. William G. Anderson. Reproduced by permission.

While many people preach to do your best and be your best, very few actually achieve these lofty goals. Dr. William Gilchrist Anderson is among the few who have. During the height of the Jim Crow era, he pushed open doors that were previously closed to black doctors at certain hospitals. His work for the civil rights movement in southwest Georgia captured the attention of the nation and brought the help of Anderson's friends: Dr. Martin Luther King, Jr. and Rev. Ralph Abernathy. Anderson has dedicated his career to pioneering work in osteopathic medicine and continued commitment to opening his profession to minorities. As the first African American to head the American Osteopathic Association, Anderson led by example. Opening the 2005 United Osteopathic Convention, Anderson stated in his speech posted on the American Osteopathic Association Web site, "We need to continue the initiative, dedication, commitment and humanism of those before us in osteopathic medicine, and continue the principles of not just treating symptoms, but treating the whole person."

Became Friends with Dr. King

William Gilchrist Anderson was born on December 12, 1927, in Americus, Georgia. His parents were John D. Sr., and Emma Gilchrist Anderson. He was born during the Jim Crow era, when laws separated blacks and whites. There were separate water fountains, restrooms, and schools. Among the indignities of the laws at the time were limiting rules that forced blacks to purchase food from the back door of restaurants; allowed them to sit in the back of buses but forced them to stand if a white person requested a seat; and restricted them to the balcony seats of movie theaters from which they were forced to exit out the back door. Though in theory the separate facilities were equal, in practice they were not. Most schools for blacks, for example, were run down and in desperate need of new books and supplies. Anderson experienced the difficulties of growing up during this stressful time for blacks, when blacks ran the risk of being beaten; having their homes or businesses torched; or worse, lynched if they offended a white person.

Despite the hardships in his life, Anderson set his sights on success. He attended the Alabama State College for Negroes, graduating with a bachelor's degree in 1949. During this time he met and married Norma Lee

At a Glance . . .

Born on December 12, 1927, in Americus, GA; son of John D., Sr. and Emma Gilchrist Anderson; married Norma Lee Dixon, November 23, 1946; children: five. *Education:* Alabama State College for Negroes, BS, 1949; University of Osteopathic Medicine and Health Services, Des Moines, IA, DO, 1956; certification in general surgery. *Military service:* US Navy, petty officer, 1944-46.

Career: Art Center Clinical Group, staff surgeon, 1967-71; Zieger Clinical Group, attending surgeon, 1971-74; Detroit Surgical Association, senior attending surgeon, consultant, 1974-84; MI Healthcare Corporation, executive vice president/chief medical officer, 1984-86; Detroit Osteopathic Hospital, director, government affairs, 1986-92; Detroit Riverview Hospital, director of medical education, 1992–; Kirksville College of Osteopathic Medicine, associate dean, 1996–; Detroit Osteopathic and Riverview Hospital, physician, educator.

Memberships: YMCA, board of directors, 1970–; Wayne County Osteopathic Association, director, 1968–, president, 1977, executive director, 1993–; MI Association of Osteopathic Physicians, director, 1975–, president, 1981; American Osteopathic Association, delegate, 1980–, trustee, 1981–, president, 1994-95.

Awards: Michigan State University, Walter F. Patenge Medal of Public Service Award, 1982; Ohio University, Phillips Meritorious Service Award, 1986, Doctor of Humane Letters, 1990; West Virginia School of Osteopathic Medicine, Doctor of Science, 1993; University of Osteopathic Medicine, Doctor of Humane Letters, 1994; American Osteopathic Association, Dale Dodson Award, 2001.

Addresses: *Home*—Southfield, MI. *Office*—Detroit Riverview Hospital, 7733 E. Jefferson, Detroit, MI 48214-2598.

Dixon. The Dixon family was close friends of the King Family. Norma's brother, James, was close to Martin Luther King, Jr., who would become the leader of the civil rights movement. King frequently visited with the Dixons. Anderson heard King practicing his sermons, and they became friends while King was a senior in high school. The two shared a desire to help people. For his part, Anderson decided to enter medicine.

Co-Founded Albany Movement

Anderson received his medical training at the University of Osteopathic Medicine and Health Sciences, in Des Moines, Iowa. He also earned certification in general surgery. He held an internship at the Flint Osteopathic Hospital, in Flint, Michigan. During his internship, Anderson grew increasingly frustrated that he could not treat white patients, and fought and won the right to do so. After completing his internship, he returned to Albany, Georgia, where he opened his own practice. While many doctors had offices but were given hospital privileges, most black physicians were relegated to black hospitals, or if there was not one in the vicinity, had no hospital privileges at all. In Albany Anderson had no hospital privileges because of his color, so he had to perform any needed surgeries in his office.

With the many injustices going on in Albany and the surrounding counties, Anderson joined the Criterion Club. The club petitioned the city government to form a biracial commission to begin the process of desegregation. The request was met with resistance. However, the group was not deterred. Soon others pushing for civil rights joined them; Charles Sherrod, Cordell Reagon, and Charles Jones—members of the Student Nonviolent Coordinating Committee (SNCC)—began approaching black residents in the area to hold voter registration drives. While many avoided the three SNCC members, young people responded to them.

The SNCC, the Criterion Club, and the local chapter of the National Association for the Advancement of Colored People (NAACP), and other groups banded together and formed the Albany Movement. Anderson, who was fairly new to organizing—though he had started an NAACP chapter at Morehouse College with King during a short time when he lived in Atlanta—was elected as the movement's president. With their new organization formed, the members rallied for real change.

Students Challenged Status Quo

In November of 1961, the federal Interstate Commerce Commission (ICC) ruled that all of the interstate transportation facilities be desegregated. That same day, nine students tested the waters by entering the whites only waiting area of Albany's Trailways bus station. When the police arrived, they left the area peacefully. They also filed affidavits with the ICC.

On November 22, 1961, which also was Thanksgiving Day, high school students, members of the SNCC, and several students from Albany State College, entered several of the whites only areas at the Trailways station, including the lunch counter. When the police arrived, all were arrested. The next day, 300 students protested their arrest and jail terms.

On November 25th, the Albany Movement held their first meeting. Their first march as a group was held on November 27th to protest Albany State College students Bertha Gobel's and Blanton Hall's expulsion from the college. Anderson led the way, and according to *Weary Feet, Rested Souls,* told the police officer, "If you strike anyone in this line, strike me first." Many were arrested that day, and supporters of the movement urged Anderson to contact King for help in continuing their struggle.

Asked King to Join Demonstrations

When King arrived in December of 1961, he thought he would give a speech, but he joined the movement's next march, and with Anderson by his side, was arrested. By mid-December more than 500 demonstrators had been taken into custody. Nevertheless, the activists continued to push for change. The Albany movement tried everything the civil rights movement came to be known for: sit-ins, marches, voter registration drives, boycotts, lawsuits, and pleas for help from Washington.

At each turn the movement supporters and King, who had brought in his newly formed Southern Christian Leadership Conference (SCLC), were met with a formidable foe in Police Chief Laurie Pritchett. With each new march, more were arrested. Though he ran out of jail space, Pritchett would just shuffle the demonstrators to other jails in the surrounding counties, where many were beaten or underfed.

Appeared on Meet The Press

The protests and boycotts continued well into 1962. During this time, as more protests were held, King was scheduled to appear on the *Meet The Press* television news program. He was in jail, and Anderson appeared in his place. His appearance turned the nation's attention to Albany. A friend of Albany Mayor Asa Kelley anonymously paid King's and Abernathy's fines, and they were released.

Federal Judge Robert Ellison issued an injunction forbidding further marches. While King decided against another march, other black demonstrators held one. When demonstrators learned that the pregnant wife of Slater King, who was the vice president of the Albany Movement, had been kicked when she brought food to jailed demonstrators, another march was held. This time, the police were peppered with rocks and the march turned violent.

King called for a moratorium on marches, and left Albany soon after. Though he considered his involvement a failure, many in Albany felt differently. Charles

Sherrod, who later became Albany city commissioner, told the *Albany Herald,* "Now I can't help how Dr. King might have felt, or…any of the rest of them in SCLC, NAACP, CORE, any of the groups, but as far as we were concerned, things moved on. We didn't skip one beat." Anderson stayed on and continued the fight.

Opened Group Practice in Detroit

Albany did remove all segregation statutes on the books in 1963, but not before Anderson was arrested and convicted on federal charges of juror intimidation and perjury, because of protests against a local white business owner who had acquitted a county sheriff of murder of a demonstrator. However, due to the many threats to his family and himself, Anderson moved to Detroit. He took a residency position at the Art Center Clinical Group. He then opened a group practice where he treated patients until 1984. He continued to make strides in his profession, even becoming the first African American president of the American Osteopathic Association.

Anderson later would focus his attention on helping others become doctors of osteopathy by developing educational programs for the Kirksville College of Osteopathic Medicine and Detroit Riverview Hospital. He joined numerous organizations, and sat on several boards. He has been honored by every major organization in his profession and has received several honorary doctorates. Posted on the American Association of Colleges of Osteopathic Medicine (AACOM) website, Barbara Ross-Lee, DO, who introduced Anderson at the AACOM luncheon where he was presented with the Dale Dodson Award, stated that Anderson "has focused not only on improving the health of his individual patients, but on improving the health of the society in which his patients live." In addition to his commitment to his profession and the rights of his people, Anderson also co-authored a book with his wife, *Autobiographies of a Black Couple of the Greatest Generation.* His commitment to his profession and to the lives of minorities has been honored with the 2001 creation of the William G. Anderson Minority Scholarship at the American Osteopathic Foundation.

Selected works

Autobiographies of a Black Couple of the Greatest Generation, Michigan Osteopathic Association, 2004.

Sources

Books

Davis, Townsend. *Weary Feet, Rested Souls, A Guided History of the Civil Rights Movement,* W.W. Norton & Company, 1998, pp. 162-176.

Who's Who Among African Americans, 18th Edition, Thomson Gale, 2005.

Periodicals

Albany Herald, November 15, 1998, supplement.

On-line

"Albany, A Major Part in Fight for Civil Rights," *The Student Voice,* Albany State College, www.asustudentvoice.com/vnews/display.v/ART/2006/02/07/43e8c133c5f34 (accessed March 15, 2006).

"Anderson to Open 2005 Unified Osteopathic Convention," *DO-online.org,* www.do-online.osteotech.org/virtual_convention.cfm?PageID=conv_05_nwsandersonopen (accessed February 1, 2006).

"Dodson Award Presentation," *American Association of Colleges of Osteopathic Medicine,* www.aacom. org/events/award-lunch/speech-anderson.html (February 1, 2006).

"William G. Anderson," *Kellogg African American Health Care Project,* www.med.umich.edu/haahc/Oralbios/anderson.htm (accessed February 1, 2006).

"William G. Anderson I, D.O., FACOS," *Kirksville College of Osteopathic Medicine,* www.kcom.edu/academia/Fac-Staff/Anderson-W.htm (accessed February 1, 2006).

"William G. Anderson Receives Honorary Doctorate," *The Communicator: The Newsletter of the University of New England College of Osteopathic Medicine,* www.une.edu/com/rsas/newsletter/ian06.html (accessed February 1, 2006).

"William Gilchrist Anderson," *Biography Resource Center,* http://galenet.galegroup.com/servlet/BioRC (accessed February 1, 2006).

—Ashyia N. Henderson

Tiki Barber

1975—

Professional football player, sportscaster

Barber, Tiki, photograph. AP Images.

Tiki Barber has set standards for professional athletes both on and off the field. Barber joined the New York Giants as a running back in 1997 and became one of the team's brightest stars. By the 2000 season, when the team went to the Super Bowl (and suffered a heavy defeat to the Baltimore Ravens) Barber played an important part in the offensive line-up. A former college sprinter, in his early professional career Barber's outstanding pace helped him disrupt the pattern of games in the later stages, but he soon became a key part of the Giants' offense. In 2005 he held the Giants career records for rushing yards (8,787), and rushing touchdowns (50), despite playing for a team that underachieved throughout most of his career. That year Barber also became the first player in National Football League (NFL) history to make 1,800 rushing yards and 500 receiving yards in a single season; his total yardage was the second highest in history. Barber was part of the NFL all-star Pro Bowl teams of 2004 and 2005 and worked as a sports broadcaster for WCBS-TV in New York City, and Fox News. In addition, with his twin brother, Ronde, he hosted a radio show and wrote books for children. Sometimes described as "the nicest man in the NFL," Barber seemed likely to have a lasting career in the spotlight.

Known as "Tiki" since early childhood, Barber was born Atiim Kiambu Barber on April 7, 1975, in Roanoke, Virginia. He and his twin brother Ronde were born more than a month premature and very underweight; nevertheless they both grew to become strong, agile athletes. He attended Roanoke Cave Spring High School where he and his brother excelled at sports, but were also academically driven. A high-school valedictorian, he went to the University of Virginia on an academic scholarship to major in business. While he maintained his focus on his studies, Barber also became an accomplished college athlete; he broke the University of Virginia's long jump record on his first jump. He was drafted to the New York Giants after graduation in 1997.

Barber's career with the Giants began quietly. Despite initial worries about moving to New York he and Ginny Cha, whom he married in 1999, soon settled in to city life. Despite some success in 1997 the Giants did not begin to improve under the leadership of Jim Fassell until 1999. In that season Barber emerged as a major

At a Glance . . .

Born Atiim Kiambu Barber on April 7, 1975, in Roanoake, VA; married Ginny Cha, May 1999; children: one son. *Education:* University of Virginia, BA, business, 1997.

Career: New York Giants, professional football player, 1997–; WCBS-TV, sports commentator, 2000; WFAN-AM-FM, fill-in host, c. 2000; Pro Bowl all-star team, member, 2004, 2005; Fox News' *Fox & Friends* morning show, occasional commentator, 2004–.

Addresses: *Office*—New York Giants, Professional Football Player, Giants Stadium, 50 Rte 120, East Rutherford, New Jersey, United States 07073.

talent, catching 66 passes in the season and showing dangerous pace. In 2000 he and Ron Dayne forged a partnership that became central to the Giants' season. Known as "Thunder and Lightning" the pair led the Giants to the National Football Conference (NFC) championship against the Minnesota Vikings. They beat the Vikings 41-0 in a game Barber has singled out as the most memorable of his career. 2000 was Barber's breakout year as a running back, but the Giants' dismal performance against the Baltimore Ravens in Super Bowl XXXV was probably a more realistic measure of the team's underlying ability. Despite holding on to trail only 10-0 by the halfway point, what followed was a collapse that became one of the worst in Super Bowl history: the Giants eventually lost 34-7.

After 2000 the Giants continued to underachieve despite having what was then considered one of the most potent offensive line-ups in the NFL. It was not until 2004 that the team began to improve, but they still struggled to hold their own. Barber told Josh Elliott of *Sports Illustrated* that he found it hard being part of a struggling team, saying that "None of what I've done matters if we're not winning." In fact Barber had a great season in 2004. At an age when many professional football players begin to show signs of age, Barber turned in the best season of his career, was selected for his first Pro Bowl team, and led the NFL in total yards from scrimmage. It was a performance he was not expected to repeat. By then he had taken to running on sand dunes to protect his knees from excessive wear; and while he had no specific injuries, the question of how long he could keep going was a regular topic in interviews.

As it happened, Barber's 2005 turned out even better. He again led the NFL in total yards from scrimmage,

and he took the Giants' record for the longest touchdown run (95 yards), a record that had been previously set by Hap Moran who managed 91 yards in 1930. He was also selected for a second Pro Bowl. The *New York Post* said in its report card for the 2005-6 season: "There was no way Tiki Barber (357-1,860, 9 TDs rushing, 54-530, 2 TDs receiving) could top last year but he did, by a mile. Broke into the superstar pantheon, quite a feat at 30 years old." In fact at 1,860 yards and 9 touchdowns rushing, his 2005 season ranked number 42 in the top NFL single season performances since 1960 and he joined the league's all-time top 50 for rushing yards. He also became the first player in the history of the NFL to achieve more than 1,800 rushing yards and 500 receiving yards in a single season.

Barber is widely thought to be one of the best running backs of his generation, but he has also been active in several other areas. In 2004 Barber and his brother published a children's book together, titled *By My Brother's Side*, which the *School Library Journal* called "a sun-drenched childhood anecdote about perseverance." The autobiographical book tells several stories from the brothers' childhood and has proved highly popular. In early 2005 he appeared in an off Broadway play in which he played Duke, a playboy. The same year, again working with writer Robert Burleigh and illustrator Barry Root, Tiki and Ronde produced another volume, *Game Day*, in which the brothers play for the Cave Spring Vikings. While Tiki takes all the glory, playmaker Ronde seems to go unnoticed until the coach plans to have the ball passed to Ronde who breaks out of his usual blocking role to win a touchdown. Writing in *Booklist*, Ilene Cooper said of the book: "What works best here is the feel-good mood—the anticipation, the excitement of the game, and the thrill of victory."

Well known as a laid-back individual with a ready smile, Barber has prepared well for the moment when his career ends. In 2005 he told *Sports Illustrated*: "I'll try to play until I'm 33 or so, and then my body will say, Enough." By then he had already become a regular analyst on Fox News's morning show, *Fox & Friends*. In an interview with *Men's Fitness* magazine he outlined his ambition for when his career as a player ends. Asked to finish a newspaper headline "Tiki Barber of the Giants …" he said: "… makes seamless transition to any of the morning football shows. I want to be the next James Brown: the head guy at a desk talking football."

Selected writings

Books

(With Ronde Barber and Robert Burleigh; illustrated by Barry Root), *By My Brother's Side*, Simon and Schuster, 2004.

(With Ronde Barber and Robert Burleigh; illustrated by Barry Root), *Game Day*, Paula Wiseman Books, 2005.

Sources

Periodicals

Booklist, September 1, 2005, p.119.
Boys' Life, February 2006, p. 8.
Men's Fitness, November 2003.
New York Post, January 10, 2006, p. 77; January 11, 2006, p. 75.
Publishers Weekly, October 3, 2005, p. 70.

School Library Journal, November 2004, p.122; January 2006, p. 116.
Sports Illustrated, December 13, 2004, p. 35; April 11, 2005, p. 26.

On-line

Pro Football Reference, www.pro-football-reference.com/ (March 7, 2006).
"Tiki Barber," *Biography Resource Center*, www.galenet.com/servlet/BioRC (March 7, 2006).
"Tiki Barber," *ESPN*, http://sports.espn.go.com/nfl/players/stats?playerId=1218 (March 7, 2006).

—Chris Routledge

Halle Berry

1966—

Actress

Berry, Halle, photograph. AP Images.

Halle Berry has become a beacon of success to women around the world. Her personal beauty and grace catapulted her into the limelight, but her persistence, strength, and ambition propelled her to success and high achievement. In 2002 she became the first African American woman to win an Oscar Award for Best Actress. While she focused her professional choices on opening doors for other African Americans, Berry inspired women of all races with her willingness to fight personal battles. Besides racial prejudice, Berry battled such difficulties as abusive relationships, thoughts of suicide, missteps with the law, and an ongoing struggle with diabetes. From each battle Berry emerged victorious, showing the world her commitment to living life according to her own terms.

Embraced her Black Heritage

Born to a white mother and black father, Berry grew up in Cleveland, Ohio. Her parents had a tumultuous relationship and separated when she was four years old. Berry struggled with the difficult feelings of being witness to her father's abuse of her mother and older sister. Raising her daughters alone, Berry's mother, Judith, a registered nurse, did her best to care for her children's needs. She sent Berry to a psychotherapist to help her deal with her feelings. Berry described how helpful her sessions were to *Redbook*: "To learn at such an early age that there is a calm and effective way to process emotions was a lesson I've never forgotten. I've continued therapy, and though it hasn't kept me from making major mistakes, it has provided me with a means to look at myself with healthy objectivity, and that keeps me grounded."

Throughout her childhood, Berry recalled, she was so shy her mother had to coax her to leave home to go downtown. Being the offspring of a biracial couple, Berry had her initial encounter with prejudice as a youngster, when her family moved from an inner-city neighborhood to suburban Cleveland. "People would call me 'zebra' and leave Oreo cookies in our mailbox," she recounted to *Elle*. When she questioned her mother about these incidents, Berry related in *Ebony*, her mother explained, "I'm white, and you are black.... What do you see when you look in the mirror? You see what everyone else sees. They don't know that you're

At a Glance . . .

Born on August 14, 1966, in Cleveland, OH; daughter of Jerome (hospital attendant) and Judith (registered nurse) Berry; married David Justice (professional baseball player), 1993 (divorced 1997); married Eric Benet (musician), 2001 (divorced 2004); children: (adopted) India. *Education*: Attended Cuyahoga Community College, Cleveland, OH, 1985.

Career: Model, late 1980s–; actress and producer, 1989–.

Awards: Miss Teen Ohio and Miss Ohio, 1985; first runner-up, Miss USA Pageant, 1986; winner of dress competition, Miss World Pageant, 1986; Golden Globe Award, 1999; NAACP Image Award, 2000, 2002, 2003; Emmy Award, 2000; Oscar Award, 2002.

Addresses: *Agent*—William Morris Agency, One William Morris Place, Beverly Hills, CA 90212. *Web*—www.hallewood.com.

biracial. They don't know who your mother is, and they aren't going to care." With her mother's support, Berry embraced being black but did not embrace the idea that being black would limit her opportunities. As Berry told *Redbook*, "I became an over-achiever."

From the time she was in grade school, Berry wanted to be an actress. She related to Laurie Werner in *USA Weekend*, "I would imitate scenes from *The Wizard of Oz*. I even had the right dog." A cheerleader, Berry also became prom queen and class president during her high school years. When she was 17 years old, Berry was surprised to learn one of her high school boyfriends had entered her name in the Miss Teen Ohio beauty pageant. Winning the title, she then entered a succession of other pageants, including Miss World, in which she won the dress competition. Berry was also named first runner-up in the Miss USA competition after her selection as Miss Ohio in 1985.

In 1986 Berry enrolled at Cuyahoga Community College in Cleveland to study broadcast journalism. When she took an internship at a local radio station, Berry discovered she disliked reporting. She left college before completing her degree to pursue modeling and study acting in Chicago. Her mother encouraged the career transition, Berry divulged to Lawrence Chua in *Elle* magazine: "When I left home to start acting, [my mother's] attitude was, 'Keep your chin up, go do it; but if you fail, home is always here.'"

Broke into Acting

While in Chicago, Berry auditioned for a role in producer Aaron Spelling's television pilot *Charlie's Angels '88*. Although the show did not materialize, Spelling was impressed with Berry's screen test. He encouraged her not to give up acting. Two big breaks in the young actress's career came with a three-week USO tour with Bob Hope and a starring role as a teenage fashion model in the 1989 television series *Living Dolls*. Berry remarked in *Ebony*, "Here I was an ex-model, a former beauty queen and when *Living Dolls* was canceled, I was playing a model. People weren't taking me seriously."

Hoping audiences would view her differently, Berry prepared for her next role as a crack addict named Vivien in Spike Lee's 1991 film *Jungle Fever* by interviewing several crack addicts and going ten days without a bath. Although her role brought her acclaim, Berry took a recurring part in the television series *Knots Landing* for financial purposes in 1991. "I'm a real miser," the actress told Werner. "I want a cushion," she added.

After Berry's 1991 appearance as a femme fatale in the motion picture *Strictly Business*, Peter Biskind wrote in *Premiere*, "Berry may still be playing somebody's girlfriend, but clearly her star is ascending." The actress almost lost the leading role of Natalie in the comedy. She recalled to Chua, "I found out that they hired me, thought I was too light-skinned, hired someone darker, realized that was a mistake, and then hired me again. And I understood that I had gone through all of this agony for two weeks just because of my skin color."

Although critics were divided in their reviews of the film, Berry's portrayal marked a turning point in her career. Her appearance in leading roles was assured with her selection as Damon Wayans' exotic dancer girlfriend in the movie *The Last Boy Scout*. Vincent Canby of the *New York Times* wrote, "The best thing in the film is Halle Berry. She is an actress who is going places." Berry researched her role in the movie by paying the owner of a Hollywood strip joint to let her dance. After the film's success, Berry commented to Biskind, "I don't want to rise to superstardom overnight, like Julia Roberts. There's no place to go but down."

"Though she is an imposing beauty...Berry's radiant looks belie the strengths that have made her a young actress worth watching," wrote Chua in 1992, after the release of the comedy *Boomerang*. Judy Gerstel of the *Detroit Free Press* lauded Berry in the film as "versatile," noting that her role as Angela was "played to doe-eyed perfection." The year *Boomerang* was released, *Ebony* profiled the young actress as an image breaker: "A down-to-earth, drop-dead gorgeous woman, Berry exudes confidence, having already shattered the Hollywood adage that models can't act."

As her film career picked up steam, Berry's personal life became the fodder for the press. Berry's difficult relationships turned into media stories. The public learned of her court battle with an ex-boyfriend over financial issues, how another ex-boyfriend hit her so hard that she lost 80 percent of the hearing in one ear, and followed the highs and lows of her first and second marriages, including her thoughts of suicide after the break-up of her first. Moreover, Berry's struggle with diabetes also came to light. Throughout each tragedy, Berry displayed her characteristic strength, dealing with the challenges, learning from her mistakes, and moving on.

Blazed Her Own Trail

Despite her personal difficulties, Berry remained focused in her professional life. She was keenly aware that she had to blaze her own trail. To that end, Berry continually sought diverse roles. She went from a hip-hop dancer in *Strictly Business* to a college co-ed in *The Program* to playing a recovering drug addict fighting for her son in *Losing Isaiah*—for which she won rave reviews. She also played historical characters, portraying Alex Haley's paternal grandmother in *Queen*, a television miniseries. And in 1995 Berry became the first African American to portray the role of the Ethiopian ruler Sheba in *Solomon and Sheba*, a made for cable television movie.

Her career building roles took her from television to film and back again, jumps that were unusual among the most successful actors in the industry. About her hopping back and forth between television and film roles—something that she was advised not to do— Berry explained in *Ebony*: "Listen, the same rules that apply to Julia Roberts don't apply to me. Black actresses don't have the same choices as white actresses." And Berry made the most of the choices she had, being cast in roles not typically played by blacks and winning critical acclaim and acknowledgment for her acting talents.

By 1998 Berry was producing and starring in the story of Dorothy Dandridge, the person who Berry "fell in love with" as a child and who had inspired Berry to become an actress for the way "she jumped off the screen," as Berry related to *Newsweek*. Dandridge's life had many parallels to Berry's own: she possessed great beauty, suffered difficult personal relationships, and experienced the injustice of racial prejudice. Director of *Introducing Dorothy Dandridge,* Martha Coolidge told *Redbook* that Berry is "a dead ringer" for Dandridge and that in her role, Berry "captured her spirit, her talent, and her sensitivity."

Berry found inspiration from playing Dandridge and she even gained a better understanding of her goals in the movie industry. Learning from Dandridge's self-destructive reaction to the prejudice and pressure of the movie industry in the 1950s, Berry resolved to fight for her career. "Getting the Dorothy Dandridge story made was a significant point in my development. It was an opportunity to play a woman who had so many obstacles in her life—obstacles I could relate to as a black actress who has to struggle in Hollywood…. The project was a major turning point for me and my career. It helped me grow as an actress and strengthened my resolve to take chances and explore new roles and new avenues," as Berry noted in *Essence*. She added in *Redbook* that from Dandridge's story she learned that "it is my responsibility to force them [Hollywood] to know what to do with me, because I think that's what ultimately killed her." For her portrayal of Dandridge, Berry won a Golden Globe Award and an NAACP Image Award in 1999 and an Emmy Award the following year.

As one of Hollywood's best-known black actresses, Berry continued to seek new, challenging roles and even returned to modeling when she signed with Revlon Cosmetics. Her relentless pursuit of interesting roles paid off. Her portrayal of Leticia Musgrove in *Monster's Ball* catapulted her to the highest accolade ever earned by a black actress. In the 2001 film, Berry played a down-on-her-luck waitress dealing with an imprisoned husband and her abusive tendencies toward her overweight son. *Variety* reported that critic Peter Travers called Berry "volcanic" and that Roger Ebert noted that Berry's performance cause him to think "about (Berry's character) as deeply and urgently as about any movie character I can remember." For her part in *Monster's Ball,* Berry won the Oscar Award for Best Actress in a Leading Role.

Berry deeply understood the importance of the award. Upon accepting the award she said: "This moment is so much bigger than me. This moment is for Dorothy Dandridge, Lena Horne, Diahann Carroll…It's for the women who stand beside me: Jada Pinkett Smith, Angela Bassett, Vivica Fox…and it's for every nameless, faceless woman of color that now has a chance because this door tonight has been opened," as her speech was quoted in *Redbook*. Berry went on to use what she told *Variety* was the "power of Oscar" to open doors for herself. "Minds are still a bit closed towards having black actors play opposite certain kinds of actors or certain parts in movies, so I've decided to take that power and try to make some of my own opportunities." Since her historic win, Berry played such different characters as a Bond girl in *Die Another Day*, a superhero in the *X-Men* films, a psychiatrist in *Gothika,* and the lead in the made-for-television movie of Zora Neale Hurston's *Their Eyes Were Watching God.* Doing so proved Brian Levant, her director in the 1994 filming of *The Flintstones,* to be correct in his assertion to *Good Housekeeping* that "the range she's capable of is phenomenal…But that's Halle: the entire package."

Selected works

Films

Jungle Fever, 1991.
The Last Boy Scout, 1991.
Strictly Business, 1991.
Boomerang, 1992.
The Program, 1994.
The Flintstones, 1994.
Losing Isaiah, 1995.
The Rich Man's Wife, 1996.
B.A.P.S., 1997.
Bulworth, 1998.
Why Do Fools Fall In Love?, 1998.
X-Men, 2000.
Monster's Ball, 2001.
Swordfish, 2001.
Die Another Day, 2002.
Gothika, 2003.
X2, 2003.
Catwoman, 2004.
X-Men: The Last Stand, 2006.

Television

Living Dolls, ABC, 1989.
Knot's Landing, 1991.
Queen: The Story of an American Family, 1993.
Solomon and Sheba, 1995.
The Wedding, 1998.
Introducing Dorothy Dandridge, 1999.
Their Eyes Were Watching God, 2005.

Sources

Periodicals

Detroit Free Press, July 1, 1992.
Ebony, February 1992; October 1992; December 1994; March 1997; November 2002, p. 186.
Elle, April 1992; October 2003, pp. 258-267.
Essence, October 1996; May 2002, p. 154; March 2005, p. 132.
Good Housekeeping, August 2002, p. 98.
Heart and Soul, April 2002, p. 56.
Jet, November 11, 1991; September 2, 1996; March 7, 2005, pp. 52-5.
Newsweek, August 30, 1999, p. 48.
New York Times, March 12, 1995, p. 15.
People, November 25, 1991; December 23, 1991; July 20, 1992; May 11, 1998.
Premiere, December 1991.
Redbook, March 2003, p. 130.
Upscale, June/July 1992; October/November 1992.
USA Weekend, November 8-10, 1991.
Variety, August 15, 2005, pp. 62-85.

On-line

The Official Site of Halle Berry, www.hallewood.com (July 21, 2006).

—Marjorie Burgess, Ashyia N. Henderson, and Sara Pendergast

Jeffri Chadiha

1970—

Journalist

Inspired by a teacher in a journalism class at the University of Michigan, former college athlete Jeffri Chadiha got his big break writing for the *Ann Arbor News*, before taking a high-profile job at the *San Francisco Examiner*, where he worked full-time covering the Oakland Raiders. After turning down a job at the *New York Times* he moved to *Sports Illustrated* as a staff writer in 2000 and joined what has the reputation of being the most influential sportswriting team in the United States. Chadiha has remained at the forefront of the organization's Web presence and has been a major contributor to *SI.com*, writing features and reports about football: its athletes, its politics, and its controversy.

Jeffri Chadiha was born in Ann Arbor, Michigan, on November 20, 1970; he has a twin brother, Jon, and a younger brother, Kizza. His father, Jonathan, is a dentist and his mother, Letha, is a professor in the School of Social Work at the University of Michigan. Chadiha attended Ann Arbor Gabriel Richard High School and after graduating in 1988 went to the University of Wyoming on a full football scholarship, playing in the defensive back position but often finding himself unable to play because of knee injuries. After a series of operations Chadiha realized that a career in football was out of the question. He transferred to the University of Michigan in 1990, and he graduated from there with a bachelor's degree in communications in 1993.

Chadiha's studies at the University of Michigan started him thinking seriously about a career in journalism. He took writing classes and found inspiration from Don Kubit, his mentor in a class on sportswriting, and from a graduate level class on magazine writing. Chadiha told *getthatgig.com* that a career in journalism appealed to him partly because "I figured, at the least, I could keep the same hours I had as a student." He landed a job as a part-time reporter at the *Ann Arbor News* covering high school sports and in 1993, after graduation, he joined the *News* full-time as a police reporter. He told *Contemporary Black Biography(CBB)* that although the police beat was tough, it was there that he learned how to talk to people, to listen to them, and how to be sympathetic as an interviewer. In particular, he felt that the experience of interviewing the relatives of victims of shootings drove home his responsibility as a journalist to respect privacy while writing a story.

At the *News,* Chadiha covered police reports for a year before switching to sports, which he covered until 1996. Even then he wasn't completely settled on a career in sportswriting, and he prepared himself to go to law school. It was only a few days before his final test for law school that he was invited to go to San Francisco to work as a sportswriter for the *San Francisco Examiner*. Uncertain about what to do Chadiha made an unusual deal with himself. Chadiha's roommate had organized a party for that night, and Chadiha told *CBB* that he used the party to help him decide which career path to follow. He decided that if he was back home before 4 a.m. he would take the take the test and go to law school; after 4 a.m. and he would go to San Francisco. He arrived home at 6 a.m., and he spent the next two years at the *Examiner* covering the

At a Glance . . .

Born Jeffri Wade Chadiha on November 20, 1970, in Ann Arbor, Michigan; partner, Whitney Stephens. *Education:* University of Wyoming 1988-90; University of Michigan, BA communication, 1993.

Career: *Ann Arbor News,* police reporter, 1993-94; sportswriter, 1994-96; *San Francisco Examiner,* sportswriter, 1996-2000; *Sports Illustrated,* reporter, 2000–.

Addresses: *Office*—c/o Sports Illustrated, 135 West 50th Street, 3rd Floor, New York, NY 10020-1339.

Oakland Raiders full-time, followed by two years covering the San Francisco 49ers.

His years at the *Examiner* brought Chadiha attention within his field. Covering the Raiders was a reporting job nobody liked; they were a "dysfunctional" team and hostile to the press. But Chadiha made a name for himself writing about the team's trials and tribulations on and off the field. After a while he came to the attention of several major newspapers: the *Chicago Tribune* and the *New York Times* both expressed interest in hiring him—the *Times* even made an offer, which Chadiha turned down. In January 2000 he was invited to submit material to *Sports Illustrated,* one of the most influential sports magazines. Chadiha's memory of the job offer from *Sports Illustrated* remained vivid: he was on vacation in Puerto Rico and collected the message out in the street on the only phone in the village.

Sports Illustrated offered Chadiha a challenge. He told *CBB* that even after holding down a job at the *Examiner* and receiving offers from the *New York Times,* he felt the need to "be more than what I was," when joining *Sports Illustrated* in April 2000. Chadiha was keenly aware that he was joining one of the largest sports media organizations in the world, and he worked hard to raise his game. Chadiha focused on improving not only the quality of his writing, but also his efforts to get the job done. He told *CBB* that sports fans often think that watching football games for a living must be a dream job, but in fact, he said "the games are the least enjoyable part ... it's the people." Chadiha honed his skills at interviewing and worked to connect with the people who bring the games to life.

Chadiha looked past play-by-plays and player biographies to offer readers more: he opened debate about the political side of sports journalism. In 2004 he

sparked controversy with comments about a pre-game skit on ABC's *Desperate Housewives*-themed intro to its *Monday Night Football* show. In the segment, black football star Terrell Owens embraced Nicolette Sheridan, star of the *Desperate Housewives* TV show. Chadiha commented in an article for *SI.com*: " What the segment did do, however, was make me wonder if America was ready to see a naked, blonde, white woman with her arms wrapped around an outspoken, controversial, highly paid black man. From what I can tell from everybody's reaction, the country definitely wasn't." Chadiha told *CBB* he received hundreds of emails about the article on both sides of the debate. The example serves as testament to Chadiha's willingness to take risks, a great strength of his reporting skills.

Chadiha's position among sportswriters is an influential one. Much of his work for *Sports Illustrated* appears on the *SI.com* Web site, which in February 2006 was ranked number 133 among most visited Web sites worldwide. Chadiha welcomed his open line of communication with his on-line audience. When asked by *CBB* he was laid back about having to compete with amateur journalists and bloggers on-line, arguing that if it encouraged people to write it couldn't be a bad thing.

It's the writing that thrills Chadiha. What gets him out of bed in the morning, he told *CBB*, is doing what he loves doing: "trying to reach people and myself." In addition to his continued work with *Sports Illustrated,* Chadiha shared with *CBB* that he intends to write books.

Sources

Periodicals

The Milwaukee Journal-Sentinel, October 28, 1998.

On-line

"Jeffri Chadiha: Inside the NFL: It's Really About Race," *SI.com,* http://sportsillustrated.cnn.com/ 2004/writers/jeffri_chadiha/11/18/chadiha.to/ (February 21, 2006).
"Jeffri Chadiha, 30, Works for Sports Illustrated Magazine. He Has a COOL JOB as Staff Writer," *www. getthatgig.com,* http://www.getthatgig.com/ sports/careers/c_staffwriter_sportsillust.html (February 21, 2006).

Other

Additional information for this profile was obtained through an interview with Jeffri Chadiha on February 10, 2006, and by email correspondence.

—Chris Routledge

Leah Chase

1923—

Chef

Leah Chase has become a New Orleans fixture as the widely respected doyenne of Creole cooking. Her restaurant, Dooky Chase's, remains an attractive landmark in the city, and was one of the first fine-dining establishments in the Crescent City that seated African-American patrons. She married into the family who first opened it, and over the years helped to establish Creole food as a legitimate cuisine in America. Her business was hard hit by Hurricane Katrina in 2005, but she was determined to return. "We had to gut the walls and put in all new equipment," she told *Milwaukee Journal-Sentinel* writer Karen Herzog several months later, and though she noted that things were "coming along," she also said that " All the rebuilding efforts here seem too slow to me. I don't have a lot of time. I'm 83 years old and would like to just do what I have to do."

Grew Up on Farm

Chase was born in 1923 in Madisonville, Louisiana, a town in the St. Tammany Parish on the Tchefuncte River near Lake Ponchartrain. Her father was a shipyard worker, but her parents and 11 siblings also farmed a plot of land that provided the family's food. Her family was Creole, a term that was first used to denote the French and Spanish settlers in the New Orleans area when it was still European-held land, but by the time she was born the word referred to the region's mixed-race population—some of whom, like Chase, had Native American blood too. Hers came from a Choctaw Indian grandmother.

The Chase family grew okra, sweet potatoes, and strawberries, and they also had a steady supply of chicken and pork from a few animals they raised. Though food from their yard was abundant, other resources were scarcer, and Chase and her sisters wore dresses made from flour sacks. As one of nine daughters, she learned to cook at an early age, taking turns with her sisters in the kitchen. The family was Roman Catholic, and because there was no high school for blacks in Madisonville, she moved to New Orleans to attend St. Mary's Academy, the city's first Roman Catholic secondary school for African-American women. She graduated at the age of 16, and for a time worked as a domestic servant before taking a sewing job in a factory. Each of these jobs was in the primary fields of employment for black women at the time, but Chase felt ill-suited to both. "I couldn't just shoot out a hundred pants pockets a day," she recalled in an interview with Nancy Harmon Jenkins for the *New York Times,* "so I went to work in this restaurant—the Coffee Pot—which was a no-no, in the French Quarter of all places. And that was a double no-no."

Waiting tables was considered a rather undignified job for a Creole, many of whom took pride in their heritage as members of the largest population of free blacks in the years before the Emancipation Proclamation of 1863 officially freed blacks from slavery. Moreover, the French Quarter—New Orleans's oldest neighborhood—had fallen on hard times by then. Many of its buildings dated back to the 1790s, and its most enduring families were descendants of the original French colonists to the area. By Chase's time, the Quarter was known for its cheap rents and lively bars. Though New Orleans was integrated to an impressive degree for a city in the U.S. South in the pre-civil rights era, many of the Quarter's older businesses held on to the strict Jim Crow laws that separated the races. But the onset of World War II had brought labor shortages, and blacks were able to find jobs in establishments previously closed to them. When Chase moved on to the posh Colony Restaurant as a waitress, it was the first time she had ever been inside a true fine-dining establishment.

Married into Restaurant Business

Chase met her future husband, Edgar "Dooky" Chase II, at a dance. His parents were fixtures in the Tremè neighborhood, the area that had been the epicenter of African-American life in the city for more than a century by then. His father, from whom he inherited his nickname, ran a small lottery-sales kiosk that also sold his wife's popular po' boy sandwiches. These were one of New Orleans's homegrown specialties, made from a crispy-crust French bread and stuffed with crawfish, fried oysters, pork sausage, or other fillings. Dooky II was a trumpeter and bandleader, and after the two wed in 1945, Chase spent the next few years traveling around the South with him and his band. They settled into a less nomadic existence when the first of their four children arrived, and by then his parents' takeout stall had become a full-fledged restaurant called Dooky Chase's. Located on Orleans Avenue, it was one of the first fine-dining establishments in the city that was open to blacks as well as whites.

When Chase's father-in-law fell ill in 1952, she and her husband became involved in running the business. "I

thought I was going to be the little hostess out front," she told Jenkins in the *New York Times* article, "but there was nobody cooking so I landed in the kitchen." Chase had some ideas for moving forward with the restaurant, but her mother-in-law had firm ideas about its menu. "I wanted to shake things up, try some new dishes like lobster thermidor," Chase explained to Jim Auchmutey in an interview that appeared in the *Atlanta Journal-Constitution.* "But folks around here didn't want that. They thought shrimp cocktail was something you drank. How were they supposed to know that stuff? They'd never been around real restaurants." In the end, Chase prevailed, and though she abandoned the idea of serving fancier food, she did expand the menu to include many classic Creole dishes, such as jambalaya, gumbo, trout amandine, and red beans and rice, a New Orleans staple that was traditionally made on Mondays and flavored with Sunday-supper pork bones. "By then, they weren't even cooking these things in the home anymore," Chase asserted in the *New York Times* interview with Jenkins, "and you never would have found them in a restaurant."

In a city with a number of world-famous restaurants, Dooky Chase's was the premier black dining establishment in the era before integration, and remained popular with the city's emerging African-American political, social, and economic leadership after the "whites-only" rules ended forever. Both Martin Luther King Jr. and Thurgood Marshall were regulars when they came to town, and Chase's dining room was also a favorite of performers Louis Armstrong, Duke Ellington, Sarah Vaughan, and Lena Horne. Pianist Ray Charles even mentioned it in his 1961 version of "Early in the Morning Blues," adding the line, "I went to Dooky Chase/To get me something to eat/The waitress looked at me and said/'Ray, you sure look beat.'"

Kept Creole Cuisine Alive

Chase eventually ridded the dining-room walls of the black and pink elephant wallpaper that dated from Dooky Chase's earliest days, and hung an impressive array of African-American art from Jacob Lawrence, Elizabeth Catlett, and others. In the 1980s, the business expanded, though the Tremè neighborhood had fallen on hard times and sometimes taxicabs refused to venture into it. Its Orleans Avenue address was near to the looming Lafitte public housing project, but Chase claimed that in six decades in business the place had never once been robbed.

Chase gained national prominence as a pioneer of Creole cuisine once New Orleans-style cooking began to gain in popularity in the 1980s. She published her first collection of recipes, *The Dooky Chase Cookbook,* in 1990. Her second title, *And I Still Cook,* came out the year she turned eighty. Chase's signature dish is Gumbo Z'Herbes, a green version of the soup traditionally served on the Thursday before Easter, a holy day on the Roman Catholic calendar. It was a kind of irony that she had achieved celebrity-chef status after so many years in the kitchen, as she recalled in an interview with Milford Prewitt for *Nation's Restaurant News,* because she began her career at a time when there were no such culinary stars of either race, but blacks commonly staffed the kitchens of restaurants across America. As she told Prewitt, she had had a conversation with French-American cooking guru Jacques Pepin, who reminded her that until recent times, few chefs in France ever achieved the same level of renown given to the restaurant itself. "I think about that when I think about when I got started, and most of the chefs in the big restaurants were black," she mused. "But they're not black anymore."

When Hurricane Katrina devastated New Orleans in 2005, there was flooding in the Tremè, and as much as five feet of water remained inside some parts of Dooky Chase's once it was over. Fortunately, Chase's grandson had acted quickly and put the restaurant's art collection in storage before the worst of the storm hit. Chase herself rode out the storm at a relative's home in Baton Rouge, which she said "was like the Underground Railroad—20 people" in a two-bedroom house, she told Mimi Read in *O: The Oprah Magazine.* "Of course I cooked for everyone. Sweetheart, who else?" She returned and moved into a Federal Emergency Management Agency (FEMA)-provided trailer across the street from Dooky Chase's, and made plans to reopen. Her famous eatery had benefited from an immense amount of community goodwill and fundraising help from as far away as New York City and Milwaukee in its efforts to rebuild. By June of 2006,

some of the million-dollar renovations had been completed, and Chase was still in her FEMA trailer. "I'm not worried about a house now," she told Herzog of the *Milwaukee Journal-Sentinel.* "I've gotta rebuild that restaurant. If I don't, this neighborhood is gone. There's only one person other than me in the neighborhood now—only one other person between here and six blocks away." Once Dooky Chase's would reopen, she said, "I think all of my street will come back."

Selected writings

Books

The Dooky Chase Cookbook, Pelican Publishing, 1990.
And I Still Cook, Pelican Publishing, 2003.

Sources

Periodicals

Atlanta Journal-Constitution, December 24, 2000, p. M1.
Milwaukee Journal-Sentinel, May 31, 2006.
Nation's Restaurant News, June 2, 1997, p. 37.
New York Times, June 27, 1990; February 23, 2005; January 11, 2006.
O: The Oprah Magazine, March 2006, p. 236.

—Carol Brennan

Bryan Ezra Clay

1980—

Olympic Decathlete

Clay, Bryan Ezra, photograph. AP Images.

Despite being rather on the small side to be the so-called best athlete in the world, at 5 feet 11 inches and 185 pounds decathlete Bryan Ezra Clay has held the Olympic silver medal (2004), the world championship decathlon title (2005), and the American decathlon title (2004, 2005). Clay first began to stand out as an athlete in high school, where dominated Hawaii's track and field events until his graduation in 1998. He moved on to a career at Azusa Pacific University, in Los Angeles, California, breaking school records in individual track and field events before moving on to the decathlon. Almost unknown nationally before the U.S. Olympic trials in July 2004, he beat world champion and American number one Tom Pappas to take a place in the Olympics. In winning his silver medal in Athens, Greece, the following month he set the fourth-highest score in Olympic history and the sixth-highest of all time. His Olympic silver medal made Texas-born Clay the first ever Hawaiian to win an Olympic track medal and the first athlete from Hawaii to make the Olympic track team since steeplechaser Henry Marsh in 1988.

Bryan Ezra Clay was born in Austin, Texas, on January 3, 1980, to a Japanese-American mother and an African-American father. From the age of five, Clay was raised in Hawaii, where he attended the James B. Castle High School (Kaneohe, Hawaii). There he excelled as a runner, breaking state records and joking with his classmates that he was going to the Olympics. In 1998, the year he graduated from high school, Clay competed in a local event in which elite athletes challenged local hopefuls in a "Celebrity 100-yard Dash." He placed fifth, with two nationally ranked athletes and a local adult sprinter behind him. The same year he set state records in the 100 meters, 110 meter hurdles, 200 meters, and long jump. Clay attended Azusa Pacific University on an athletics scholarship. Azusa Pacific is a small Christian college where he majored in social work. Azusa Pacific was also attended by Dave Johnson, the 1992 Olympic decathlon bronze medalist. Clay graduated in 2003 and married Sarah Smith in 2004; their son, Jacob Ezra, was born on July 1, 2005.

Olympic success never comes easily, but Clay's journey to Athens was harder than most. Though a talented high school athlete he had to contend with dirt tracks, poor facilities, and a lack of funding throughout his

At a Glance . . .

Born Bryan Ezra Clay on January 3, 1980, in Austin, Texas; married Sarah Smith, 2004; children: Jacob Ezra. *Education:* Azusa Pacific University, Los Angeles, CA, BA, social work, 2003. *Religion:* Christian.

Career: NAIA decathlon champion (7,373 pts), 2000; NAIA long jump champion, 2001, 2002; NAIA pentathlon champion, 2002; USA decathlon championship runner-up (8,482 pts), 2002; World Indoor heptathlon silver medalist (6,365 pts), 2004; USA Outdoor decathlon champion, 2004, 2005; Olympic decathlon silver medalist (8,820 pts), 2004; World Outdoor decathlon champion (8,723 pts), 2005.

Awards: World Indoor heptathlon silver medal, 2004; Olympic decathlon silver medal (Athens, 2004); World Championship decathlon gold medal (Helsinki, 2005).

formative years. Clay's high school coach, Martin Hee, struggled to keep the track from turning to mud and bought equipment with his own money. Funding for track and field lagged well behind football in Hawaii so that on the island of Oahu, where Clay grew up, only two of the twenty-two public schools had rubberized tracks at the time of the Athens games. After moving to California, Clay enjoyed better facilities, so much so that he continued to train at Azusa Pacific after his graduation in 2003.

In addition to years training on outdated facilities, Clay had to contend with balancing the need to train with the need to earn money. In the early part of his career finding time to train was always difficult. But when it became clear that he could make a career of track and field athletics, his then fiancée Sarah Smith agreed to support Clay as he trained for the Olympics in Athens. The couple lived on her income from teaching kindergarten. Clay was also helped by the sponsorship of a small group of Hawaiian businessmen.

Clay was first given the idea of competing in the decathlon by high school coach Hee, but was further inspired by Chris Huffins, Olympic decathlon bronze medalist in 2000, whom he met at a track clinic in Hawaii. It was Huffins who introduced him to his college coach Kevin Reid. At college Clay excelled at long jump and was twice the National Association of Intercollegiate Athletics (NAIA) long jump champion. But it was during his time at Azusa Pacific that Clay began to focus on the decathlon, which includes the 100 meters, long jump, shot put, high jump, 400

meters, 110-meter hurdles, discus throw, pole vault, javelin throw and 1,500 meters and is scored by allocating points to each athlete in each discipline. Coached by Reid in 2000, Clay was the NAIA decathlon champion and in 2002—a year before graduation— he came in second at the United States championship competition. In all Clay won 23 NAIA All-America awards. At the Olympic trials in 2003 he went up against Tom Pappas, then world champion, who was favored to take the gold medal in Athens the following year. Clay's performance at the trials was outstanding: he set a personal best of 8,660 points to knock Pappas into second place. In individual events he set personal records in shot put, discus, pole vault and javelin.

In Athens in summer 2004 Clay was still relatively unknown. His small stature meant that Pappas, a tall, powerful athlete, remained the American favorite. In the event, Pappas was forced to retire when he injured his foot in the pole vault on the second day. But Clay's performance was probably enough to have beaten him anyway. Coming in second to Czech athlete Roman Sebrle, whose gold medal score of 8,893 was the highest in Olympic history, Clay scored a total of 8,820 points, a personal best, the fourth-highest score ever in an Olympic games, and the sixth-highest of all time; he was also just 71 points away from Dan O'Brien's American record. After Athens, Clay became a celebrity in his home state. On August 25, 2004, the *Honolulu Advertiser* declared in a headline: "It's Clay Day!" But Clay, a committed Christian, believed his faith helped him to stay focused on his sport. He told the *BPSports* Web site: "I'm not out there for the money or the fame or the glory," Clay said. "I'm out there to do God's will and allow Him to work through me."

Clay built on his success in Athens, improving his performance in the build-up to the World Championships in Helsinki, Finland, in 2005. Arriving as one of the favorites Clay's main competitor was reigning Olympic champion Sebrle. He managed to put in one of his best ever decathlon performances, setting personal bests in the shot put and the 400 meters. His throw of 72 meters in the javelin was not only a personal best, but a World Championships record for a decathlon javelin throw. Despite a poor performance in the 1500 meters in terrible weather conditions, Clay finally took the gold over Sebrle with 8,732 points and a margin of 211 points, one of the largest winning margins of all time.

Clay's strongest events are the 100 meters, long jump, the 110 meter hurdles and the discus. He has also competed in pentathlons and heptathlons; he was the NAIA pentathlon champion in 2002 and the World Indoor heptathlon silver medalist in 2004. As world decathlon number one, and arguably the world's finest athlete, in 2006 Clay's next target is the Olympic Games in 2008, where he has the chance to add to his outstanding tally of track and field successes.

Sources

Periodicals

Honolulu Advertiser (Hawaii), May 13, 2003; August 25, 2004.
Honolulu Star Bulletin (Hawaii), July 18, 2004; August 25, 2004.
USA Today, July 17, 2004.
Washington Post, August 23, 2004: p. D13.

On-line

Bryan Clay, www.bryanclay.com (March 14, 2006).
"Bryan Clay," *USA Track and Field*, www.usatf.org/athletes/bios/Clay_Bryan.asp (March 14, 2006).
"Bryan Clay: World's Greatest Athlete?" *Hawaii High School Athletic Association* www.hhsaa.org/page_server//PrepNews/HomegrownReports/2BE61395AE56559BFD41179CF5.html (March 14, 2006).
"Clay Reigns Supreme in Decathlon," *BBC Sport*, http://news.bbc.co.uk/sport1/hi/athletics/4139432.stm (March 14, 2006).
"Decathlete Bryan Clay Counts on Prayer Support," *BPSports,* www.bpsports.net/bpsports.asp?ID=4603 (March 14, 2006).
"What People Are Saying About Bryan Clay," *Hawaii High School Athletic Association*, www.hhsaa.org/page_server/PrepNews/HomegrownReports/4660ED1D33714D4DFD41205E1B.html (March 14, 2006).

—Chris Routledge

Kenneth L. Coleman

1942—

Information technology executive

Despite working in an industry notorious for being dominated by white executives, Ken Coleman has held some of the most senior positions in Silicon Valley. Before his retirement in 2001 Coleman was Executive Vice President of Silicon Graphics, Inc. (SGI), a $2.3 billion goliath of the computing industry. Named as one of the top 25 blacks in technology by *Black Enterprise* in 2001, after leaving SGI, Coleman was expected to retire to his retreat on the island of Maui and perhaps join the boards of one or two corporations. Instead Coleman made a surprising move—at the age of 61, he founded a software startup company called ITM to provide company CIOs (Chief Information Officers) with software to help them run their businesses. The step down from major corporation to startup was hard enough, but as *Black Enterprise* explained, what made Coleman's achievement with ITM so remarkable was that it was "a rare tech startup launched by an African American with significant investment, counsel, and management expertise from other blacks in the industry."

Kenneth L. Coleman was born on December 1, 1942, in Centralia, Illinois. He attended the University of Ohio and graduated with a bachelor's degree in industrial management in 1965 before beginning an MBA, which he completed in 1972. His studies were interrupted by military service: Coleman served as a United States Air Force Captain between 1968 and 1972, including a tour of duty in Vietnam. He married Caretha Coleman and they have five children: Kennetha, Karen, Kimberly, Kristen, and Kenneth.

Coleman began working in the technology sector when he joined Hewlett Packard as a personnel manager in 1972. He worked for the company for 10 years, during which time he worked as a corporate staffing manager and as Northern European personnel manager. One of his major achievements at Hewlett Packard was to have played an important part in the development of the personal computer business. It was during Coleman's tenure at the company that HP became a major player in the emerging PC market. Coleman moved from Hewlett Packard to Activision, a software startup that was one of the success stories of the early PC gaming market. He was vice president for human resources and later vice president for product development at Activision. Coleman joined Silicon Graphics, Inc. (SGI) in 1987 and eventually became one of its highest-ranking executives. An article in *Black Enterprise* points out that in his 14 years at the company he was running "global sales, services, and marketing for the $2.3 billion computer systems giant and managing more than 4,000 employees in 37 countries."

Coleman's success in an industry that has been traditionally hard to break into for African Americans has been outstanding. Among IT executives he ranks as one of the most successful across the sector and one of the most successful black executives of the 1980s and 1990s. A comment he made to *Black Enterprise* in 2001 hints that the key to his success is to have continually re-educated himself: "Your past has less to do with your future success than your knowledge to deal with and manage change. It's more about what you know now than what you did 20 years ago." In an industry as fast moving and unforgiving as technology,

At a Glance . . .

Born Kenneth L. Coleman on December 1, 1942, in Centralia, Illinois; married Caretha; children: Kennetha, Karen, Kimberly, Kristen, Kenneth. *Education:* Ohio State University, BS, industrial management, 1965, MBA 1972. *Military Service:* United States Air Force, Captain 1968-72.

Career: Hewlett-Packard Corporation, corporate staffing manager, personnel division, then Northern European personnel manager, 1972-82; Activision Inc, vice president, human resources, vice president, product development, 1982-87; Silicon Graphics Computer Systems, senior vice president of global services and senior vice president of administration and business development, 1987-01; ITM Software, co-founder, chairman, and CEO, 2002–.

Memberships: State of California M(athematics) E(ngineering) S(cience) A(chievement) (MESA), board member 1984-85; board member, Bay Area Black United Fund 1984-85; member, University of Santa Clara Industry Advisory Committee, 1984-85; member, Ohio State Business Advisory Board 1984-85; member and past president, Peninsula Association of Black Personnel Administrators, 1975–; industry advisor, Bay Area Black MBA Association; board member, San Francisco Exploratorium, Ohio State University College of Business Dean's Advisory Council; board member, Children's Health Council; board member, The Community Foundation of Santa Clara County; board member, University of California, San Francisco.

Awards: Award for Excellence in Community Service, San Jose CA, 1981; "Top 50 Blacks in Corporate America," *Black Enterprise,* 2000; Marketing Opportunities in Business and Entertainment award, 2001; Ohio State University Distinguished Service Award; National Alliance of Black School Educators Living Legend Award; American Leadership Forum of Silicon Valley Exemplary Leader Award; One Hundred Black Men of Silicon Valley Lifetime Achievement Award; Silicon Valley Junior Achievement Business Hall of Fame.

Addresses: *Office*—ITM Software, 161 East Evelyn Ave, Mountain View, CA 94041.

Coleman has demonstrated his adaptability more than once. He entered the industry with an interest in computers, though he does not consider himself a "techie," but has since been influential in several expanding technical markets. Where his real skill seems to lie, however, is in assessing the needs of businesses and providing them with products and support to meet those needs. At SGI he developed consulting and customer support services, presiding over a growth in sales of more than $250 million.

Even as he approached retirement Coleman was thinking of new products and new business opportunities. Though widely expected to retire to his home in Maui, Coleman began instead to think about setting up a new company. Along with several other former SGI executives Coleman became a founder of ITM, a company specializing in management information software designed specifically for IT managers. ITM was founded in the fall of 2002. In the aftermath of the dotcom collapse it was not easy to raise money, or to convince cash-strapped technology companies that they needed a new software tool. But by 2004 Coleman and his board had raised $12.8 million in venture capital. Coleman had also made an effort to attract African-American investors, allowing them to invest as little as $50,000, an unusually low sum for a startup tech company. By 2005 the company had attracted high-profile customers such as Intuit, SGI, and Lifescan, a division of Johnson and Johnson.

Coleman has given several interviews in which he offers advice to black Americans trying to break into the IT industry and in corporate America in general. Part of his secret is his energy and enthusiasm for new challenges, as well as his commitment to delivering on promises. But there is one piece of advice that sums up Coleman's successful approach. He told *Black Enterprise* in 2000: "We must be willing to take risks."

Sources

Periodicals

Black Enterprise, February 2000; March 2001; November 2004.

On-line

ITM Software, www.itm-software.com (February 7, 2006).
"Kenneth L. Coleman," *Biography Resource Center,* www.galenet.com/servlet/BioRC (February 7, 2006).
"Kenneth L. Coleman," *ITM Software Team,* www.itm-software.com/html/mgmntKen.shtml (February 7, 2006).

—Chris Routledge

Erroll B. Davis, Jr.

1944—

University administrator, executive

As one of the first African Americans to hold a top-level post in the utilities industry, Erroll B. Davis, Jr. guided Alliant Energy Corp. through a period of expansion and financial stability. While doing so, he gained a strong appreciation for the importance of education, especially for minorities historically denied access to the best schools. This commitment to education led to a late-career shift from the corporate boardroom into the halls of academia, where Davis began applying his considerable administrative skill as chancellor of the University System of Georgia system in 2006.

Erroll Brown Davis, Jr. was born on August 5, 1944, and grew up in a working-class neighborhood in Pittsburgh, Pennsylvania. While he had a close relationship with his parents, Erroll Sr. and Eleanor, his strongest influence as a child was his grandfather, John Boykin, a Georgia farmer who had transplanted to Pittsburgh and worked as a chauffeur. Davis was an academic standout from an early age. He graduated from high school at age 16. He then worked his way through Carnegie-Mellon University, becoming the first member of his family to graduate from college. He received his Bachelor of Science degree in engineering from Carnegie-Mellon in 1965 at the age of 20. He moved to Chicago for graduate school, receiving a Masters degree in finance from the University of Chicago in 1967. After finishing his schooling, Davis spent two years as an Army officer during the Vietnam War, though he never saw action outside of the United States. He married his seventh grade sweetheart Elaine, and started preparing for his business career.

In 1969 Davis landed a finance job with Ford Motor Company in Detroit. He worked for Ford until 1973, when he left for position in Rochester, New York with Xerox Corporation, where her served until 1978. At Xerox, his focus was on strategic financial planning. That year, Davis was recruited by Wisconsin Power and Light Company (WPL), a utility based in Madison, Wisconsin, for a position in corporate finance. He originally planned to stick with WPL for just a few years, then move on to a bigger company. "Unfortunately, they kept promoting me and ruining my game plan," Davis joked in a July 2005 *Wisconsin State Journal* article.

Davis was quoted in a February 2006 interview with the *Wisconsin State Journal* as saying that he never planned on being CEO. "I didn't take any particular steps that were focused on being CEO," he was quoted as saying. "My focus was to do the job I was given to the best of my ability. I continued to do well in my positions and continued to get promoted." Planned or not, his rise to the CEO ranks was relatively swift. Over the next 12 years, Davis climbed the ladder steadily at WPL. He became executive vice president in 1984, president in 1987, and chief operating officer in 1988. In 1990 he was named president and CEO of WPL's parent company, WPL Holdings, Inc., which in addition to the utility company owned Heartland Development Corp., a subsidiary involved in affordable housing development, energy, and environmental services in the United States and Mexico. By this time, Davis was gaining widespread recognition for his managerial skill. He received the Distinguished Alumnus Award from the

University of Chicago's Graduate School of Business in 1993. He also received a Bronze Medal in *Financial World's* "CEO of the Year" competition that year.

While his star was rising in the corporate world, Davis was also developing a keen interest in higher education. He served on the board of regents of the University of Wisconsin from 1987 to 1994. In 1989 he became a lifetime member of the Carnegie Mellon board of trustees, serving as chair for several years. Under Davis' direction, two ambitious diversity programs were launched at Carnegie Mellon. One focused on high school upper classmen in an effort to increase the number of minority students qualified to attend elite colleges. The other was aimed at closing the gender gap in computer science by making the curriculum more attractive to high school girls. Davis also served for a time on the board of trustees of his other alma mater, the University of Chicago.

A November 1994 profile in *Ebony* noted that Davis stood out as one of the very few high-ranking African American's in the utilities industry. The article called Davis the "first Black to head a *Business Week* 1000 company and reportedly the only Black CEO of a major public power utility...." Over the next decade, Davis continued to stand out.

In 1998 WPL merged with two Iowa-based utility companies, Interstate Power Co. and IES Industries, to create a new entity, Alliant Energy Corporation. Davis took the lead in shepherding the company through the merger process, and was tapped as Alliant's first CEO and president. From June of 2002 to June of 2003 Davis served as chair of the board of directors of the Edison Electric Institute, the nationwide association of shareholder-owned electric utility companies. In 2004 he was elected to the U. S. Olympic Committee (USOC) Board, where he sought to improve the USOC's image, which had been stained by scandal in recent years. Through this period, Davis continued to rack up an impressive collection of honors and awards. In 2002 *Fortune* magazine listed him as one of the "50 Most Powerful Black Executives in America." He was the recipient of the Carnegie Mellon Alumni Distinguished Service Award in 2004. He was named one of the "75 Most Powerful Blacks in Corporate America" by *Black Enterprise* magazine in 2005.

In 2005 Davis announced that he was retiring from Alliant Energy, though he planned to retain his role as chair of Alliant's board. Even as he announced his retirement, few expected that Davis would be spending much time in his rocking chair. In addition to his work in the Olympic movement, Davis was still serving on numerous corporate boards of directors, the Federal Reserve Bank of Chicago's Seventh District Advisory Council, and actively pursuing his own philanthropic endeavors through the Davis Family Foundation, which he and Elaine had established a decade earlier.

Davis' so-called retirement did not last long. In December of 2005 it was announced that he would take over as chancellor of the University System of Georgia, making him the first African American to hold the job on a permanent basis, and, perhaps more significantly, marking a triumphant return to the state where just a couple of generations earlier his family had eked out a modest living as farmers. Upon assuming his new job in February of 2006, Davis took charge of a statewide system of 35 pubic colleges and universities serving

253,500 students, employing 35,000 faculty and staff, and with an annual budget of about $5 billion. Davis assumed his new role with a concrete goal in mind. As he told the *Gwinnett Daily Post*: "If education is to be effective, it has to be effective for everyone. I think that's the key to a vibrant middle class." Davis seemed primed to make his goal a reality.

Sources

Periodicals

Atlanta Journal-Constitution, December 11, 2005, p. A1.
Capital Times (Madison, WI), August 23, 2004, p. 1D.
Diverse Issues in Higher Education, December 29, 2005, p. 10.
Ebony, November 1994, p. 70.
Florida Times Union, December 22, 2005, p. B1.

Wisconsin State Journal, July 24, 2005, p. C1; February 1, 2006, p. 45.

On-line

"Errol Davis Biography," *University System of Georgia,* www.usg.edu/chancellor/bio/davis_bio.pdf (August 3, 2006).
"Errol Davis Biography," *United States Olympic Committee,* http://usocpressbox.org/usoc/pressbox.nsf/(staticreports)/Breaking+News/$File/ErrollDavis.pdf?Open (August 3, 2006).
"New University System Chancellor Visits Georgia Gwinnett College," *Gwinnett Daily Post,* www.gwinnettdailypost.com/index.php?s=&url_channel_id=32&url_subchannel_id=&url_article_id=11664&change_well_id=2 (August 3, 2006).

—Bob Jacobson

Quinton de' Alexander

19(?)—

Fashion designer, philanthropist

Fashion designer Quinton de' Alexander knew from a young age that he was a singular individual. When he was only eight years old, he gave away the train set his parents had been sure he would love and begged his father to buy him a sewing machine he found at a garage sale. With persistence, de' Alexander taught himself to sew on that machine, and after a short time was earning money by selling the clothing he designed. Influenced by his father's style and dedication to his community, de' Alexander developed a grace and elegance not only in the clothes he made, but also in his own sense of style and presentation. His personal flair, combined with almost inexhaustible energy, would enable him to succeed in a very competitive business and inspire him to use that success to support a huge variety of charitable causes.

De' Alexander was born in the culturally rich city of New Orleans, Louisiana, and grew up near Bourbon Street in the heart of that city's bustling French Quarter. His father, William, worked for the city's sanitation department and his mother, Yvonne, cooked in a restaurant. Even with both parents working hard, the family sometimes ran short of money. To help out, de' Alexander and his brothers spent many happy hours fishing to bring catfish home for dinner.

Growing up in New Orleans, de' Alexander was captivated by the festive atmosphere of Mardi Gras and the many parades and shows for which the city was famous. He grew to love the beautiful clothes and the glamour of the spectacle. He was also influenced by his father, who took his role as a city employee seriously. Along with working at his job, William de' Alexander also took a leadership role in his church and worked as a precinct captain to help with elections. He was also always stylishly dressed, and de' Alexander admired his father's sharp fashion sense. He began to believe that by dressing elegantly and carrying himself with dignity he could rise above the racism he saw around him.

De' Alexander loved nice clothes, and unlike most children he knew, he much preferred a nice suit to a new toy as a gift. He soon began to feel that he could make beautiful clothes himself. When he was eight years old, he found a sewing machine for sale at a garage sale and persuaded his father to buy it for him. Though his father at first tried to persuade him that boys did not sew, he eventually gave in, and young Quinton took his sewing machine home and began to teach himself to sew and design. His first project was making potholders and curtains for his mother's kitchen. By the time he was fourteen, he was not only designing and sewing his own clothes, but making money selling his creations for both men and women.

While developing his design career, de' Alexander also enjoyed his school years. He was tall and athletic and excelled in football, basketball, and track. He also participated in school theatrical productions where his talent and stage presence often earned him leading roles. At the age of seventeen he wrote, produced, choreographed, and designed the costumes for his own musical revue called, *Oh, What a Night*, highlighting songs from currently popular shows like *Fame* and *Dream Girls*. That same year, he also staged his first fashion show at the prestigious New Orleans Country Club.

When de' Alexander was still a boy, his parents had divorced and his father had moved to Chicago. By the time he was in high school, de' Alexander was a regular visitor to the Midwestern metropolis, both to visit his father and to attend fashion conventions and shows. He finished his high school education by graduating from Chicago's Cabrini/Hales Franciscan Alternative High School.

While the carnivals of New Orleans had been a good place to begin his fashion career, de' Alexander felt that he would need to move to a larger city to develop his career. He showed his designs at fashion conventions, where boutique owners and designers alike were impressed with his dramatic and sophisticated clothing. De' Alexander soon settled permanently in Chicago and began to sell his designs through the city's upscale clothing stores, establishing his own design house, Chez de' Alexander, in 1987.

Within a few years, de' Alexander had become one of the nation's top fashion designers, hosting regular black-tie, or formal dress, fashion shows so elaborate that they were often described as "extravaganzas." Usually held in exclusive Chicago venues such as the DuSable Museum of African History, de' Alexander's fashion shows frequently have dramatic themes, such as his 2000 show which was a pageant of Biblical history. For many years, de' Alexander has been a featured designer in the famous Ebony Fashion Fair, a cross-country African American fashion show sponsored in cities throughout the United States by *Ebony* magazine since 1958.

Though the world of high fashion traditionally favored the young, thin, and wealthy, de' Alexander did not design his clothing for such a limited audience. He took pride in creating "nice clothes everybody can wear," as he explained to *CBB*. His elegant gowns and suits were as flattering to older and larger people as to tall, thin runway models.

Although the cost of de' Alexander's original designs made them generally available only to those in the upper class, he took care to honor his own working-class roots by involving himself in his community. A generous philanthropist in the Chicago area, de' Alexander has raised money for a wide variety of causes, such as the Lupus Foundation, La Rabida Children's Hospital and Child Abuse Center, and the DuSable Museum. But de' Alexander gave much more than money to the organizations closest to his heart. He served on the board of directors of Concerned Citizens Inc./Mothers House, an organization that supports single mothers, and devoted time and energy to other organizations for at-risk parents, such as the Illinois Department of Human Services (Teen Parent Services-Central) and Real Fathers Real Men.

De' Alexander combined fashion and philanthropy in inventive ways. He regularly offered free seats at his exclusive fashion shows to those who could not otherwise afford to attend. To bring some glamour and fun into the lives of young single mothers, he arranged "spa days" with makeovers and modeling lessons, presenting a designer prom dress to the teen mom with the best grades. He created similar programs for older people, building self-esteem in those whom society often ignores by staging fashion shows where seniors model designer originals.

Another side of de' Alexander's community work was inspired by his own solitary struggle to learn the skills he needed to succeed in the field of fashion design. Through an organization he founded called Creativity United, Inc., de' Alexander helped aspiring artists to gain a foothold in all facets of the design industry. Creativity United also hosted the Midwest Fashion and Beauty Designer Awards, an annual event recognizing the achievements of both established and beginning designers.

In spite of his success, de' Alexander has continued to run his design business in a very personal way. He operated his house of design, Chez de' Alexander, out of his former residence in Chicago. Along with his demanding work schedule and his tireless charitable work, de' Alexander has kept alive his love of the theater. Twice a year he and his partner Ellis Foster staged musical shows for which de' Alexander frequently designed the choreography, costumes and sets. In his free time, de' Alexander enjoyed collecting antiques and continued to sew all of his own clothes.

Sources

Periodicals

Chicago Defender, April 3, 1999, p. 21; October 26, 2000, p. 13; November 11, 2000, p. 17; December 2, 2000, p. 18; May 19, 2001, p. 21; October 18, 2001, p. 15; April 15, 2004, p. 9.
Ebony, February 2005, pp. 137-40.
Jet, October 23, 2000. pp. 12-18; October 1, 2001, pp. 32-9.

On-line

"Ebony Show Returns with Panache," *Fresno Bee,* www.fresnobee.com/lifestyle/story/8394619p-9228060c.html (accessed March 1, 2006).

Other

Additional information for this profile was obtained through an interview with Quinton de' Alexander on March 9, 2006.

—Tina Gianoulis

Sean Garrett

1979—

Songwriter, music producer, vocalist

Not long after multiple Grammy Award-nominated songwriter Sean Garrett decided he wasn't going to take "no" for an answer, his meteoric success ensured that he wouldn't have to. Known for writing chart-busting hit songs, Garrett has no shortage of A-list artists saying "yes" to making hits with his help. Garrett collaborated with such talents as Bon Jovi, Beyoncé, Kanye West, Jennifer Lopez, Janet Jackson, Ciara, Nelly, Chris Brown, Mary J. Blige, Jamie Foxx, Ricky Martin, Fantasia, 112, Christina Milan, Donell Jones, Amerie, Mario Winans, and Christina Milian in 2005, placing his singles in the #1 position on every music chart in the country. Garrett is considered an innovator, standing at the crossroads of R&B, Pop, and Hip-Hop, writing and producing music that fans across genres are excited about. Garrett wrote three hit songs in 2004: "Goodies," "Lose My Breath," and the hit single "Yeah!," which he co-wrote for Usher's multi-platinum *Confessions* album. The single "Yeah!" won BMI's 2005 Urban Song of the Year Award. Garrett penned five songs on the Destiny's Child album *Destiny Fulfilled*. In 2006 Garrett started off the year by occupying the top three spots on the Billboard Hot 100 Chart with his "Grillz" by Nelly, "Run It!" by Chris Brown, and "Check On It" by Beyoncé.

Garrett was born in 1979 in Atlanta, Georgia, and spent his early years in Philadelphia. His mother was the first to notice that her young son had musical talent. To nurture that talent she entered Garrett as a singer in local talent contests. He loved performing and quickly decided he would become an entertainer. It took him some time before he figured out exactly what kind of

entertainer he would be; but, as he noted in an interview with *Contemporary Black Biography (CBB)*, he "enjoyed every minute" of his explorations.

During his teen years, Garrett's father, a military man, moved the family to Germany, where they lived in Munich, Mainz, and Nuremberg. These years were difficult ones, but they greatly influenced Garrett's music, and he learned a lot about family. "Each time we moved we were all at a different place in our lives," he told *CBB*. "My father would be concentrating on his new job. My mother worked for the government, so she would be dealing with having to leave her friends and work, and my brother and I would be leaving all our friends again. Sometimes it was difficult, and I'm a little emotional, so it does come through in the music." For Garrett, his music provided an escape. Through his family's moves Garrett kept on singing and writing, all the while listening to such performers as Michael Jackson, New Edition, and Bell Biv DeVoe. Understanding the importance of great songwriting in addition to great vocals, Garrett studied the work of songwriters like Barry White, Quincy Jones, R. Kelly, Lenny Kravitz, and Babyface. Garrett wanted to cover all his bases and he had the talent to do it.

By the time Garrett turned 17 he had penned plenty of songs and was looking for a recording contract. Over the next few years, he came very close to making it. He traveled to Europe and won a brief contract with Ariola/BMG; soon, he had nearly inked a deal with Warner Brothers in the United States, but the deal fell through and he was left without a recording deal. These

At a Glance . . .

Born Sean Garrett in 1979, in Atlanta, Georgia. *Education:* Attended the University of Maryland.

Career: Signed with Ariola/BMG, Europe, late 1990s; worked as a mortgage broker, early 2000s; HITCO, Atlanta, GA, songwriter and producer, 2004–.

Awards: BMI Urban Song of the Year, 2005, for "Yeah!"

Addresses: *Office*—HITCO Music Inc., 500 Bishop Street NW, Suite A4, Atlanta, GA 30318-4380. *Agent*—d.baron Media Relations, Inc., 1411 Cloverfield Blvd., Santa Monica, CA 90404.

two near-brushes with fame left Garrett somewhat disillusioned, and he decided to make a move to pursue a more secure career. He described the experience on a Web site maintained by his agent, d. baron Media: "After that whole experience, I took a couple of years off, went to college and had a lucrative job as a mortgage broker but I quickly realized that I was a creative person and you can not keep creative people in a structured setting; it's just not going to happen, especially when they feel other things going on in their hearts." Leaving his brief career in business, he returned to honing his skills as a singer and songwriter. He credits the death of his mother in 2003 as the event that made him get really serious about his career. Garrett had always been very close to his mother. Her death gave him determination and made him unwilling to accept obstacles in his path. That's when Garrett decided that "no" would not work if he wanted to achieve the level of success he'd always wanted. It didn't take long for Garrett's resolve to pay dividends.

In 2004 Garrett received a double stroke of luck, penning a ballad for Motown artist Latif and watching his new single "Yeah!," performed by celebrated artist Usher, become one of the biggest hits of the year. The song was nominated for three Grammy Awards and was named BMI's 2005 Urban Song of the Year. Buoyed by the success of these songs, Garrett was soon sought after as a hit maker by the industry's top talent. Drawing praise from his peers, this musical genius makes the job look easy. His fan base continues to widen as continues to write and now produce.

Success has brought challenges as well as rewards. Garrett said that one of the big surprises was how his success made some people around him change. "They think you've changed," Garrett said, "when the truth is, they've changed." Despite earning accolades following his first hit with Motown, Garrett keeps himself grounded. He knows the importance of family and has a good sense for handling the business side of his career. "You can't play with your craft," Garrett told *CBB*. "I know I have to deliver." With so much industry recognition so quickly, big things are expected of Garrett, but he has his own predictions for his future. "God is ahead," he said. "The things that God did for me come with a price as far as helping people. I want to help someone else. I want to help them become me, and do what I've done." For now, he's doing just that for newcomers in the business. Garrett is executive producer for young artists like 17-year-old Detroit native Tierra Marie, and he has written eight songs for her upcoming debut album.

Selected works

Singles

"Yeah!," 2004.
"Goodies," 2004.
"Grillz," 2004.
"Loose My Breath," 2004.
"Gimmie That," 2005.
"Ain't No Way," 2005.
"Enough Crying," 2005.
"Check On It," 2006.
"Run It," 2006.

Sources

On-line

"Songwriter Sean Garrett Poses Triple Threat on the Charts," *BMI,* www.bmi.com/news/200601/20060130a.asp (August 8, 2006).
"Sean Garrett," *d. baron Media Relations, Inc.*, www.dbaronmedia.com/index.php/artists/seangarrett/news/020805 (August 8, 2006).

Other

Additional information for this profile was obtained through an interview with Sean Garrett on March 15, 2006.

—Sharon Melson Fletcher

Bernie Grant

1944-2000

Politician, activist

Bernie Grant was arguably the most important black politician in British history. A passionate advocate for social justice and the rights of minorities, Grant was known for an outspoken style that made some of his staid colleagues in Parliament uncomfortable. While that style made him some enemies over the years, it earned him even more admirers, particularly among Britain's ethnic and immigrant communities, for whom he was a leading voice in the halls of government.

Bernard Alexander Montgomery Grant was born on February 17, 1944, in Georgetown, Guyana (known at the time as British Guiana). His parents, Eric and Lily, were both schoolteachers. They named their son after two British World War II generals whom they admired. Grant attended a series of government-run schools, and then enrolled at St. Stanislaus College, a Jesuit school in his hometown of Georgetown. As a young man, he worked at a desk job with the Demerara Bauxite Company in Guyana.

Quit College in Face of Discrimination

The Grant family moved to Britain in 1963, and Bernie took a job as a clerk with British Railways. From 1965 to 1967 he studied at Tottenham Technical College. From there, he moved on the Heriot-Watt University in Edinburgh, Scotland to study engineering, but he dropped out of the program in protest in 1969 when he learned that the school's work experience program in South Africa was offered only to white students.

Having abandoned his engineering aspirations, Grant went to work as an international telephonist (also called a switchboard operator.) He quickly became involved in the labor movement, working with the Union of Post Office Workers to improve conditions for himself and his coworkers. Labor organizing was soon a consuming passion for Grant. In 1971 he joined the Socialist Labour League (which later became the Workers Revolutionary Party), a far-left political group. Three years later, however, he switched over to the mainstream Labour Party, and rapidly worked his way up the local organizational ranks. His first election to public office came in 1978, when he became a member of Haringey (the London borough that includes the Tottenham area) Council. Within a year he was named Deputy Leader of the Council. In 1978 he also took a full-time position with the National Union of Public Employees (NUPE), the main British labor union representing those who work in the public sector.

From the start of his involvement in the labor movement, Grant was particularly concerned with racial inequities. He was one of the founders of the Black Trades Unionists Solidarity Movement (BTUSM), and from 1981 to 1984 he worked full time for that organization. In 1985 Grant was elected Leader of the Haringey Council, making him the first-ever black leader of a local unit of government in British history. Grant got his first taste of nationwide publicity that year, when he expressed sympathy for young rioters in the Broadwater Farm area of Tottenham who were protesting against perceived police harassment and excessive violence. Media outlets across Britain attributed to Grant the remark: "What the police got was a bloody good hiding." While he claimed that the remark was reported out of context, Grant was widely criticized in the national press for his position. However, he refused to back down, even after the Tories—the common nickname for the Conservative Party, Britain's other major political party—and about 1,000 white Tottenham union members demanded that he resign from Parliament. The local Tottenham police chief came to Grant's defense, pointing to his long-standing role as a peacekeeper in the community, but his reputation nevertheless suffered. The *Sun* newspaper dubbed him "Barmy Bernie," (Crazy Bernie) according to the *BBC News,* a nickname that stuck for the rest of his career.

In the wake of the Broadwater Farm incident, Grant became increasingly frustrated by the Labour Party's lukewarm support, and its ongoing failure to field black candidates for Parliament. He was quoted in an October 1985 *New York Times* article as saying that race is "the one issue that the so-called extreme left and the right wing get together on quite happily…. They both adopt the position that we're all one class, the working class, and there is no race problem here, which of course is arrant nonsense." He called white, liberal Members of Parliament hypocrites for supporting the struggles of black people only up to the point where

they started threatening their hold on those Parliamentary seats, which represented largely minority constituencies.

Elected to Formerly All-White Parliament

Grant was elected to Parliament in 1987, becoming one of the first black members of British national government, along with four other blacks elected that year to the institution that had had all white members for the previous 65 years. He secured the nomination for his seat, which represented Tottenham, by toppling incumbent Norman Atkinson, the former treasurer of the Labour Party. Grant attracted a great deal of attention, both positive and negative, when he entered his first ceremonial opening of a parliamentary session clad in traditional African garb. Grant wasted no time positioning himself as the Parliament's most vocal advocate for racial justice. He was a founder of the Parliamentary Black Caucus, inspired by the U.S. Congressional Black Caucus, and he worked to forge ties with black leaders and politicians around the world. He traveled widely, especially to regions with largely black populations, such as Africa and the Caribbean. In 1990 traveled to South Africa, along with American activist Rev. Jesse Jackson, to visit Nelson Mandela on the day he was released from his 27 years in prison. He also spent eight days in Iraq that year as head of a peace mission organized by the Afro-Asian Solidarity Movement. The following year, he toured northern Africa, including a visit to Libya.

In Parliament, Grant was outspoken and at times confrontational in his campaign against such race-based issues as police harassment, fair housing, educational equity, health care access, resources for inner-city neighborhoods, and public policy pertaining to refugees. He explained his 1990 vote against Britain's participation in the Gulf War in terms of race, arguing that the reason the United Nations was considering kicking Iraqis out of Kuwait but not considering kicking Russians out of Lithuania was entirely a matter of skin color. "If we are talking about white people invading a white country, United States and British forces would never be involved as they are in the Gulf today," Grant was quoted as saying in a 1990 *Independent* article.

Even within his own Labour Party, Grant often found himself doing battle against the majority. Other black politicians, for whom Grant was a trailblazer, embraced the moderate direction taken by the Party under Prime Minister Tony Blair. Grant, on the other hand, remained true to his populist, labor activist roots. He was dismayed by his party's Centrist policies, and sought to raise consciousness among his peers about issues affecting minorities in Britain. While he was often disenchanted with the workings of the government, he commanded the respect—albeit grudging in many cases—of his peers. He was made chair of the All Party

Group on Race and Community, and of the British Caribbean Group. In 1990 Grant founded the Standing Conference on Racism in Europe. In 1997 he was named to the Select Committee on International Development. Grant also served on the Home Secretary's Race Relations Forum in 1998. In addition to these posts, Grant was one of the leading voices for the Africa Reparations Movement in Britain. He took the lead in organizing major conferences among politicians, activists, and scholars to forge a pan-European black agenda.

Played Peacemaker Role Late in Career

While Grant was widely regarded as a firebrand who shot from the hip, he also demonstrated skill as a diplomat who knew how to defuse potentially explosive situations. This skill was on display in 1993, when he intervened in the matter of Joy Gardner, a Jamaican immigrant who died of asphyxiation during a raid by immigration officers. Gardner's death outraged the black immigrant community in Britain, and the event brought tensions between minorities and those hostile to immigrants to a boiling point. Grant, who was widely perceived as being anti-police, was able to step in and convince angry protestors not to escalate the situation. The officers were eventually acquitted of all charges stemming from Gardner's death.

Grant's health began to decline in the late 1990s. In 1998 he suffered through both heart bypass surgery and kidney failure. Nevertheless, he continued to serve in Parliament, remaining as feisty as ever, at least to the degree his health allowed. In his final year of service, he worked to establish a major arts facility in Tottenham, the International Centre for the Performing Arts. Unfortunately, he did not live to see the project's completion. Grant died on April 8, 2000. Some 5,000 colleagues and admirers attended his funeral, including high profile British athletes and musicians.

His views may have mellowed a bit in his final years in Parliament; by then, Grant was renowned more for his integrity and effectiveness than for his anger and outspokenness. Upon Grant's death the entire British establishment was singing the praises of a man who was once viewed as a dangerous and reckless voice of the far left. Prime Minister Tony Blair called Grant "an inspiration to Black British communities everywhere," according to *Chronicle World*. It is not an exaggeration to say, as was said at the funeral, that Bernie Grant changed the course of British history.

Sources

Periodicals

Ebony, March 1988, pp. 76-84.
Guardian (London), April 10, 2000, p. 20.
Independent (London), April 10, 2000, p. 6.
New Statesman, April 17, 2000, p. 24.
New York Times, October 28, 1985.
Times (London), April 10, 2000, p. 19.

On-line

"Bernie Grant a Controversial Figure," *BBC News,* http://news.bbc.co.uk/2/hi/uk_news/politics/706403.stm (July 10, 2006).
"The First Black Parliamentarians in Our Times," *Chronicle World,* www.chronicleworld.org (July 10, 2006).
"History: Black Pathfinders in Modern British Politics—The Hon. Bernie Grant and Lord David Pitt," *Chronicle World,* www.chronicleworld.org (July 10, 2006).
"Labour MP Bernie Grant dies," *BBC News,* http://news.bbc.co.uk/1/hi/uk_politics/706394.stm (July 10, 2006).
"Bernie Grant Archives," *Archives Hub,* www.archiveshub.ac.uk/news/04060901.html (July 10, 2006).

—Bob Jacobson

Denyce Graves

1964—

Opera singer

Graves, Denyce, photograph. AP Images.

Mezzo-soprano Denyce Graves has realized *USA Today*'s prediction that she would become one of the twenty-first century's operatic superstars. As Bizet's sultry, passionate Carmen, she won glowing reviews worldwide. Jerry Schwartz noted in the *Atlanta Journal-Constitution* that critics have called her Carmen "one of the most stunning performances ever of that storied role." The *Wall Street Journal* called her "the hottest Carmen on the opera circuit today," and Martin Feinstein, former general director of the Washington Opera, stated simply, "she is the definitive Carmen." But in an industry where singers often get pigeonholed by particular roles, Graves resisted being limited. "I'm more than Carmen," Graves noted in the *Los Angeles Times* in 1999. She is indeed. Graves' goal for herself, as she told the *Philadelphia Tribune,* is "artistic independence."

Rose to Opera Stardom Early

Following a three-year apprenticeship with the Houston Grand Opera, where she made her debut as Hansel in *Hansel and Gretel* in 1989, Graves took the operatic world by storm. She has sung with tenor legends Placido Domingo, Luciano Pavarotti, and Jose Carreras. She has appeared on the stages of the world's most famous opera houses, including the Vienna State Opera, La Scala in Milan, and the Royal Opera in London's Covent Garden. Cultivating her role as Carmen in Minnesota from 1991, Graves made her debut at New York's Metropolitan Opera to critical acclaim in the fall of 1995, in the title role of *Carmen.*

Reviewers have been effusive in their descriptions of Graves's voice. In 1997 Tony Kornheiser wrote in the *Washington Post*, "Denyce Graves's voice is spectacular. It's so clear and clean you feel you can see through it." Herbert Kupferberg described it as "sumptuous but mercifully light and flexible" in Parade in 1994 and in a 1994 article for *American Record Guide*, David Reynolds called it "a full and voluptuous instrument indeed." Others were more specific. Reviewer Anthony Tommasini wrote in the *New York Times* in 1995 that Graves has "a classic mezzo-soprano voice with dusky colorings and a wide range, from her chesty low voice to her gleaming top notes." Schwartz described it as "quite distinctive—rich, burnished, deep." He concluded, "Her wonderfully tasteful musicianship allows it to project with a directness that few singers in any age have been able to manage."

Emerged from Difficult Childhood

Denyce Antionette Graves was born March 7, 1964, to Charles Graves and Dorothy (Middleton) Graves-Kenner. The middle child of three, Denyce and her siblings were raised by their mother on Galveston Street in southwest Washington, D.C. Charles Graves walked out on his family when Denyce was not yet two and his youngest daughter not yet born. Dorothy Graves worked hard to support her family, first as a laundress and then as a clerk typist at Federal City College—now the University of the District of Columbia. "Our neigh-

borhood was tough and chaotic... and very poor," Graves told Marilyn Milloy of *Essence*. "Violence, drugs, hopelessness, despair—it was all there. Yet with all that, my mother held her ground and built a solid foundation for our little family."

Dorothy Graves built that foundation on a bedrock of love, discipline, and faith. She was strict, making sure her children had no spare time in which to find trouble. Regular chores and homework filled much of their after-school time, and Dorothy took care of the rest by scheduling various activities for the evenings, such as sewing, report writing, gospel singing, and church attendance. "Thursday night was always for our singing group. I loved to sing early on," Graves told *Essence*. Popular music was forbidden in the Graves home, as were certain television shows that Dorothy felt portrayed blacks in a demeaning manner. As a result of this sheltered upbringing, Denyce was neither familiar with nor especially interested in whatever was considered "cool" at the time. Consequently, she stood out as different from her peers. Classmates called her "Hollywood" merely because she was aloof. Her mother balanced the discipline with encouragement. She told her children they were special, that their throats and brains had been kissed by God, that they could do anything.

Graves's first mentor was her elementary school music teacher, Judith Grove, who, through a series of job changes, followed her to Friendship Junior High and on to high school. Impressed by the girl's commitment to hard work and her serious attitude toward music, in 1977 Grove encouraged her to apply to Duke Ellington School of the Arts, a public performing arts high school in Georgetown. Graves won admittance by passing an audition. Although her mother had serious qualms at the prospect, Graves did not.

Found Refuge in School

She felt immediately at home at Ellington. She no longer stood out; all the students there were committed, working toward similar goals. She recalled in an article in the *Washingtonian*, "I felt that I could finally breathe. There have been few things in my life where I said 'This is it,' but when I walked through that door, there was a rightness in my bones about it."

While a student at Ellington, Graves saw her first opera. She was 14. Attending a dress rehearsal at the Kennedy Center for Beethoven's *Fidelio*, she was captivated. Some time after that, a teacher gave her a recording of Marilyn Horne singing an aria from the opera *Cavalleria Rusticana*. Playing the aria until she had it memorized, Graves determined to become an opera singer.

Graves finished high school in just two years, graduating in 1981. She was offered scholarships to several colleges, but chose the Oberlin College Conservatory in Ohio. The school had offered only a partial scholarship, so she worked several jobs to make ends meet. At Oberlin she studied under renowned voice teacher Helen Hodam. Reaching mandatory retirement age in 1984, Hodam left Oberlin to teach at the New England Conservatory of Music in Boston, and Graves followed her there. Working up to three jobs at a time to support herself, it would take her four more years to graduate. She earned her Bachelor of Music in 1988.

Before she graduated, Graves entered the Metropolitan Opera Regional Auditions in 1986. She won. "I had to win," she told the *New York Times*. "I was four months behind in my rent. I couldn't pay for the rented dress I was wearing." When she got to New York to sing in the finals, however, she was stricken with a mysterious throat ailment. It got worse as she sang. Forced to withdraw from the competition, she saw 11 specialists before the problem was diagnosed as a treatable thyroid condition. Disheartened, she took a secretarial position and did not sing again for a year.

Launched Career

Then Graves received a series of phone calls that would change her life. The Houston Grand Opera called to invite her to audition for its opera studio, a young artists training program. The disaster of the Metro finals was too fresh an experience, and Graves said thank you, but her singing days were over. Houston called again a couple of months later and renewed the offer. Her answer was still thanks, but no thanks. Six weeks passed and Houston called a third time. This time, friends persuaded her that this was meant to be, so she flew to Texas to audition. She had not sung in more than a year. She took her time warming up, and then sang Carmen's seguidilla. *New York* quoted Graves as saying of the experience, "That day I sang better than when I was well and in good voice. It was a revelation from God."

Graves spent three years in Houston. She told *Essence* that her life changed completely. "My job there was to do supporting roles or cover for other mezzos as well as grunge work—singing in the malls at Christmas time, things like that," she said. "But I also met the great tenor Placido Domingo, and from that point on things began to happen." Impressed with her talent and drive, Domingo became her mentor.

Her debut in a lead role came in 1989 in Houston, as Hansel in *Hansel and Gretel*. Graves was invited to sing in the Tucker Foundation's 1990 Gala Concert, which was broadcast nationally in 1991 on PBS's Great Performances. Building on her Houston apprenticeship, she has proven herself a major talent ever since. She has sung leading roles in all the most respected opera houses in the world.

Wins Worldwide Acclaim with Carmen

Although she had sung other roles early in her career, her characterization of Carmen generated the most

excitement. By early 1996 she had sung in more than 30 productions of that opera. Hailed by enthusiastic critics as "the world's reigning Carmen," it has become her signature role. In a 1995 review in the *New York Times*, Tommasini wrote, "She is a compelling stage actress who exude[s] the sensuality that any Carmen must have but few do." Tim Page observed in the *Washington Post*, "We do not merely listen to her Carmen, we experience it; she not only sings the role of the fiery Gypsy girl, she embodies her." She made her much-anticipated debut at New York's Metropolitan Opera in 1995 as Carmen. Linda Killian noted in the *Washingtonian* in 1996, "Whenever an opera house anywhere in the world thinks about doing a production of Carmen, Graves is at the top of the list. She has reached the point where she says no to Carmen as often as she says yes." The reason, Killian explained, is that "Domingo and others have warned her that she mustn't become typecast, that she needs to expand her repertoire and her voice by doing other roles." Graves explained the benefit of other roles to her voice in *New York*. "Mozart and bel canto—I swear to God, they make your voice better. They're difficult, especially for a voice like mine. My voice is broad. It's fat. I need to work to line it up, to make it skinny. With Carmen you have to watch out. It's so theatrical. It can take the sheen off the voice and get it out of line, make it hard."

And she has found various roles, including Baba the Turk in Stravinsky's *The Rake's Progress*, Charlotte in Massenet's *Werther*, and Dalila in Saint-Saens's *Samson et Dalila*. In 2005, Graves introduced a new role to the stage in the world premier of *Margaret Garner*, the story of a slave girl, at the Michigan Opera Theatre in Detroit. She has sung at the White House on numerous occasions and performed with Placido Domingo on his *Concert for the Planet Earth*, which was broadcast worldwide from the United States summit on the environment in Rio de Janeiro in 1992. Her performances have also been featured on PBS several times.

Carefully Crafts Image

Graves is conscious of being a role model for black children, just as Leontyne Price was an early inspiration for her. She is also grateful to those who broke the operatic color barrier before her. Her own struggles to reach the top, she told *Ebony*, "are nothing in comparison to the suffering of those people who allowed me to be in the position that I'm in today." In spite of her meteoric rise to stardom, Graves has encountered racism, and believes she has lost out on roles because she is African American. And, having pursued a career in what has been traditionally an elitist art form dominated and controlled by whites, she has been criticized by blacks for wanting to be "white." Responding to those who would try to pigeonhole her as one thing or another, Graves had this to say to the *Atlanta Journal-Constitution* in 1996: "Anyone who thinks the world of international opera is any easier for black people than anything else has never been there. But bitterness can eat a hole in your soul." Killian noted in *The Washingtonian* that Graves strives to leave race aside as she hones her craft. She wrote, "Graves does not want to be a black opera singer. She wants to be an opera singer who happens to be black."

In 1990 Graves married classical guitar importer David Perry. They met the year before while performing with the Wolf Trap Opera Company in Virginia. Perry was a lutenist in the orchestra. He travels with Graves much of the time, handling details for her and calming her nerves before performances by playing classical guitar for her. Perry created Carmen Productions to promote Graves' career through television and recording projects. "My husband is a rock in this whole crazy turbulence of a career," Graves told the *Christian Science Monitor*. They have a home in Leesburg, Virginia.

Having reached the top, Graves's struggle continues. "The key in this business is not only about getting your foot in the door," she told *Essence*, "it's about demanding such a standard of excellence from yourself that you stay in the room. The ultimate goal, in my opinion, is for people to flock to the theatre not only to see *Carmen*, but to see Denyce Graves." To enhance her career, Graves added steady bookings for concerts, recitals, and recordings to balance her work. More than just a way to keep her "in the room," these activities served another purpose. As quoted in *Afro-American Red Star*, Graves said, "I think it's important to use the voice in different ways. A steady diet of opera is very heavy for the voice."

Graves understands the power of her talent. She made a national name for herself. President and Mrs. Bush requested that she sing at a national memorial service held at the Washington National Cathedral after the terrorist attacks in 2001. She branched out from the music industry to become what *Opera News* described as "sort of a diva-as-mini-corporation." She launched perfume and jewelry lines, and was subject of a 2003 PBS documentary called *Denyce Graves: Breaking the Rules*. Appointed a Cultural Ambassador for the United States in 2003, Graves also represents the State Department on international missions of peace. If her career thus far is any indication, Denyce Graves will remain in the limelight for years to come.

Selected discography

Concert For Planet Earth, Sony Classical, 1993.
Otello, Deutsche Grammophon, 1993.
Hamlet, EMI, 1993.

Recital Denyce Graves: Heroines de l'Opera romantique Francais, FNAC Music, 1993.
Angels Watching Over Me, NPR Classics, 1998.
Denyce Graves: A Cathedral Christmas, PBS Productions, 1998.
Voce di Donna, BMG/RCA Red Seal, 1999.
Memorial, Carmen Productions, 2001.
Lost Days: Music in the Latin Style, BMG/RCA Red Seal, 2003.
Denyce Graves: French Opera Arias, Virgin Classics, 2004.
Kaleidoscope, Carmen Productions, 2004.

Sources

Periodicals

American Record Guide, September/October 1994.
Atlanta Journal-Constitution, November 16, 1997, November 17, 1997.
Christian Science Monitor, July 24, 1996.
Cincinnati Enquirer, February 21, 2003.
Classic FM, November 2002.
Ebony, February 1996.
Essence, September 1996.
Glamour, December 1997.
Los Angeles Times, January 21, 1996; September 5, 1999.
New York, September 11, 1995.
New York Post, January 10, 2003.
New York Times, December 28, 1997, October 14, 1995, October 9, 1995.
Opera News, September 2001.
Opera Night, May/June 1998.
Parade, May 29, 1994.
People Weekly, October 23, 1995.
Reader's Digest, February 1997.
Tampa Tribune, February 10, 2003.
Theatre Bio, Suzanne Stephens Arts Services, June 1998.
Wall Street Journal, April 4, 1995.
Washingtonian, December 1996.
Washington Post, January 19, 1997, June 8, 1996, October 9, 1995, March 26, 1995, February 24, 1991, September 28, 1989.

On-line

"Denyce Graves: Breaking the Rules," *The National Music Education Site: WHYY*, www.whyy.org/education/denycegraves/about_show.html (July 12, 2006).

—Ellen Dennis French and Sara Pendergast

Bunnatine "Bunny" Greenhouse

1944—

Army procurement officer, whistleblower

Bunny Greenhouse's story would be compelling enough even if she had never become caught up in controversy. She rose from a childhood in poverty to become one of the highest-ranking civilians working for the US military. It was her decision to follow her conscience and blow the whistle on alleged abuses in military contracting, however, that put Greenhouse in the news. By exposing apparent favoritism in the awarding of millions of dollars in Army contracts to well-connected companies, Greenhouse touched a nerve in the highest levels of the American defense industry and government. Her integrity may have cost her her career.

Learned Drive from Family

Bunnatine (Bunny) Greenhouse was born Bunnatine Hayes on July 22, 1944. She grew up in the poor, segregated, cotton town of Rayville, Louisiana in the Mississippi River delta. What her parents, Chris and Savannah Hayes, lacked in education—Chris, a cotton processor by trade, did not make it past second grade—they made up for in perseverance and drive. They instilled in each of their six children a sense of self-confidence that yielded amazing results. Greenhouse's older sister, a scholar in linguistics and literature, became one of the first black professors at Louisiana State University. An older brother also earned a PhD and taught at Baton Rouge's Southern University. Her

most illustrious sibling, however, made his mark outside of the academic realm. Younger brother Elvin Hayes led the Washington Bullets to the 1978 National Basketball Association championship, and has been included on nearly every list ever compiled of the greatest basketball players of all time.

Greenhouse graduated as valedictorian of her high school class, and went on to graduate at the top of her class from Southern University in 1965, taking only three years to earn a degree in Mathematics. That year, she married her college sweetheart, Aloysius Greenhouse. Foreshadowing her own career, her husband became an army procurement officer. His job, which entailed overseeing the purchase of various supplies and services, took him to postings across the United States and over to Europe. Bunny moved around with him, taking jobs teaching math at the high school and college levels. The only substantial period they were apart was during Aloysius's two tours of duty in Vietnam, for which he earned the Silver Star. Bunny returned to teach at her hometown high school in 1967, the year the school was integrated. The white students there had never encountered a black teacher before.

"At the time, I didn't quite know what to make of a black person who didn't have a hoe in their hand," one former student from that period, Miriam Lane Davey, was quoted as recalling in an October 2005 *Washing-*

At a Glance . . .

Born Bunnatine Hayes on July 22, 1944, in Rayville, Louisiana; married Aloysius Greenhouse, 1965; three children. *Education:* Southern University, BS, mathematics, 1965; University of Central Texas, MS, Business Management, 1982; George Washington University, MS, Engineering Management, 1995; Industrial College of the Armed Forces, MS, National Resources Strategy, 1996.

Career: Math teacher, college instructor, several states, 1965-81; Dynalectron Corporation, Ft. Worth, TX, contract administrator, 1981-83; Dallas/Ft. Worth Airport Board, contract administrator, 1983; US Army, procurement advisor, Seckenheim, Germany, 1983-86; Director of Contracting, Carlisle Barracks, PA, 1986-87; procurement analyst/advisor, various stations, 1987-91; Chief, Analysis and Evaluation Offices, Pentagon, 1991-95, Chief, Procurement Management Review Team, 1996, Deputy for Armaments and Munitions, 1996-97; US Army Corps of Engineers, Principal Assistant Responsible for Contracting, 1997-2005.

Memberships: National Contract Management Association; Project Management Institute; Armed Forces Communications and Electronic Association; Defense Systems Management College Alumni Association.

Awards: Outstanding Young Women of America, 1975.

Addresses: *Office*—US Army Corps of Engineers, 441 G. Street, NW, Washington, DC 20314-1000.

ton Post article. "She had been somewhere else, she was cosmopolitan, she was sophisticated. It really changed my viewpoint...."

Began Career in Government

After 16 years as a teacher, Greenhouse undertook a career shift in 1981, entering government service as an Army procurement official. Starting at the bottom of the bureaucratic ladder as a Department of Defense procurement intern, she specialized in the minute details of contracting, working long hours while also raising three children. She used that experience to land a job as supervisor of contract pricing and administration with Dynalectron Corporation in Fort Worth,

Texas. She remained in that position until 1983. Along the way, she somehow found the time to go back to school, earning a master's degree in business management from the University of Central Texas in 1982. In 1983 she took a position as contract administrator with the Dallas/Fort Worth Airport Board, but before the year was over she had moved on to a new job as a US Army procurement advisor based in Germany. Back in the United States in 1986, she advanced to a series of progressively higher posts within the Army's procurement system over the next several years. From 1991 to 1996 she served in high-ranking civilian procurement positions at the Pentagon. As she worked her way up the ladder, Greenhouse picked up two additional master's degrees: one in engineering management from George Washington University and one in national resources strategy from the National Defense University at the Industrial College of the Armed Forces.

In 1997, Lt. Gen. Joe Ballard, the first black chief engineer at the Army Corps of Engineers, hired Greenhouse to the position of Principal Assistant Responsible for Contracting (PARC), the highest procurement post at the Corps and one of its highest civilian offices. In this job, Greenhouse oversaw the handling of billions of dollars worth of government contracts. In addition to her impressive credentials, Ballard favored Greenhouse for the job for another reason—he hoped to break up the "old boys network" of informal contracting arrangements that tended to result in the awarding of lucrative contracts to a handful of favored, well-connected companies.

For her first few years on the job, Greenhouse received dazzling performance reviews, toiling behind the scenes to save taxpayers millions of dollars. As the war in Iraq heated up, however, Greenhouse became troubled by how some of the Corps' biggest contracts were being awarded. A stickler for rules that existed to ensure a fair playing field for all companies competing for contracts, Greenhouse saw a pattern of favoritism emerging in dealings with Halliburton, the company formerly run by Vice President Dick Cheney. In March of 2003 the Corps awarded—over Greenhouse's objection–a Halliburton subsidiary, Kellogg Brown & Root (KBR, which is now its official name), a five-year, no-bid contract worth $7 billion to repair oil fields. Later that year, she complained when Corps leaders approved KBR's charges for fuel imports to Iraq after the Pentagon's own auditors said the charges were inflated by more than $61 million. The following spring, Greenhouse questioned the extension—with no bids entertained from other companies–of an expiring Halliburton logistics contract in the Balkans.

Blew the Whistle

Greenhouse's complaints of favoritism toward Halliburton made her a pariah in the military community. Suddenly Greenhouse, whose work had been rated as exemplary throughout her career, was threatened with demotion on the basis of poor performance. Rather than back down, Greenhouse decided to fight back. She went public with her assertions, and Army brass made good on their threats of demotion. In June of 2005, Greenhouse testified at a Senate Democratic Policy Committee hearing about KBR's favored treatment and overcharges. Two months later, she was removed from her PARC position and reassigned (senior executives cannot be fired) to a lower-level, lesser-paying post. Rather than accept defeat, Greenhouse hired a lawyer and contested the demotion, arguing that it was a clear-cut case of reprisal for her outspoken objection to shady contracting decisions. In November, allegations based on Greenhouse's statements were forwarded to the US Department of Justice, which was considering opening a formal investigation. Meanwhile, KBR and Halliburton continued to rack up government contracts, in spite of ongoing investigations of mishandling, bribery, and overcharges related to earlier contracts in Iraq and elsewhere.

As of early 2006, it was not clear whether Greenhouse would prevail in her attempt to salvage her career. One thing was clear, however: Greenhouse's actions shone a light on military contracting practices, which, taxpayers can only hope, will make future abuses more difficult to perpetrate.

Sources

Periodicals

Associated Press, August 7, 2005.
New York Times, August 29, 2005; November 15, 2004.
Time, November 1, 2004, p. 64.
Vanity Fair, April 2005, p. 138.
Washington Post, August 29, 2005, p. A11; October 19, 2005, p. C1.

On-line

"A Background Trip with the PARC," *US Army Corps of Engineers,* www.hq.usace.army.mil/cepr/asp/walking/parc.asp?strCat=9 (April 28, 2006).
National Whistleblower Center, www.whistleblowers.org/html/greenhouse.htm (April 28, 2006).
"Ordeal of a Whistleblower," *Alternet,* www.alternet.org/story/24885 (April 28, 2006).

—Bob Jacobson

Aaron Hall

1964—

Singer

Few modern performers can legitimately claim to have helped launch a musical genre. Aaron Hall is one such artist. As an original member of the band Guy, and later as a solo artist, Hall was one of the originators of the soulful R&B offshoot known as New Jack Swing. His career and personal life have seen some ups and downs since the heyday of New Jack in the late 1980s and early 1990s, but Hall's voice remains one of the signature sounds of the New Jack style.

Aaron Hall was born August 10, 1964, in the Bronx, New York. Growing up in the tough housing projects of New York, he both witnessed and experienced his share of violence. As a young man he was shot and stabbed. In the mid-1980s he saw his mother struck and killed by a drunk driver on Christmas Day.

Hall was working in a Brooklyn shoe store when another original Guy member, Tim Gatling, heard him singing in the stockroom and suggested that they connect with Teddy Riley, a neighborhood acquaintance who already had his foot in the door of the music industry, having produced songs for such well-known rappers as Doug E. Fresh, Kool Moe Dee, and Heavy D. Together, Hall, Riley and Gatling formed the band Guy in 1987. Guy quickly signed with Uptown Records, the original label of such eventual stars as Jodeci and Mary J. Blige. Gatling soon left the band and was replaced by Hall's brother Damion.

Guy was an instant sensation among urban audiences, and is generally credited with being one of the driving forces behind the creation of the style known as New Jack Swing. The band's first two albums, *Guy* (1988)

and *The Future* (1990), became classics of the new genre. The soundtrack to the 1989 Spike Lee film *Do the Right Thing* included a Guy song, "My Fantasy." Guy also appeared briefly in the 1991 movie *New Jack City*, as a band playing on New Year's Eve.

In Guy, Hall's role was to lay rough-edged vocal verses over a foundation of swing beats provided by bandmate and producer Teddy Riley. In the fall of 1991, at the height of their fame, Guy split up. The breakup of Guy was somewhat mysterious at the time, but years later members of the band explained that the split was their way of escaping from the restrictive and exploitative first contract they had signed as eager newcomers to the music industry. Following the breakup, MCA representative Louil Silas signed Hall as a solo artist. Silas brought Hall along when he started his own label, Silas, under the MCA umbrella.

Hall launched his solo career with the top-selling R&B single "Don't Be Afraid," which was featured on the soundtrack of the 1992 motion picture *Juice*. His first solo album, *The Truth,* was released the following year on the Silas/MCA label. The album's initial single, "Get a Little Freaky," represented an attempt "to resurrect the 'Nasty Man' persona from his tenure in … Guy," according to a November 1993 *Billboard* article. The single did not perform particularly well, and Silas conceded that it had been a mistake to release that track first. Another cut, however, "I Miss You," became a surprise hit, and the album was an overall success. Meanwhile, former bandmate Riley went on to form BLACKstreet, whose debut album was a big seller.

Despite the initial success of his solo career, the 1990s

At a Glance . . .

Born Aaron Hall on August 10, 1964, New York City; children: Aaron IV (with model Gloria Velez).

Career: Member of New Jack Swing band Guy, 1987-1991, 1999-2000, 2005–; appeared in film *New Jack City,* 1991; launched solo career in 1993 with recording *The Truth* (Silas/MCA); co-founded Head Start Music Group label, 2005.

Addresses: *Agent*—Universal Attractions, 145 West 57th St., 15th Floor, New York, NY 10019.

were a rocky decade for Hall, especially in his personal life. In 1994 his son, also named Aaron, died soon after birth. Not long after, Hall, already in his 30s, entered a relationship with model and dancer Gloria Velez, who was just 16 years old at the time. Velez, who has appeared in many hip-hop videos over the years, gave birth at age 17 to Aaron Hall IV. The couple went through a bitter and highly public breakup soon after, with Velez gaining full custody of Aaron IV. Velez has been quite vocal about Hall's shortcomings as a father, calling him a "deadbeat dad" and maintaining that he has not contributed financially or otherwise to Aaron IV's upbringing. She has also accused Hall of physically abusing her. Hall has always denied these allegations and argued that his attempts to contact Velez to arrange for child support have been rebuffed.

In 1996 Hall pleaded guilty to assault charges for hitting an ex-girlfriend, and was sentenced to five years of probation. A few years later he was ordered to undergo two years of anger management training. He ended up serving 11 months in Rikers Island when he failed to show up on time for one of the sessions. Despite all the trauma, Hall managed to turn out another strong solo album for MCA in 1998, *Inside of You.* Guy reunited briefly at the end of the decade to record the album *Guy III,* (MCA, 2000), but the reunion did not prove lasting, in part due to Hall's ongoing legal problems.

In the spring of 2004, Hall announced plans for a comeback on a new label of his own creation. The label was formed in partnership with entrepreneur Dwayne Corbitt, a former basketball player with business interests that included real estate and a children's programming/animation production company, Headstart/Legendary Entertainment. To Hall, establishing his own label represented a form of liberation. "I'm not a slave anymore...," he was quoted as saying in a May 2004 *Billboard* magazine article. "Ever since

I got shafted in my MCA deal, I know I had to do my own thing or not at all." Hall also expressed his intention to sign other acts to the new label, including the urban rock rapper J. Naugh-T. Meanwhile, that summer Geffen records released *The Best of Guy,* part of its "20th Century Masters: Millennium Edition" series, in recognition of the band's crucial contribution to modern R & B.

Hall's new album, *Adults Only,* came out in 2005 on the Head Start Music Group label. On the disc's first track, "Intro," the singer explains that *Adults Only* would be Aaron Hall's final project. Citing a lack of respect he had received from his peers and the media over the last several years, Hall announced that he was henceforth adopting a new persona, to be known as E. Kane. His next recording project, according to Hall, would be called *E. Kane the O.G.* As fans awaited the arrival of Mr. Kane, Mr. Hall did not disappear entirely. Guy, featuring its heyday lineup of Riley and the Hall brothers, reunited for a series of live performances from late 2005 through the first half of 2006 as part of a nationwide "New Jack Revival Tour" that drew enthusiastic audiences in several major cities. The reunion fueled rumors that a fourth Guy album was forthcoming. New Jack Swing may no longer be new, but plenty of listeners apparently still appreciate the swing.

Selected discography

Albums with Guy

Guy, MCA, 1988.
The Future, MCA, 1990.
Guy III, MCA, 2000.
The Best of Guy, MCA, 2004.

Solo Albums

The Truth, Silas/MCA, 1993.
Inside of You, Silas/MCA, 1998.
Adults Only: The Final Album, Head Start, 2005.

Sources

Periodicals

Billboard, November 20, 1993; December 4, 1999, p. 80; May 1, 2004, p. 28.
Black Enterprise, July 27, 2004.
Jet, September 6, 1996, p. 59.

On-line

"Aaron Hall Working to Overcome Tough Times with Guy Reunion, New Persona," *MTV News,* www.mtv.com/news/articles/1508850/20050902/story.jhtml.

"Guy," *Red Entertainment Agency,* www.redenter-
tainment.com/Guy/Guy.htm.

—Bob Jacobson

Lalah Hathaway

1969—

Vocalist, songwriter

Hathaway, Lalah, photograph. WENN/Landov.

Lalah Hathaway set herself apart from the hard-edged hip-hop trends of the 1990s with a subtle vocal style rooted in her jazz training and in the classic soul vocals of her father Donny Hathaway. Her smooth voice brought her many admirers, for she was equally at home in styles ranging from R&B ballads and up-tempo numbers to pop standards and jazz. She appeared on more than 100 recordings and concert performances by other artists. After a featured vocal slot on a major jazz release, pianist Joe Sample's *The Song Lives On,* Hathaway re-entered the spotlight in 2004 with the critically lauded album *Outrun the Sky.* She remained a strong concert draw through the middle 2000s.

Hathaway's unique voice didn't fit readily into any particular niche in an increasingly fragmented music industry. But Hathaway accepted the limitations and rewards that came with her stylistic versatility. "It's all music to me," Hathaway explained to Richard Harrington of the *Washington Post.* "I've always recognized that I'm somewhat different as a musician and singer because I understand that [mine is] a singular voice—it's my voice and nobody else has it. Doesn't

make me better than anyone else, just makes me singular."

Lalah Hathaway has good musical genes. She was born in Chicago, Illinois, in 1969, just before her father, Donny Hathaway, began his ascent to international fame thanks to a series of duets with singer Roberta Flack. Donny Hathaway was trained in both classical and gospel traditions, and Lalah's mother Eulaulah was an opera singer. The major event of her youth was her father's death in 1979 after he fell 15 floors out the window of a building; it was generally accounted a suicide. "I was only ten years old when it happened, but it was very traumatic," Hathaway recalled to Deborah Gregory of *Essence.* "I had been very close to my father. Now I carry the pain inside; sometimes I feel it, sometimes I don't, but I'll have to deal with it for the rest of my life."

She was enrolled in a high-school music program that focused on classical music, but teachers decided that her low, rather quiet voice wasn't suited to opera. She also grew up during a golden age of R&B female vocals, listening to singers like Chaka Khan, and in the 1980s she came under the spell of the fusion jazz that was making inroads into urban radio, hearing instru-

At a Glance . . .

Born in 1969 in Chicago, IL: daughter of Donny Hathaway, a soul music vocalist, and Eulaulah Hathaway, an opera singer. *Education:* Berklee College of Music, Boston, 1990.

Career: Recording artist, various record labels, 1990–.

Addresses: *Label*—Sanctuary Records, Sixth Floor, 369 Lexington Ave., New York, NY 10017. *Web*—www.lalahhathaway.com.

mentalists like guitarist Pat Metheny and the group Weather Report. The eclectic atmosphere of Boston's Berklee College of Music fit Hathaway well, and her vocal talents bloomed. "I met a lot of great musicians, and the musician I am was informed by that," she told Harrington. Major-label talent spotters turned their ears in Hathaway's direction, and she was signed to Virgin as a sophomore. While her classmates were traveling to vacation spots for spring break during her senior year in 1990, she was recording her debut album, *Lalah Hathaway.*

Critics praised the album, and Hathaway garnered high-profile club dates around Boston and beyond. She moved to Los Angeles in 1991. "[H]er voice is limpid, smooth, and bracing, with just a hint of sultriness," noted David Hiltbrand of *People.* "You have only to listen to 'Obvious' or 'I'm Coming Back' to realize that she has a very sure, remarkably mature flair for phrasing." Radio programmers were less friendly than critics, however, and the album stalled out in the middle ranges of *Billboard* magazine's R&B chart. The jazz component in R&B was on the decline by the early 1990s, and, noted Eric Snider of the *St. Petersburg Times,* "It's readily obvious that there's plenty more of the jazz singer waiting to come out" in Hathaway's voice.

The next phase of Hathaway's career seemed to bear out her jazz tendencies. Her sophomore release *A Moment* came out on the Virgin label in 1994 and failed to attract much attention with its combination of ballads and funky numbers intended to reach a younger demographic. Meanwhile, Hathaway's reputation in the jazz world was growing. She recorded and toured with key jazz instrumentalists and producers, including keyboardist Herbie Hancock, saxophonist Grover Washington Jr., and bassist Marcus Miller, whose band she joined shortly after graduating from music school. In 1992 she began touring with former Crusaders pianist Joe Sample, and her schedule was busy through the 1990s even though she didn't record again under

her own name after 1994. Hathaway's jazz phase culminated the 1999 Joe Sample/Lalah Hathaway release *The Song Lives On,* which cracked the top five of *Billboard's* Contemporary Jazz chart. "I think she's found her niche," jazz DJ Jay McLaughlin told Sonia Murray of the *Atlanta Journal-Constitution.* "I don't know a lot of R&B singers that can just come over and start singing jazz. And be received like she has been."

Still, Hathaway was frustrated by her lack of R&B exposure and wasn't ready to give up on the genre. "It seems like this music has forsaken the whole art of A&R [artists-and-repertoire], watching an artist develop, and having a story to tell with a beginning, middle, and end," she told Murray. "Especially for black girls who want to do something other than shake [their] butts." Later, asked by Renee Graham of the *Boston Globe* why there had been such a long break between her solo albums, she was even blunter: "Because the music industry sucks," she said. "It's in a constant state of flux. I signed two deals, the record labels folded, a partner moved away or decided to do something else." And the stark split between hip-hop and retro neo-soul troubled Hathaway. "From my own experience with soul music, there's a couple of extremes out there," she told Graham. "If you're in the middle, there's nowhere to even take the music to be heard. The window of opportunity is just closing and closing."

Hathaway did find work in the early 2000s, continuing her long association with Marcus Miller and appearing on albums by Take 6, MeShell NdegeOcello, and Mary J. Blige. In the summer of 2004 she performed "Forever, for Always, for Love" on the Luther Vandross tribute album *Forever, for Always, for Luther.* The song gave Hathaway a Number One urban adult contemporary single and was also included on her third solo release, *Outrun the Sky,* which appeared in late 2004. The album once again garnered substantial critical praise. *Ebony* gushed that "Effortlessly, she pulls listeners into her universe with rich vocals, lush lyrics, and full-bodied rhythms." Stylistically the album made use of the full range of Hathaway's talents, with rock, blues, gospel, jazz, and even country influences, and Hathaway made autobiographical songwriting contributions of her own with songs such as "Boston."

The album made it into the hip-hop/R&B top 40 and brought Hathaway a fresh round of exposure. She rejected the idea of an electronic duet with Donny Hathaway (comparable to "Unforgettable," in which diva Natalie Cole's voice was joined with that of her late father Nat "King" Cole) but contemplated among various other future projects, an album of Donny Hathaway covers with her sister Kenya, a member of the band on television's *American Idol.* She was also planning a new solo album featuring fresh compositions of her own, and it seemed possible that what she needed to reach top-level stardom was material that revealed the real Lalah Hathaway.

Selected discography

Albums

Lalah Hathaway, Virgin, 1990.
A Moment, Virgin, 1994.
(With Joe Sample) The Song Lives On, GRP, 1999.
Outrun the Sky, Sanctuary, 2004.

Sources

Periodicals

Atlanta Journal-Constitution, August 6, 1999, p. P3;
   July 21, 2005, p. P5.
Billboard, April 16, 1994, p. 28.
Boston Globe, September 19, 1990, p. 76; September 23, 2005, p. D18.
Ebony, October 2004, p. 45.
Essence, February 1991, p. 32.
Jet, January 10, 2005, p. 28.
People, September 24, 1990, p. 21.
St. Petersburg Times, April 19, 1991, p. 25; June 17, 1994, p. 27.
Washington Post, February 10, 2006, p. T6.

On-line

Lalah Hathaway, www.lalahhathaway.com (March 25, 2006).
"Lalah Hathaway," All Music Guide, www.allmusic.com (March 25, 2006).
"Lalah Hathaway," Soul Tracks, www.soultracks.com/lalah_hathaway.htm (March 25, 2006).

—James M. Manheim

Endesha Ida Mae Holland

1944-2006

Educator, playwright

"I love sharing my stories with my students," educator and playwright Endesha Ida Mae Holland once told *People* magazine. "I tell them about me and let them know that no matter what barriers are put in their way, they can make it."

Overcame Rough Beginnings

Holland knows about barriers. She was born on August 29, 1944, in Greenwood, Mississippi, a place she later called "a testament to African-American inferiority," as the *New York Times* noted. "I was always conscious of our inferiority, until the civil rights movement came." Before it came, Holland lived with her mother and never knew her father, "though there were three men who would come by and say they were my daddy," she disclosed to *People*. Her mother took in ironing (and, as *Nation* reported, became renowned "for pressing so sharp a crease in a pair of trousers that they could stand up by themselves"), then became a midwife referred to by the community as "the second doctor."

At the age of 11, Holland was baby-sitting for a white toddler one day, when the mother of the young child led Holland to her husband's bedroom to be raped. Holland is rather philosophical about the experience: "It happened to a lot of girls," she explained in *People*. "There was a saying that a white man didn't want to die unless he'd had a black girl."

By age 13, Holland quit school and earned rent money for her mother and siblings as a prostitute (she charged her white customers double), until she followed a stranger into an office of the Student Nonviolent Coordinating Committee (SNCC) in 1962. She saw black women working at typewriters, which so inspired the 18-year-old Holland that she began volunteering at the SNCC office. She traveled extensively across the nation for the civil rights movement; she worked with Martin Luther King, Jr., and was jailed more than a dozen times. *New York Times* writer Glenn Collins reported that the other civil rights workers were warned that Holland was a scandalous person; however, "the workers were all inexperienced in going to jail, [and] I was a veteran: I knew how to survive there…. I'd been there so often for stealing and fighting. I felt like a queen in jail. The workers really needed me, and I used to protect them." Holland considered being jailed for her civil rights work as a real moment of glory.

Despite "inspir[ing] her children to make something of themselves by seizing opportunities she never had," as *Time* magazine recorded, Holland's mother was nervous about her daughter's activism, with good reason: her house was firebombed in 1965. Holland came home to see her mother, in flames, die at her own front door. Holland maintained to *People* magazine reporters: "Neighbors saw who did it but were afraid to say…. I think the firebomb was meant for me." She suspected that the Ku Klux Klan was punishing her for her civil rights work.

Told Her Story on Stage

Holland left Mississippi in 1966 and headed north. Not

At a Glance . . .

Born Ida Mae Holland on August 29, 1944, in Greenwood, MS; died January 25, 2006, in Santa Monica, CA; daughter of a midwife; married in 1963 (divorced, 1966); married second husband (a professor; divorced); married third husband (divorced); children: Cedric. *Education*: University of Minnesota, BA, 1979, MA, 1984, PhD, 1986.

Career: Quit school to become a prostitute, c. late 1950s; Student Nonviolent Coordinating Committee (SNCC), Greenwood, MS, office volunteer, 1962, and civil rights worker, 1963-66 (jailed 13 times); co-founder, African-American studies program at University of Minnesota; founder, Women Helping Offenders (prison-aid program); State University of New York at Buffalo, American Studies department, professor, 1986-1993; University of Southern California, School of Theatre, playwright-in-residence, then professor emeritus, 1993-2006.

Awards: Lorraine Hansberry Award for best play, 1981, for *The Second Doctor Lady*; Helen Hayes Award for best nonresident play for *From the Mississippi Delta*; October 18 declared as Dr. Endesha Ida Mae Holland Day in Greenwood, MS, 1991.

long after, she was accepted as a student at the University of Minnesota, a new world for her. In addition to helping start an African-American studies department, Holland initiated Women Helping Offenders (WHO), a prison-aid program that occupied a great deal of her time and even paid her a salary. In 1983, Holland took Endesha as her first name in order to honor her African heritage.

Taking a play-writing class as an "easy" way to satisfy degree requirements, Holland wrote a story called *The Second Doctor Lady* about her mother. When she read it in class, "everyone was weeping." This is the play Holland eventually expanded into *From the Mississippi Delta*. She also completed master's and doctoral degrees and had all the street people she had met throughout her travels attend her graduation in 1985. She told *People*: "The whores and pimps and junkies were there.... When they called my name, the entire auditorium rose to its feet."

From the Mississippi Delta was performed regionally both in the United States and in London before it opened Off-Broadway in late 1991. The play has been

widely reviewed and, as *Time* noted, "blends folktales, childhood memories, salty down-home sociological observations and blues and gospel standards with Holland's unabashed 'confessions.'"

Critics generally applauded Holland's play. A reviewer for *Variety* wrote, "Conceived in straightforward storytelling terms, the play is an extraordinary work of autobiography by someone who struggled against the twin evils of racial bigotry and poverty in the Mississippi delta in the '40s." Margaret Spillane, writing in *Nation*, contended that Holland's play "contains two of the most astonishing dramatic moments I have ever seen onstage": the rape of eleven-year-old Phelia, and her mother, Aint Baby, presiding over the birth of a couple's thirteenth child. Spillane also asserted: "Aint Baby regards her midwife's certificate not as an emblem of superiority over her neighbors but as a means to guarantee that their community will carry on.... [And] when Phelia uses her cap-and-gowned moment of glory to name every single person from the Delta and beyond who ever extended love and wisdom to her, she seems to rise atop a pyramid made of their names, their unseen lives unearthed by the act of naming."

Became Beloved Teacher

Holland taught American Studies at the State University of New York (SUNY) at Buffalo beginning in the mid-1980s. The *New York Times* described her as "a large, authoritative woman with an expressive face and a powerful presence," and the head of the American Studies department, Professor Elizabeth Kennedy, told *People* magazine that Holland "create[d] an electric atmosphere in the classroom" and noted that her courses were so popular that many more students tried to get into them than could be admitted.

Holland relished the new order in her life provided by her position. She overcame the barriers of poverty and low expectations, but never disavowed her background. Indeed, *New York Times* writer Collins recounted that "she [wasn't] embarrassed by the intrusion of her raunchy past into her current life." Rather, she profited from it by dramatizing her life for the stage. "I've had an extraordinary life," Holland claimed in the same article; "I'm not ashamed of my life, and I'm proud to say that I've changed.... Young people need to know that they can do wrong things and yet still change and grow."

In 1991, the town of Greenwood, Mississippi, designated October 18 as Dr. Endesha Ida Mae Holland Day. Receiving the key to the city on the steps of Greenwood's city hall, Holland remarked, "The last time I was on those steps I was on my way to jail." Commenting on the turnaround, Mississippi's governor Ray Mabus said that Holland's history "serves as a model for all people, to show that with determination we can overcome obstacles for a better life." For Holland, the only obstacle that she could not overcome was ataxia, a degenerative neurological disease that slowly eroded her physical abilities over the last 15 years of her life. In 1993 she left SUNY-Buffalo and took a position as playwright-in-residence and then professor emeritus at the University of Southern California's theatre program. She passed away on January 25, 2006, at her home near Los Angeles.

Selected writings

The Second Doctor Lady, 1979, performed by the Negro Ensemble Company, first produced in London at the Young Vic Theatre; revised as *From the Mississippi Delta* (two-act autobiographical drama), produced Off-Broadway at Circle in the Square, November 1991.

From the Mississippi: A Memoir, Simon & Schuster, 1997.

Sources

American Theatre, vol. 23, no. 4, April 2006.
Boston Globe, June 4, 1991.
Buffalo News, April 5, 1998.
Chicago Tribune, January 14, 1990.
Ebony, June 1, 1992.
Los Angeles Times, May 8, 1994.
Nation, July 1, 1991.
New York Times, June 9, 1991; November 5, 1991; November 12, 1991; February 1, 2006.
New Yorker, September 5, 1988.
People, December 2, 1991.
Star Tribune (Minneapolis), February 12, 1993.
Time, November 25, 1991.
Variety, June 10, 1991; February 6, 2006.
Wall Street Journal, February 13, 1991.

—Fran Locher Freiman and Tom Pendergast

Donald L. Hollowell

1917-2004

Attorney

Donald L. Hollowell was a distinguished civil rights attorney who successfully argued several notable court cases that helped end segregation in the American South. As a lawyer for the National Association for the Advancement of Colored People (NAACP), Hollowell quickly rose to prominence for his expert legal strategies and confidence in the courtroom. He knew Martin Luther King Jr.—on one occasion even securing King's release from a Georgia state prison—and was an ally and confidant of many other notable leaders in the civil rights struggle. "Not only did he have courage, but he had a brilliant legal mind," onetime NAACP President Julian Bond wrote of him in a tribute published a few years before his death, *The Sacred Call,* according to *Atlanta Journal-Constitution* writer Julie B. Hairston. "He outstripped, out-argued, out-appeared these famous so-called great constitutional lawyers who had erected this barrier of segregation throughout the South. They had the reputation, but Hollowell had the goods."

Hollowell was born in Wichita, Kansas, in 1917. As a teen, he was told to quit school by his father in order to work full-time to support the family, and Hollowell enlisted in the U.S. Army instead. He served six years with the famous Tenth Cavalry, an all-black regiment dating back to 1866 whose members were dubbed "Buffalo Soldiers" by the Kiowa Indians. During his stint in the service, Hollowell earned a high school diploma, and upon his discharge enrolled at Lane College, a historically black college in Jackson, Tennessee. He was a starting quarterback on its Dragons football team, but re-enlisted in the military when the

United States entered World War II in late 1941. He saw combat in Europe and reached the rank of captain.

Hollowell returned to Lane after the war, and graduated in 1947. He earned a law degree from the law school of Loyola University in Chicago in 1951, and moved to Atlanta, Georgia, that same year. It was an era of deeply institutionalized racism in the American South, and Hollowell was one of just a dozen black lawyers in the city. Deeply interested in challenging the series of local ordinances known as the Jim Crow laws that relegated African Americans to the status of second-class citizens, he became involved in several notable court cases seeking to end discrimination. His first major case came in 1955, when he served as lead attorney on *Ward v. Regents.* He argued on behalf of Horace T. Ward, an African-American applicant to the University of Georgia School of Law who had been rejected for admission. The University barred black students at all levels, and the case attracted widespread attention. A federal court sided with the school, however, in ruling that Ward had not fulfilled the necessary entrance requirements.

Hollowell knew Martin Luther King Jr., and was asked to help out when King was arrested at a 1960 protest, and then sentenced to four months on a misdemeanor charge involving his driver's license. Hollowell secured King's release from Reidsville State Prison thanks to arguments presented to the Georgia Court of Appeals, but future instances when King was jailed would require White House intervention. When asked what King was like as a client, Hollowell replied that the legendary civil

At a Glance . . .

Born Donald Lee Hollowell on December 19, 1917, in Wichita, KS; died of heart failure on December 27, 2004, in Atlanta, GA; son of a janitor; married Louise Thornton (a professor of English). *Education:* Lane College, Jackson, TN, BA, 1947; Loyola University, JD, 1951. *Military service:* U.S. Army, Tenth Cavalry, c. 1935-41; served again in the U.S. Army during World War II; reached rank of captain; 1941-45.

Career: Attorney, Atlanta, GA, 1951-65; argued cases with the National Association for the Advancement of Colored People (NAACP), 1955-65; Equal Employment Opportunity Commission (EEOC), Southeastern office, director, 1966-85; Voter Education Project, president, 1971-86.

rights leader was "always cooperative," he said in a *Fulton County Daily Report* interview. "He'd have his own decision, but we never had any problem with having him to go along with what we were suggesting in the situation."

Hollowell mounted a second challenge to the University of Georgia's discriminatory policies when he took on another test case, this one involving two gifted students, Charlayne Hunter and Hamilton Holmes, who applied for admission to the undergraduate division of the school in 1959, but were turned down. Again, the University maintained that they had been rejected by admissions officers for reasons other than the color of their skin. *Holmes v. Danner* went to trial in U.S. District Court in December of 1960, and this time the judge ruled in the students' favor. Hunter and Holmes's first week of classes made national headlines because of the riots that erupted on campus, and Hollowell and his wife received harassing telephone calls and even death threats. Holmes went on to become the first black graduate of Emory University's medical school, and Hunter the pioneering broadcast journalist Charlayne Hunter-Gault.

Hollowell won other successful desegregation cases, including one involving public transportation in Macon, Georgia, and another that forced Grady Memorial Hospital in Atlanta to hire African-American doctors

and served as a landmark decision that integrated hospitals across the United States. With the ostensible end of the civil rights struggle that came with the passage of the Civil Rights Act of 1964 and the following year's Voting Rights Act, Hollowell moved on to a federal appointment. There were a number of new government agencies created to enforce the anti-discrimination laws, and one of them was the Equal Employment Opportunity Commission (EEOC), which monitored the workplace. In 1966, U.S. President Lyndon B. Johnson appointed Hollowell as the first director of the EEOC's Southeastern office, a job he held for the next nineteen years.

A respected civic leader in Atlanta, Hollowell was known as the top civil rights lawyer in Georgia, and one of the best in the South. In both his private practice and federal job, he worked to train a younger generation of civil rights attorneys. One of them was Vernon Jordan, who served as director of the National Urban League and advisor to two U.S. presidents, Jimmy Carter and Bill Clinton. Hollowell remained active in various civil rights organizations, and served as president of the Voter Education Project from 1971 to 1986. During his tenure, the number of registered African-American voters climbed from 3 million to 5.5 million.

Hollowell's wife, Louise Thornton Hollowell, was a professor of English at Morris Brown College. The couple, who had no children, never moved out of the Atlanta house they purchased in 1961. Hollowell died on December 27, 2004, of heart failure at the age of 87. His funeral at Morehouse College was a three-hour affair in which he was eulogized by more than twenty speakers, including Hunter-Gault, Jordan, and United Nations Ambassador Andrew Young. Hollowell's one-time law-firm partner, Marvin Arrington, told the gathering that Hollowell was a hero in the civil rights struggle whose legal brilliance helped end desegregation in the South. "Every time you drink out of a water fountain that doesn't have 'black' and 'white,'" Arrington said, according to the *Atlanta Journal-Constitution*, "you ought to say 'Thank you, Don.'"

Sources

Periodicals

Atlanta Journal-Constitution, February 24, 2000, p. JD5; December 29, 2004, p. A1; January 1, 2005, p. C1.
Fulton County Daily Report, December 30, 2004.

—Carol Brennan

Clint Holmes

1946—

Singer, composer

Holmes, Clint, photograph. Ethan Miller/Getty Images for CineVegas.

Casino entertainer Clint Holmes doesn't fit the Las Vegas mold. Whereas many casino headliners put together glitzy, heavily choreographed shows built around their own versions of familiar popular songs, Holmes has used his headliner status to develop original material, including a musical, *Comfortable Shoes,* based on his own experiences as a biracial American. After a career marked by ups and downs, Holmes has become an icon of Las Vegas entertainment with a long-running engagement as headliner at Harrah's casino. Holmes's musical director at Harrah's, Bill Fayne, has called him "the world's greatest unknown," according to the *Las Vegas Review-Journal.*

Influenced by Jazz and Classical Music

Clinton Holmes was born in Bournemouth, England, on May 9, 1946. His father Eddie, an American GI stationed in England, enjoyed singing jazz, and his mother Audrey was a trained opera singer. Holmes grew up in the small town of Farnham, New York, southwest of Buffalo. As a youth he sang and absorbed

musical lessons from both parents, stating on his Web site that "my mom taught me how to sing correctly and my dad taught me how to enjoy it." Outside of music, Holmes had a hard childhood. He was rejected by both white and black classmates, and the father of his planned high school prom date refused to let her attend with him.

Holmes played in rock bands in high school and majored in voice at Fredonia State College (now the State University at Fredonia). Racial prejudice continued to dog him when he visited the family of a college girlfriend. "I flew from Buffalo to Long Island to stay at their house, only to wake up the next morning to hear her mother screaming, 'I didn't send you to college to shack up with a nigger. I want him out of the house,'" he recalled to Mike Weatherford of the *Review-Journal.* But he did well in school and broke into the music business with a series of gigs in Buffalo nightclubs.

The US Army furthered Holmes's musical training after he was drafted. He played trombone in the Army Band, sang in the Army Chorus, and, at his own request, was picked to sing "Alfie" at a celebration honoring his commanding officer for a promotion. The

At a Glance . . .

Born Clinton Holmes on May 9, 1946, in Bournemouth, England; son of Eddie Holmes, an American serviceman and jazz singer, and Audrey Holmes, a British opera singer; married Brenda; children: Brent, Brittany, Cooper. *Education:* Attended Fredonia State College, Fredonia, NY. *Military service:* US Army, mid-1960s; performed in Army choirs and bands.

Career: Singer and composer, mid-1960s–; moved to Washington, DC, after military discharge and performed in Eastern states, 1970s; *The Late Show Starring Joan Rivers,* cast member, 1986; *Entertainment Tonight,* correspondent, late 1980s; *New York at Night* (television program), host, early 1990s; Atlantic city casinos, later 1990s; Las Vegas, performer, 1999–.

Selected awards: Emmy award, for *New York at Night;* Buffalo, NY, Musical Hall of Fame; Casino Legends Hall of Fame; Best Singer in Las Vegas award.

Addresses: *Office*—Harrah's Las Vegas, 3475 Las Vegas Blvd South, Las Vegas, NV 89109; *Web*—www.clintholmes.com.

officer must have been impressed, for Holmes soon received a three-grade promotion to sergeant and joined the Army Chorus in a White House performance. Stationed in Washington, DC, he stayed on in the city after his discharge and landed more nightclub work. During his ten years based in Washington, he married, and he and his wife, Brenda, began raising three children. He began working with a New York agent, and his performing orbit spread up and down the Eastern seaboard. On one occasion he was booked into a club in the Bahamas, where he trotted out a routine in which he impersonated pop star Johnny Mathis. Mathis's producer Paul Vance happened to walk by, heard the routine, and invited Holmes to visit him back on the mainland.

Song Had Second Wind

That meeting resulted in Holmes's recording of "Playground in My Mind," a sweet novelty tune written by Vance and featuring Vance's son, Phillip, on a children's chorus with the words "My name is Michael; I have a nickel." The record was released in June of 1972 and went nowhere. In November, however, a radio programmer in Wichita, Kansas, decided that the

song's sentimental mood and background chorus suited it to the holiday season. The song generated heavy phone requests from listeners as it spread across the Midwest and then throughout the country, and an amazed Holmes, who hadn't particularly liked the song, was rushed into a Los Angeles studio to record a *Playground in My Mind* album. Airplay for the single kept going after the holidays, and it rose to the number two position on *Billboard's* pop singles chart for the week of June 16, 1973.

Holmes correctly guessed that he hadn't had much to do with the song's success. "'Playground' was an excellently made record, but it could have been almost anybody singing it," he told the *Super Seventies* Web site. "It didn't have to be me; therefore, it was not a career-making record. It didn't bear the stamp of Clint Holmes. I think that's why, even today, a lot of people remember the song but not the fellow who sang it." Indeed, follow-up singles flopped, and Holmes seemed destined to be branded as a one-hit wonder.

His next chance at the national spotlight came about in 1986, when comedienne Joan Rivers asked him to join her as sidekick on the then-young Fox network's *The Late Show Starring Joan Rivers.* The show lasted only two years, but that was enough to showcase Holmes in material he felt comfortable with and to sharpen his skills in interacting with other artists. After the show's demise he soon landed a slot as musical feature and events correspondent on the syndicated *Entertainment Tonight* television program. That lasted another two years, and then, in the early 1990s, Holmes was given a show of his own: he hosted *New York at Night* on New York's WWOR-TV, serving as both interviewer and performer. The show brought Holmes an Emmy award.

Wrote Autobiographical Musical

Holmes's growing visibility led to several casino residencies in Atlantic City in the 1990s, and he starred in a production of the musical *Pal Joey* at the Claridge Theater there. His Atlantic City revue *Sophisticated Rhythms* was an unusually elaborate one, featuring a live five-piece backing Holmes in music ranging from songs of jazz legend Cab Calloway to contemporary material. But Holmes had still bigger ambitions on his mind. By 1995 he had written more than 20 songs for *Comfortable Shoes* and was looking for backing to bring the show to Broadway. The musical incorporated the scenes of prejudice Holmes had faced as a result of his biracial background. It had a successful premiere in 1996 at the Paper Mill Theater in Milburn, New Jersey, but financing for its New York run fell apart at the last minute. Holmes found himself dealing with unemployment and with the death of his father.

An offer to star in a revue at the Golden Nugget in Las Vegas helped turn things around for Holmes, who moved to the fabled capital of gambling and nightlife in 1999. The musical atmosphere of Las Vegas proved to be a congenial one for Holmes, who received crucial encouragement from star comedian Bill Cosby when the two worked together early in Holmes's Vegas career. Holmes was tabbed by the city's convention bureau to write a Las Vegas theme song, "L.V.," as a counterpart to such markers of urban identity as "Chicago" and "New York, New York." The song gained a measure of familiarity as it began to be used in the city's massive New Year's Eve celebrations, and Holmes moved on to a headliner slot at the giant Harrah's casino.

Holmes did not give up on *Comfortable Shoes*, and the show was given a full production in 2002 in Chicago, with former Broadway *Lion King* lead Christopher Jackson in the role of Holmes. A review quoted in the *Las Vegas Review-Journal* took the position that *Comfortable Shoes* had noble intentions but "needs a lot more work for a national future." Undaunted, Holmes began to incorporate his own music into his Vegas shows, and in the process he began to develop a product that became more and more distinctive. The *Review-Journal's* Weatherford praised Holmes's "risk-taking" performances, noting that "at least a third of the show consists of original songs by Holmes and his musical collaborators. This is tricky but crucial, if Holmes wants to showcase his distinct musical heritage." The show included numbers from *Comfortable Shoes*, and by the mid-2000s he was a Las Vegas fixture, bouncing back from a bout with colon cancer in 2004. Among other honors, the main theater at Harrah's was renamed the Clint Holmes Theater.

Selected works

Albums

Playground in My Mind, Epic, 1973.
Edges, Valley Vue, 1997.
Clint Holmes Live, 2001.
If Not Now When, 2005.

Plays

Comfortable Shoes (musical), 2002.

Sources

Periodicals

Jet, August 1, 1994, p. 35.
Knight Ridder/Tribune News Service, July 21, 1995.
Las Vegas Review-Journal, October 6, 2002, p. J1; April 11, 2003, p. J4; December 24, 2004, p. A3, J4.
Record (Bergen County, NJ), April 5, 2002, p. 37.
Star-Ledger (Newark, NJ), September 15, 1996, p. 5.

On-line

Clint Holmes, www.clintholmes.com (May 2, 2006).
"Clint Holmes Biography & News," *Harrah's Las Vegas*, www.harrahs.com (March 24, 2006).
"'Playground in My Mind': Clint Holmes," *Super Seventies*, www.superseventies.com/1973_8singles.html (March 24, 2006).

—James M. Manheim

Ebony Hughes

1948—

Women's health educator, healthcare advocate, entrepreneur, registered nurse

Ebony Hughes dedicated herself to women's health education and community health advocacy. She co-founded two obstetrical home health agencies and was honored in 2004 with the American Heart Association's Sister-to-Sister Award for her work in African-American women's healthcare. Hughes focused on educating staff and patients about their rights and responsibilities, patient education, and navigating the health care system. As a conference speaker and educator, she shared her expertise in community health, teaching strategies, and the skills communities need to ensure greater access to quality healthcare. Hughes's concern for the well-being of others extended worldwide. As a childbirth and CPR instructor, Hughes provided training to medical staff and community workers in Russia, Hungary, Ukraine, and Albania.

Hughes was born on February 8, 1948, in the Pittsburgh Hill District of Pittsburgh, Pennsylvania, where she grew up with a twin brother, James, and a sister. The Hughes children saw many rough times from an early age after their parents divorced. It was a struggle for their mother, Ruth, as she raised her kids alone. Despite hard times, Hughes remained focused on her future and finished high school in 1966. She entered the University of Pittsburgh that year to study psychology and stayed one year. Hughes had grander ideas about the role she could play in helping to make the world a better place. In 1967 she became a VISTA Volunteer.

VISTA (Volunteers In Service To America) is a national program of citizens who spend a year working at a community organization helping to solve the problems of poverty. Hughes was assigned to work at Thresholds, a community day care center on the North side of Chicago that worked with adults with mental health issues. This was Hughes's first opportunity to work with such a diverse community of people, all facing common issues of health and poverty: American Indians, Blacks, and whites from the Appalachians all sought help at the centers. Hughes gained a wealth of on-the-job training. "We did it all," Hughes said in an interview with *Contemporary Black Biography* (*CBB*), "We did the painting; we got the furniture; we developed social programs that recruited patients from the state hospitals who were near discharge." As Hughes wrapped up her year with VISTA she realized how much she liked Chicago and valued the relationships she had developed during her stay. She also liked being on her own, but she also needed to focus on a career.

That year a chance meeting with the aunt of a young man Hughes was dating turned Hughes's interests towards nursing. She had never considered the field until the woman explained the benefits of such a career. "She told me that hospitals will always need nurses, and that I could go anywhere in the world," Hughes said. "And I had always wanted to travel. Three months after that conversation I was enrolled in the Cook County School of Nursing, in the RN program." While there Hughes and fellow nurses started a black student nurses association. Hughes served as the group's president during its second year. She graduated in 1972 and began work in the psychiatric unit of Cook County

At a Glance . . .

Born Ebony Hughes on February 8, 1948, in Pittsburgh, PA; married Charles Howard, 1972 (separated, 1981); children: Kesi, Ahmed. *Education:* Cook County School of Nursing, Chicago, IL, RN, 1972.

Career: VISTA Volunteers, Chicago, IL, community volunteer, 1967-68; Cook County Hospital, Chicago, IL, psychiatric nurse, 1972-78; Magee-Womens Hospital, Pittsburgh, PA, charge nurse, 1982-95; Healthy Start, Pittsburgh, PA, charge nurse, 1995; Magee-Womens Hospital, Braddock and Duquesne, PA, case manager, 1995-96; Magee-Womens Hospital, Pittsburgh, PA, community nurse educator, 1996–.

Memberships: American Heart Association. American Cancer Society.

Awards: Lamaze International, Lamaze International Award, 1998; National Organization of Black Law Enforcement Executives, William H. Moore Award for Excellence, 2003; American Heart Association, African-American Heart Health Awareness Award, 2004.

Addresses: *Office*—Magee-Womens Hospital, 300 Halket St, Pittsburgh PA 15213-3108.

Hospital. "With 2,000 beds it was one of the largest hospitals in the country, and we saw everything," Hughes told *CBB.*

A few months later Hughes married Charles Howard. The couple soon moved to Atlanta, where they lived for several years. Hughes later returned to Pittsburgh after her separation from her husband in 1981, taking a position as charge nurse in labor and delivery at Magee-Womens Hospital. There she met another nurse with similar ambitions as her own. The two opened Options, the first for-profit maternal home health agency in the Pittsburgh area. Several years later she and a new partner founded a second agency, but at the time it was difficult for small agencies to compete with hospitals in the area. They too were now offering the same services to their patients, essentially cutting out the small providers. In the meantime Hughes continued to work at the hospital until she took an early retirement in 1995.

Her retirement ended after two months as she began work briefly as a charge nurse with Healthy Start, a new program targeted to women in the African-American community with high-risk pregnancies. The program operated six sites in areas that were high-risk for Sudden Infant Death Syndrome and had a high rate of black infant mortality. The program offered women home and prenatal visits, birth control counseling, childbirth classes, and referrals to food banks.

The following year a doctor Hughes knew from her days at Magee-Womens urged her to apply for a new position with the hospital's ambulatory care department. The job involved perinatal (the time before and just after women give birth) outreach work in the high-risk, low-income areas of Braddock and Duquesne, outside Pittsburgh. Several doctors were starting a family practice there that would offer adult, pediatric, and prenatal care. "We counseled women and teens on birth control and safe sex, and provided them with prenatal care," Hughes said. The clinic also conducted couples counseling and health fairs. It was the work here that first led to Hughes's role as an advisor and board member for health and community organizations around Pittsburgh.

In 1996 Hughes received a job offer from the Womancare program at Magee-Womens International, a department of Magee-Womens Hospital. The program was partnering with medical providers in former Soviet Union countries and Hughes would be a good fit on the team. Hughes, excited about the opportunity, accepted the position. The hospital was setting up resource centers in these countries to teach women about basic women's health care. In addition, the fall of communism had revealed a severely antiquated health care system that lacked well-trained personnel and basic necessities. Medical personnel from the old Soviet bloc traveled to Magee-Womens to take classes in proper sterilization, infection control, and other training vital to proper patient care. "Those countries didn't even have disposable equipment to use," Hughes told *CBB.* "There was nothing for a pap smear. These are things that we in the United States take for granted."

Over the next decade Hughes spread her message, training health care providers and patients. As a childbirth expert she worked with groups to open health centers in Moscow, a badly needed resource for pregnant women and general women's health care. She was later invited back to give childbirth training in Minsk, Belarus. Hughes found the job and travel to be fascinating as she worked with the Romas (better known as the gypsies, although the term carries a negative connotation) in Gyor, Hungary, Afghan refugees in Moscow, and medical personnel in the Ukraine and Albania. On these trips Hughes introduced the concept of partner support during pregnancies, promoted the concepts of family health care centers and better communication between mothers and daughters.

In the United States Hughes coordinated programs such as Families in Motion, a walking program designed to encourage families to exercise, and worked with the GIFTS program, a group providing incarcerated women with cervical and breast health education and screening. An admired colleague at Magee-Womens Hospital, Hughes continued to open doors and ease the way for women and health care professionals to learn about the things that keep women healthy.

Sources

On-line

"Ebony Hughes to Receive the 2004 Sister-to-Sister Award," *Western Pennsylvania Hospital News,* www.pghhospitalnews.com/archives/?page=1&articleID=146 (March 1, 2006).

"Lamaze International Awards," *Lamaze International,* www.lamaze.org/about/awardhistory.asp (March 3, 2006).

"Vista Web by Friends of VISTA," *VISTA,* www.friendsofvista.org (March 1, 2006).

Other

Additional information for this profile was obtained through an interview with Ebony Hughes on April 14, 2006.

—Sharon Melson Fletcher

Judith D. Jackson

1950—

Social worker, service organization administrator

Inspired by her parents' daily example of hard work and volunteerism, Judith D. Jackson chose to dedicate her career to social service. Jackson has participated in the development of several important social service programs. Through her work with the National Association of Black Social Workers, she has worked to build black community and improve the lives of all African Americans. And her service at such organizations as the Children's Aid Society, Franklin Wright Settlement, and the Detroit Youth Foundation has concentrated on strengthening families and especially the lives of children.

Learned Service at Home

Judith Dianne Jackson was born in the small Indiana town of Marion on July 1, 1950. Her father Clayton R. Jackson worked as a nurse's aide and physical therapist at the local Veteran's Administration hospital, where her mother Amy also worked as a baker. Jackson's family had been part of Indiana's thriving black population for generations, and her parents were active members of the community. Her father retired from his job at age sixty-two and devoted his later years to a variety of civic activities, such as joining the boards of the public library and the local Urban League. Her mother also eventually left her baking job to work for the Purdue University extension program, going into the community to teach home management skills, a job which her daughter would refer to as "social work without the degree."

Though Marion was not strictly segregated, young Judith and her brother and sister grew up in largely African American working-class communities. Her family was not wealthy, and her father sometimes worked two jobs to support them. However, the Jacksons always had the necessities of life, and Judith felt safe and secure in the nurturing environment of her home. She liked school, and was strongly influenced by her parents' expectations that she would do well. Because she enjoyed French, she joined the French club and went on a summer trip to Switzerland to study the language. She was also selected for membership in the National Honor Society.

During her junior year in high school, Jackson participated in a summer leadership program called Girls State, where students elect representatives to a mock legislature in order to learn about citizenship and government. Jackson was elected Superintendent of Education, a position that required her to give her first speech before a large crowd. Though she was nervous, her father's supportive presence in the audience gave her courage, as his support in her life would give her courage throughout her career.

Because she was raised in a protected environment, it was not until she was in high school that Jackson began to experience the effects of racism. There, she saw most black students being steered away from academic study towards the vocational track, where they were taught lower level courses and shop classes to prepare them for working class jobs. Jackson's parents had higher ambitions for their children, however, and worked to make sure they enrolled in the high-level academic classes which would prepare them for college.

Began to Study Social Work

Though neither Amy nor Clayton Jackson had had the opportunity to graduate from college, they expected all of their children to continue their education and obtain college degrees. Judith Jackson attended Indiana University, where she earned her bachelor's degree in sociology in 1972. In addition to her studies, she was also active in her sorority, Alpha Kappa Alpha, becoming president of her local chapter. One of her sorority sisters was Pearlie Evans, a dynamic social worker and political activist who became an important influence on Jackson's career. Evans lived in St. Louis and worked in the district office of Representative Bill Clay, who in 1968 had become the first African American elected to

Congress from the state of Missouri. She not only inspired Jackson to seek a leadership position within AKA, but to continue her education by entering graduate school. Jackson followed Evans' advice and entered the prestigious school of social work at Washington University in St. Louis.

Jackson had become somewhat politically active during high school, working on the presidential campaign of Democrat Eugene McCarthy, and she did her internship for her master's degree working in Congressman Clay's office in St. Louis. There she learned about the ways that political policy can affect social programs. Throughout her graduate school career, she continued her political activity, working on the campaign of John Bass, the first elected comptroller of the state of Missouri, among other projects.

Upon receiving her master's degree in social work policy and planning, and community organizing in 1974, Jackson became the first African American MSW to be hired at Lutheran Social Services. During the two years she worked there, she conducted therapy groups and helped develop a diversion program to help first-time offenders find alternatives to jail time for small crimes.

Worked in Private and Public Agencies

In 1976, Jackson moved to New York City and got a job with the Children's Aid Society there. Working under a federal grant, Jackson helped develop a program to reunite families who had been forced to place children in foster care because of social and economic difficulties. However, Children's Aid received much of its funding from the state based on the number children in foster care. Therefore, the organization did not offer much support for Jackson's program, which had the goal of removing children from foster care and placing them back with their families. In 1976, she left Children's Aid to take a job with the State of New York Department of Mental Hygiene.

For the next four years, Jackson worked with developmentally disabled clients, developing community residence programs and group homes in order to improve the lives of the developmentally disabled and change public attitudes about developmental disabilities (formerly called retardation). She rose quickly in the organization, starting as an intake worker, evaluating clients and deciding what kind of treatment and services they needed, and was soon promoted to supervisor. However, she found that she did not enjoy working for a large state bureaucracy; in 1980, she moved to Detroit to take a job with Family and Neighborhood Services, a social work organization in Wayne County, Michigan.

While working at Family and Neighborhood Services, she met Dr. Gerald K. Smith, an educator and social worker who had spent many years developing youth programs. Smith had been deputy director of Family and Neighborhood Services, but he left the organization just as Jackson joined it. However they were both active members of the National Association of Black Social Workers (NABSW) and got to know each other through that organization.

Became Director of Michigan's Oldest Settlement

Smith was director of Detroit's Franklin Wright Settlement. The settlement house movement began during the late 1800s and was one of the first progressive social work programs. Social workers worked and often lived in the houses, where they not only offered support services to the most vulnerable members of society, but also worked for reform to improve conditions for poor working people. Franklin Wright Settlement, the oldest settlement house in the state of Michigan, continues to provide a wide variety of services to the community. In 1982, Smith hired Jackson as deputy director of Franklin Wright Settlement. She worked there for more than ten years, becoming executive director in 1990. The Settlement, like Jackson's earlier work with Children's Aid, places great importance on offering support to keep families together.

In 1999, Gerald K. Smith began to organize a new youth project, and he asked Judith Jackson to work there as his vice-president. An outgrowth of a project first started by the W.K. Kellogg Foundation, the Detroit Youth Foundation aimed to mobilize community support in order to encourage the development of young people. Rather than only focusing on preventing or solving the problems of the young, Detroit Youth hoped to promote positive values, such as education and leadership. Under Smith and Jackson's leadership, the program has opened a building called Youthville Detroit, filled with activities for young people. As well as recreational opportunities, Youthville also offers supportive organizations and opportunities to learn a wide variety of skills young people can use to improve

their lives, from organizing and grant-writing to technology.

Along with her ongoing social service work at Detroit Youth, Jackson has continued to be involved with the National Association of Black Social Workers, becoming president of the organization from 2002 through 2006. During her tenure, she continued the group's mission of working to make a difference within the African American community, not only as social workers, but as members of the community working for the liberation of black people. Under Jackson's administration, NABSW bought a small house in Washington, D.C., setting up its office in the nation's capitol in order to work more effectively to influence public policy.

Though she has been central in improving the lives of thousands over the course of her career, Jackson's most cherished work is within her own family, and the accomplishment that gives her the most pride is the growth and development of her own son, Evan Clayton Jackson.

Sources

On-line

Detroit Youth Foundation, www.detroityouth.org (May 9, 2006).
National Association of Black Social Workers. www.nabsw.org (May 9, 2006).
"Judith D. Jackson." *Washington University Magazine,* http://magazine.wustl.edu/Winter00/classmates.html (May 9, 2006).
Trujillo, Renee. "Social Workers From Black America Promote Welfare, Survival in Belize." *Reporter,* www.reporter.bz/index.php?option=content&task=view&id=524&Itemid=2 (May 9, 2006).

Other

Information for this profile was obtained through an interview with Judith D. Jackson on May 12, 2006.

—Tina Gianoulis

Mae Jackson

1941-2005

Social worker, politician

Mae Jackson made a name for herself as mayor of Waco, Texas. When she died suddenly on February 11, 2005, she left many friends and admirers stunned and grieving. Chet Edwards, Waco's Democratic representative to the state House of Representatives, voiced the feelings of many when he said, "Our city has lost a caring, dedicated leader, and many of us have lost a dear personal friend. Waco is a better community today because of Mae Jackson's unselfish public service, and for years to come, her warm spirit of loving thy neighbor will inspire all of us."

A social worker by profession, Jackson continually exceeded the duties of her job in her efforts to improve the society she lived in. An enthusiastic advocate of volunteer work, Jackson not only promoted volunteerism, but also volunteered many hours of her own time to a wide variety of community organizations. As the first African American to be elected mayor of the City of Waco, Jackson proved to be an energetic and confident leader. In addition, her straightforward honesty and generosity were an inspiration to those who knew and worked with her.

Mae Jackson was born on September 10, 1941, in the east central Texas town of Teague. Despite the difficulties of growing up in a segregated Southern town during the 1940s and 1950s, Jackson determined a successful course for her life. Jackson learned the value of education early. Her father worked as a school principal, and her mother was a teacher; with their encouragement, Jackson became an enthusiastic student. In 1958 she graduated as valedictorian of her class at Booker T. Washington High School, and the

following fall she left Teague, moving south to start college in the city of Houston.

College served Jackson well in the changing times. Jackson earned her Bachelor of Science degree at Texas Southern University, a historically black institution. After graduating from TSU in 1962, Jackson moved south to the city of San Antonio to continue her studies in graduate school at Our Lady of the Lake University. Jackson chose OLLU because of its masters program in social work. Jackson had been drawn to the idea of serving others as a young girl, and chose social work as her career.

Worked in Civil Rights Movement

While Jackson studied to earn her Masters of Social Work degree, the civil rights movement took on more and more momentum. Inspired, Jackson moved to Washington, DC, in order to join the movement. There she started work with the National Council of Negro Women (NCNW), a progressive women's service organization that had been founded in 1935 by African-American educator and activist Mary McLeod Bethune. In 1957, presidency of the NCNW had passed to another energetic black organizer, Dorothy Height. Height would become Jackson's mentor.

Height was president when Jackson went to work with the NCNW. The two had much in common. Like Jackson, Height was a social worker who believed passionately in justice and community. Also like Jackson, Height was a member of Delta Sigma Theta sorority and had served as its national president from

At a Glance . . .

Born Mae J. Jackson on September 10, 1941 in Teague, TX; died February 11, 2005, Waco, TX; married Dillard Huddleston; children: three. *Education:* Texas Southern University, BS, 1962; Our Lady of the Lake University, MSW, 1965; University of Texas at Arlington, PhD, 1985.

Career: Caseworker in state and private social service agencies; Governor's Commission for Women, vice chair, 1985-87; Texas Board of Pardons and Paroles, Executive Board member, 1991-1997; City of Waco, City Council, District 1 representative, 2000-2003; City of Waco, mayor, 2003-2005.

Selected memberships: Delta Sigma Theta Sorority, Incorporated, life member; Emily's List, Majority Council; National Association of Negro Women; National Federation of Democratic Women; National Association of Social Workers.

Selected awards: Robert L. Gilbert Community Service Award, 1987; Waco Chamber of Commerce and General Motors, Athena International Award, 1991; Bluebonnet Girl Scout Council, Women of Distinction Award, 1994; Texas Association of Social Workers, Lifetime Achievement Award, state and local, 2003; Texas Democratic Women, Outstanding Officeholder Award, 2005 (given posthumously).

1947-1956. Jackson had joined Delta Sigma Theta while a student at TSU, perhaps attracted by the sorority's reputation for service to the community.

Height became a friend to Jackson during her years in Washington. Along with her job at the NCNW, Height was also an administrator at the Harlem YWCA in New York City, where she worked hard to provide a place of safety and empowerment for young black women. Inspired by Height's work, Jackson would become an advocate for the YWCA throughout her career. Together, Height and Jackson also worked on a program called "Wednesdays in Mississippi," where interracial teams of women from the North made weekly trips to racially torn Mississippi to offer help and support to those working for civil rights in the Southern state.

Began Active Career in Waco

After working with the NCNW in Washington for two years, Jackson returned to Texas. She remained a member of the NCNW for life and continued the type of activist public service she had learned from working with Height. Over the next several decades Jackson lived in the city of Waco, Texas, and did enough work to fill several careers. As a caseworker, she provided direct social services to clients in need, focusing especially on children's mental health and supporting at-risk families. She also taught various elements of social work at a number of colleges and universities, among them Baylor University, McLennan Community College, Paul Quinn College, and the University of Texas at Austin and at Arlington. In addition, she volunteered her services in many community organizations, including Center for Action Against Sexual Assault, the Laura Edwards Day Care Center, the Mental Health Association, the Waco Boys Club, and the Waco Symphony Association. For ten years, she was producer and host of KWTX-TV's *Minority Forum.*

Jackson even found time in her busy schedule to return to school and earn her doctoral degree. In 1985, she received her PhD from the University of Texas in Arlington. Even her thesis, titled "A Structural and Functional Analysis of Voluntary Governing Boards in Not-For-Profit Human Services Agencies," showed the continuing value she placed on volunteer work.

Jackson's lifetime of service work did not escape the notice of those in political power. In 1985 Texas Governor Mark White appointed her as vice chair of the Governor's Commission for Women, a position she held for two years. In 1991, Governor Ann Richards, a progressive politician known for appointing women and minorities to government positions, named Jackson to the Texas Board of Pardons and Paroles. She served as a member of the Executive Board until 1997.

Entered City Government

Her work within these governmental organizations led Jackson to believe that she could further her goals of improving her community by serving in Waco's city government. In 2000 she ran for and won the position of District 1 representative on the Waco City Council. Jackson's personal experiences of racism and poverty, and her experiences working in a broad range of organizations allowed her to build bridges between people with very different goals and beliefs. She served two terms as an effective council member before running for the office of mayor in 2004, winning easily against four other candidates.

In May 2004, Jackson became the first elected black mayor of Waco. Her chief goal as mayor was to make Waco a better place for all its citizens by improving basic services, such as water quality, and promoting economic development with increased tourism and a renovated downtown area. She continued to build bridges by initiating the Community Vision Project, an outreach program designed to get input from all communities about the needs of their citizens.

On February 11, 2005, Jackson was taken to the hospital with chest pains. She died the same day, possibly due to a blood clot near her lungs or heart. Her husband and three children survived her. She had remained active and vibrant until the day of her death, defending the rights of the vulnerable and promoting strong, stable, and just communities.

Sources

Periodicals

Houston African American, February 23, 2005, p. 7.
Waco Tribune, February 13, 2005.

On-line

"African American History in the West Vignette: Mae J. Jackson," *University of Washington,* http://faculty.washington.edu/qtaylor/aa_Vignettes/jackson_mae.htm (February 13, 2006).
"Jefferson Awards: Mae Jackson-Huddleston." *KWTX,* www.kwtx.com/unclassified/1347637.html (February 13, 2006).
"Wake to Be Held Monday for Late Waco Mayor Mae Jackson." *KWTX,* http://www.kwtx.com/home/headlines/1258847.html (February 13, 2006).
Wiggins, Mimi, "Mayor Mae Jackson, 63, Dies Suddenly," *Baylor University,* www.baylor.edu/Lariat/news.php?action=story&story=22623 (February 13, 2006).

—Tina Gianoulis

Harry E. Johnson

1954—

Attorney, administrator

Attorney Harry E. Johnson has made preserving African-American heritage an important part of his career. Not content with simply building a successful law career, he has also dedicated his time to a variety of projects to empower black youth, and to ensure the legacy of one of the most important architects of the 1960s civil rights movement. As president of the Washington, DC, Martin Luther King, Jr. National Memorial Project Foundation, Johnson continues to work to place a tribute to the civil rights leader among the other important memorials in the nation's capitol.

Johnson was born on September 29, 1954, in the Mississippi River port city of St. Louis, Missouri. He learned the value of civil service early from his parents, Sara L. Pegues Johnson, a secretary at the St. Louis Board of Elections, and James J. Johnson, a police officer and tax collector. Young Harry was an active and industrious young man who worked at a variety of part time jobs from the time he was eleven years old. He delivered newspapers, sold drinks at the St. Louis Opera's outdoor concerts, and waited tables in restaurants, not because his family needed the extra money, but simply because he enjoyed being productive.

His parents divorced when he was nine, and Johnson was further influenced towards ideals of service to the community by the supportive men around him. Mentors such as James Buckley, a family friend, and Nathaniel Jackson, a neighborhood coach, always seemed to have time and attention to give to the young men in their lives. The values that he learned from them ensured that Harry Johnson would grow up to be such a man himself.

The Johnsons were Roman Catholic, and young Harry went to Catholic schools for most of his education, beginning with his early years at the small parochial school of St. Barbara's. When it was time to enter high school, he applied and was accepted at Christian Brothers College (CBC), a rigorous Catholic military academy. Though CBC was demanding, Johnson enjoyed the challenge, and during his high school years, he made the decision to attend college. With the help of financial aid, he went south to New Orleans to enter Xavier University of Louisiana, an historically black Catholic college established in 1925.

Johnson earned his bachelor's degree in political science at Xavier in 1977, and then returned home to St. Louis, where he attended graduate school at Washington University. He was pursuing a master's degree in public administration when he decided to go to law school. A law degree would not only help him if he decided on a political career; it would allow him the independence of working for himself. He attended Texas Southern University's Thurgood Marshall School of Law. After completing his education, Johnson decided to stay in Texas and set up his private law practice in Houston. In addition to working as an attorney, he also worked as an adjunct, or part time, lecturer at Thurgood Marshall.

While a student at Xavier, Johnson had joined Alpha Phi Alpha, the oldest black fraternity in the United States. Greek-letter fraternities and sororities, or brotherhood and sisterhood organizations, for white students had been first created as the new nation was

At a Glance . . .

Born Harry Edward Johnson on September 29, 1954, in St. Louis, Missouri; married Karen, 1980; children: Jennifer, Harry, Jr. and Nicholas. *Education:* Xavier University, BA, political science, 1977; Thurgood Marshall School of Law, Texas Southern University, JD, 1986.

Career: Private law practice, 1986–; Thurgood Marshall School of Law, Texas Southern University, adjunct professor of law, 2000-04; Martin Luther King, Jr. National Memorial Project Foundation, president and chief executive officer, 2005–.

Selected memberships: National Bar Association; American Bar Association; National Association for the Advancement of Colored People; Alpha Phi Alpha, national president, 2001-2004; Big Brothers and Big Sisters, National Board of Directors, 2001–.

Addresses: *Office*—7457 Harwin Drive, Suite 390, Houston, TX 77036.

forming in 1776. Fraternal clubs offered support and promoted academic excellence among their members.

During the 1800s and early 1900s, only a few courageous African Americans were able to obtain higher education. Many of these attended historically black colleges and universities, while others went to the few white institutions that granted them admittance. It was seven such students, who entered Ithaca, New York's Cornell University in 1905, who founded Alpha Phi Alpha. They saw that the isolation and discrimination that many black students experienced made a successful college career almost impossible, and they hoped that supportive national organizations could enable more African Americans to graduate.

Alpha Phi Alpha was followed by other national black Greek-letter fraternities and sororities, forming a national network of encouragement and cooperation for black students. In fact, this black Greek system has continued to offer career and social support to its members long after graduation. Many African Americans remain proud members of their fraternities and sororities throughout their lives. Along with providing support to members and promoting academic excellence, organizations such as Alpha Phi Alpha also sponsor a wide variety of community and social service programs.

Like many members, Harry Johnson remained an active member of his fraternity, and, from 2001 through 2004, he took a leadership role as national president of Alpha Phi Alpha. During his presidency, Johnson introduced a number of creative programs to build the fraternity's active membership and to develop its relationship to the community through mentorship and volunteering. He also helped coordinate the efforts of the black Greek system by participating in the National Pan Hellenic Council of Presidents, which includes the leadership of all nine historically black fraternities and sororities.

When Johnson left the presidency of Alpha Phi Alpha in 2004, it was to devote more energy to a project that was very near to the fraternity's heart. In 1984, one year after the establishment of the Martin Luther King national holiday, members of Alpha Phi Alpha had begun to work towards the creation of a national monument honoring the murdered civil rights leader. King was not only one of the most influential and visible leaders of the civil rights movement, but he had also been a member of Alpha Phi Alpha since attending graduate school at Boston University during the early 1950s. The members of Alpha Phi Alpha believed that a memorial honoring King's accomplishments and belief in non-violent resistance would be appropriate as the first African-American national monument.

It took many years of fundraising and lobbying, but in 1996, President Bill Clinton signed a bill proposing the monument, and in 1998 both houses of Congress passed a resolution authorizing four acres on the National Mall in Washington, DC, for the construction of the monument.

While serving as president of Alpha Phi Alpha, Johnson became dedicated to the creation of the memorial, and when he left the presidency of the fraternity, it was to take on the job of president and chief executive officer of the Martin Luther King, Jr. National Memorial Project Foundation. While still conducting his private law practice, Johnson continues to develop creative projects to publicize and raise funds for the memorial. Groundbreaking for the Martin Luther King, Jr. National Memorial is set for the end of 2006, and the monument, which will sit between the Jefferson and Lincoln Memorials on the National Mall, is scheduled to be completed in 2008.

Sources

Books

Brown, Tamara L. with Gregory S. Parks and Clarenda M. Phillips, editors, *African-American Fraternities and Sororities: The Legacy and the Vision,* University of Kentucky Press, 2005.

Periodicals

Jet, December 4, 2000, p. 46.
Oakland Post, February 20, 2002, p. 4.

Sacramento Observer, November 24-November 30, 2005, p. G1.

On-line

"Executive Staff," *Build the Dream,* www.mlkmemorial.org/site/c.hkIUL9MVJxE/b.1190565/k. A274/Executive_Staff.htm (March 15, 2006).

"Harry E. Johnson, Esquire," *GM,* www.gm.com/company/gmability/community/mlk/news/bios/johnson_bio.html (March 15, 2006).

"Interview with Harry E. Johnson," *Tavis Smiley Show: PBS,* www.pbs.org/kcet/tavissmiley/archive/200502/20050210_transcript.html (March 15, 2006).

"Meet Some of the MLK 'Dream Builders': Keeping the Dream Alive for the Ages," *Onyx Magazine Online,* www.onyxmagazine.com/aspx/feature_mlkmemorial.aspx (March 15, 2006).

Other

Information for this profile was obtained through an interview with Harry E. Johnson on March 20, 2006.

—Tina Gianoulis

Hank Jones

1918—

Jazz pianist, composer

Jones, Hank, photograph. Michael Buckner/Getty Images.

One of the great survivors of jazz piano, Hank Jones has adapted his playing to a huge variety of styles over a career that has lasted more than 75 years. Through it all, Jones maintained a distinctive personal style at the keyboard, one sometimes described as harplike. While many jazz pianists cultivate a percussive style, striking the keys of the instrument sharply, Jones's playing is liquid and elegant. He has accompanied a host of the great names among jazz instrumentalists and vocalists for several generations, appeared on classic jazz recordings, and released many successful albums under his own name.

Henry "Hank" Jones was born in Vicksburg, Mississippi, on July 31, 1918. His father was drawn north by the chance to work in the auto industry, and the family—father, mother, and seven children—moved into a large house in Pontiac, Michigan. The whole family was musical. Jones's father was a blues guitarist (and a Baptist deacon on Sundays), his mother sang, and his siblings studied music. One of Jones's younger brothers, Elvin, became a highly influential jazz drummer, and another, Thad, a noted trumpeter. All kinds of

music filtered through the house: the young Jones heard jazz pianists such as Thomas "Fats" Waller and Earl "Fatha" Hines, soaked up gospel music in his Pontiac neighborhood, and sat down with the family to listen to Sunday broadcasts by the Detroit Symphony Orchestra.

Jones's own first musical training came in the form of classical piano lessons, but he and his brothers were soon playing along to 78 rpm records by piano virtuoso (and trio specialist) Art Tatum. Jones began his career performing for school dances at the age of 13. Jones joined various Detroit bands and traveled around the Great Lakes with what were then called "territory" bands, regional ensembles that often incubated new styles. In 1944, Detroit saxophonist Eli "Lucky" Thompson suggested that Jones move to New York and recommended him for a spot in the band of trumpeter Oran "Hot Lips" Page.

Jones did well from the start. He had the skills to survive in New York's competitive jazz environment. "People heard me and said, 'Well, this is not just a boy from the country—maybe he knows a few chords,'" Jones told Ben Waltzer of the *New York Times*.

At a Glance . . .

Born Henry Jones on July 31, 1918, in Vicksburg, MS; father a Baptist deacon and blues guitarist; family moved to Pontiac, MI; one of seven children; two brothers, Elvin and Thad, became jazz musicians.

Career: Musician, 1931–; CBS television, staff pianist, 1959-74; *Ain't Misbehavin',* Broadway musical, pianist and music director, late 1970s.

Awards: ASCAP Jazz Wall of Fame, 2003.

Addresses: *Label*—Justin Time Records, 5455 Paré, Suite 101, Montreal, Quebec, Canada, H4P 1P7.

Whether because of his classical training or just because he had a superior ear, Jones quickly learned to function in various styles that were current in New York jazz of the 1940s. He studied the music of bebop pianist Bud Powell and picked up the then-radical new bebop style, with its complex harmonies and its virtuoso improvisations based on the harmonies, rather than the melodies, of a piece's opening material. He developed a special flair for accompanying singers, backing bebop vocalist Billy Eckstine early in his career and, after a stint with the roster of the Jazz at the Philharmonic concert series, settling in for a six-year run as Ella Fitzgerald's accompanist in 1947.

In the 1950s, with jazz clubs flourishing in New York City, Jones was ubiquitous in live appearances and on records. He worked at various times with Charlie Parker (1952's "Cosmic Rays" was a classic example of Jones's cool under the pressure of Parker's intense improvisations), tenor saxophonist Lester Young, vibraphonist Milt Jackson, and numerous other musicians whose paths crossed his because he was serving as the de facto house pianist at the jazz label Savoy. Jones joined clarinetist Artie Shaw's Gramercy 5 group in 1954, appearing on some of the last recordings Shaw made before his sudden retirement. Perhaps the biggest jazz classic to which Jones contributed his keyboard skills was saxophonist Cannonball Adderley's 1958 release *Something Else,* with an all-star lineup that included Miles Davis on trumpet.

Jones also released highly regarded recordings under his own name, often in a small-group format. These included *Urbanity* (1953), *The Jazz Trio of Hank Jones* (1955), and *The Hank Jones Quartet/Quintet* (1955), of which Waltzer wrote that "the pianist is attached to the soloist like a sidecar to a motorcycle. He balances and grounds the horn players, helping to navigate their improvisation." Jones's productivity was partly due to his avoidance of the substance abuse

problems that plagued many of his contemporaries. "I've always tried to live cleanly," he told Michael Anthony of the Minneapolis *Star Tribune.* "I didn't fall into the bad habits a lot of the guys got into: the smoking, the drinking, the narcotics. I've tried to take care of myself."

Jones's stability, and his knack for adapting himself to varying musical surroundings, extended his career to a remarkable length. In 1959 he became staff pianist for the CBS television network, providing piano music and accompanying larger groups for any program—from *The Ed Sullivan Show* to *Captain Kangaroo*—that needed jazz accompaniment, and for the dancers and even trained animal acts that came through the door at CBS to audition for a spot on a talk show. In the late 1970s Jones moved to Broadway, serving as musical director and pianist for the Fats Waller-themed musical *Ain't Misbehavin'* and expanding on Waller's tunes in late-night shows at the nearby Ziegfeld Restaurant after the curtain came down.

After the end of the show's run in the early 1980s, Jones began collecting Social Security checks but this did not signal the end of his musical career. A remarkable series of recordings under his own name began with *Moods Unlimited* in 1982 and continued through critically acclaimed projects that demonstrated the range of his abilities. He recorded duo-piano music with his Detroit-born contemporary Tommy Flanagan. His familiarity with Fats Waller's music served as the basis for *Handful of Keys* (1993), and other releases encompassed a broad sweep of jazz history. With bassist Charlie Haden he recorded an album of pieces, *Steal Away,* based on African-American spirituals; he recorded with West African musicians; he accompanied singer Abbey Lincoln in an album of duets; and he joined his brother Elvin on an album of music by the late Thad Jones, the third Jones brother who had helped shape modern jazz.

In 2003 Jones bounced back from an aortic aneurysm and resumed a busy concert schedule. In 2005 he was featured on two albums, *For My Father* and saxophonist Joe Lovano's *Joyous Encounter.* Slowing down wasn't part of his plans. "Every appearance that I do, I want to be better than the last one," he told Frank Spignese of the *Daily Yomiuri* in Japan, where he traveled for shows at Blue Note jazz clubs in Tokyo and Osaka in 2006. "Every solo that I take, I want to be better than the previous one. I want to improve to the point where I can't improve anymore. I don't think that will ever happen. You keep pushing that horizon back a little farther. If you keep making the effort, you'll show some progress."

Selected works

Albums

Urbanity, Verve, 1953.

Bluebird, Savoy, 1955.
The Hank Jones Quartet/Quintet, Savoy, 1955.
The Jazz Trio of Hank Jones, Savoy, 1955.
The Talented Touch, Capitol, 1958.
Arrival Time, RCA, 1962.
This Is Ragtime Now, Paramount, 1964.
Happenings, Impulse, 1966.
Just for Fun, Original Jazz Classics, 1977.
Bop Redux, Muse, 1977.
Groovin' High, Muse, 1978.
Great Jazz Trio at the Village Vanguard, vols. 1 and 2, East World, 1980.
Moods Unlimited, Evidence, 1982.
The Oracle, EmArcy, 1989.
Lazy Afternoon, Concord Jazz, 1989.
A Handful of Keys: The Music of Thomas "Fats" Waller, Verve, 1992.
Upon Reflection: The Music of Thad Jones, Verve, 1994.
(with Charlie Haden) *Steal Away,* Verve, 1994.
Master Class, 32 Jazz, 1997.
Favors, Verve, 1997.
Compassion, Black & Blue, 2002.
For My Father, Justin Time, 2005.

Sources

Books

Contemporary Musicians, volume 15, Gale, 1995.
Stokes, Royal W., *The Jazz Scene: An Informal History from New Orleans to 1990,* Oxford, 1991.

Periodicals

Billboard, May 14, 2005, p. 46.
Daily Yomiuri (Japan), March 2, 2006.
Entertainment Weekly, April 22, 1994, p. 59.
Jet, April 21, 2003, p. 36.
New York Times, June 24, 2001, p. AR28.
Star Tribune (Minneapolis, MN), February 23, 2003, p. F10.

On-line

"Hank Jones" (interview), *All About Jazz,* www.all-aboutjazz.com/php/article.php?id=678 (April 9, 2006).
"Jazz Profiles from NPR: Hank Jones," *National Public Radio,* www.npr.org/programs/jazzprofiles/archive/jones_h.html (April 9, 2006).

—James M. Manheim

Calestous Juma

1953—

Technology policy analyst

"Evolutionary technological change," conservation of biodiversity, biotechnology for sustainable economic development, "biodiplomacy," "ecological jurisprudence," global climate change, and the creation of a "knowledge-based economy" for Africa—these are among the concepts that Dr. Calestous Juma has developed and examined during his distinguished career in science and technology policy. From his early years as East Africa's first science and environmental journalist and founder and director the African Centre for Technology Studies (ACTS)—Africa's first independent think-tank—through his career with the United Nations (UN) and as a Harvard University professor, Juma's influence has been felt in Africa and around the world.

A prolific author, the major focus of Juma's research has been the interrelatedness of technological innovation, particularly biotechnology, sustainable development, and environmental protection. His research interests also include evolutionary and systems theory, institutional change, international trade, and globalization.

Founded ACTS

Calestous Juma was born on June 9, 1953, in Busia, Kenya, the son of John Juma Kwada and Clementina Okhubedo Juma. At the age of 21, Juma went to work as a schoolteacher in Mombasa, Kenya. Subsequently he became a journalist for the *Nation* newspaper in Nairobi and initiated the first-ever regular coverage of environmental issues in the local media. In 1979 Juma

was hired as a researcher at the Environment Liaison Center (ELC) in Nairobi. There he edited the ELC's trilingual journal, *Ecoforum,* which was distributed globally. The publication covered issues such as food production, energy utilization, and the management of genetic resources.

Eventually Juma moved to England to pursue advanced studies. He earned his doctoral degree in science and technology policy studies in 1986 from the University of Sussex. For his dissertation Juma formulated his concept of "evolutionary technological change" to explain how cultures with different social traditions and economies adapted to new technologies.

Returning to Nairobi, Juma founded ACTS in 1988 and served as its executive director until 1995. As Africa's first non-profit research institute for examining the role of technology in development, ACTS concentrated on science, technology, and environmental policies for sustainable development.

Questioned the Patenting of Life

Juma first garnered widespread attention with his 1989 book *The Gene Hunters.* It was one of the first examinations of the patenting of life forms, particularly plants. Juma claimed that crop improvements made by farmers over thousands of years constituted the "heritage of humanity." He questioned the ethics of private ownership of biological specimens and collections and argued that patenting of genetic material, with royalties paid to plant breeders and geneticists, was really the work of farmers. Juma demonstrated how patenting crops had led to a loss of genetic diversity and the transfer of food production from individual farmers to large corporations.

With co-editor Vicente Sánchez, Juma coined the term "biodiplomacy" to describe a strategy for economic development that would meet global food and medical needs. Their strategy encompassed innovation, biotechnology, and trade in natural products, while maintaining biodiversity and traditional knowledge systems. In his 1996 book, *In Land We Trust*, Juma introduced the concept of "ecological jurisprudence" to describe the relationships between property rights and conservation. By 1990 Juma also was researching and writing about the effects of global climate change on Africa.

In 1995 Juma was named executive secretary of the 174-member UN Convention on Biological Diversity. Three years later he became special advisor to the Center for International Development at the John F. Kennedy School of Government at Harvard. In 2000 he was named director of the Center's Science, Technology and Globalization Project. In 2002 Juma became professor of the practice of international development at the Kennedy School's Belfer Center for Science and International Affairs (BCSIA). He also held visiting appointments at the UN University in Tokyo, Japan, and the University of Strathclyde in Scotland, and served as chancellor of the University of Guyana.

Coordinated UN Millennium Project Task Force

Among Juma's major concerns have been the application of modern biotechnology to the massive healthcare requirements of Africa and the development of sustainable African agriculture and industries that could compete in the global economy. At the World Summit on Sustainable Development in 2002, Juma launched a study of satellite technology for mapping Earth's population and natural resources. In a 2002 interview titled "What Difference Does a Summit Make?" Juma told Jeanie Barnett of the BCSIA: "Partnerships between governments, business and community are now the key to a sustainable future. No single institution will be able to solve all of the world's problems like air and water pollution, sanitation, health, and growing enough food for the burgeoning human population. Solving these problems will require the resources and technical expertise of many people in government, industry, academia and civil society." Juma also studied issues of biotechnology, sustainable development, and geographical information sciences in his committee work for the National Academy of Sciences. In 2006, he urged Kenya to develop programs in wildlife biotechnology to protect endangered species.

Juma served as co-coordinator of the UN Millennium Project's Task Force on Science, Technology and Innovation. He was lead author of the influential 2005 report *Innovation: Applying Knowledge in Development*. In it, Juma outlined his blueprint for sustainable development in Africa, using African universities for the promotion and utilization of science and technology. In his writings, Juma called for the development of a new kind of African university, with an emphasis on community-based technological innovations and business partnerships. He has called upon the scientific community to become integrally involved in government and UN policy decisions. In addition to numerous articles on a wide variety of topics, Juma edited the *International Journal of Technology and Globalization* and the *International Journal of Biotechnology*. As of 2006, his latest book, *Taming the Gene: Biotechnology in the Global Economy*, was forthcoming.

In May of 2005, Juma told the *Earth & Sky Radio Series*: "The new vision for development is to ensure that we can advance human welfare while at the same time protecting the environment…. [N]one of this can be achieved without a renewed investment in science and technology, a better understanding of ecosystem dynamics, and new ways of designing goods and services…. [T]his places the universities in a very strategic location, institutionally, in that technical institutions will have two fundamental roles. One is generating new knowledge. And the second is serving as engines of community development in their own rights." Juma appeared particularly well poised to become a leader on these issues.

Selected writings

Books

The Quest for Harmony: Perspectives on the New International Development Strategy, ELC, 1980.
(With David Stuckey) *Power Alcohol in Kenya and Zimbabwe: A Case Study in the Transfer of a Renewable Energy Technology*, United Nations, 1985.
(With Norman Clark) *Long-Run Economics: An Evolutionary Approach to Economic Growth*, Pinter, 1987.
Biological Diversity and Innovation: Conserving and Utilizing Genetic Resources in Kenya, ACTS, 1989.
The Gene Hunters: Biotechnology and the Scramble for Seeds, Princeton University, 1989.
(With J. B. Ojwang, eds.) *Innovation and Sovereignty: The Patent Debate in African Development* ACTS, 1989.
(With S. H. Ominde, eds.) *A Change in the Weather: African Perspectives on Climatic Change*, ACTS, 1991.
(With Vicente Sánchez, eds.) *Biodiplomacy: Genetic Resources and International Relations*, ACTS, 1994.
(With John Mugabe and Patricia Kameri-Mbote, eds.)

Coming to Life: Biotechnology in African Economic Recovery, ACTS, Zed, 1995.
(With J. B. Ojwang, eds.) *In Land We Trust: Private Property, Environment and Constitutional Change*, Initiatives Publishers, Zed, 1996.
(With Karen Fang) "Bridging the Genetic Divide," in *Genetically Modified Foods: Debating Biotechnology*, Prometheus, 2002.
(Editor) *Going for Growth: Science, Technology and Innovation in Africa*, Smith Institute, November, 2005.
(With Lee Yee-Cheong) *Innovation: Applying Knowledge in Development*, Earthscan, 2005.

Periodicals

"International Ecosystem Assessment," *Science*, Vol. 286, October, 22, 1999, pp. 685-686.
"How Not to Save the World," *New Scientist*, Vol. 175, No. 2362, September 28, 2002, p. 24.
"The Way to Wealth," *New Scientist*, Vol. 185, No. 2482, January 15, 2005, p. 21.
"Harsh Lessons from Togo," *Boston Globe*, February 21, 2005.
"Biotechnology in a Globalizing World: The Coevolution of Technology and Social Institutions," *Bioscience*, Vol. 55, No. 3, March 2005, pp. 265-272.
(With Lee Yee-Cheong) "Reinventing Global Health: The Role of Science, Technology, and Innovation," *The Lancet*, Vol. 365, No. 9464, March 19-25, 2005, pp. 1105-1107.
(With Vanessa Timmer) "Taking Root: Biodiversity Conservation and Poverty Reduction Come Together in the Tropics," *Environment*, Vol. 47, No. 4, May 2005, pp. 24-44.
(With Allison DiSenso) "Political Parties as Tools of Democracy," *Daily Nation* (Kenya), January 11, 2006.

On-line

"'Satan's Drink' and a Sorry History of Global Food Fights," *FT.com*, https://registration.ft.com/registration/barrier?referer=&location=http%3A//news.ft.com/cms/s/10b5a072-9911-11da-aa99-0000779e2340.html (March 23, 2006).

Sources

Periodicals

Bioscience, November 1990, pp. 785-786.

On-line

"Calestous Juma," *BCSIA*, http://bcsia.ksg.harvard.edu/person.cfm?item_id=258 (January 24, 2006).
"Calestous Juma: Curriculum Vitae," *Friedman School of Nutrition Science and Policy, Tufts University*, http://nutrition.tufts.edu/pdf/conferences/agri_biotech/cvjuma.pdf (March 23, 2006).

"Calestous Juma," *Kennedy School of Government Faculty,* http://ksgfaculty.harvard.edu/Calestous_Juma (January 26, 2006).

"Calestous Juma: What Difference Does a Summit Make?" *BCSIA,* http://bcsia.ksg.harvard.edu/publication.cfm?program=CORE&ctype=media_feature&item_id=303&ln=qanda&gma=49 (March 23, 2006).

"Dr. Calestous Juma, Ph.D.," *Pew Fellows Directory,* www.pewmarine.org/pewFellowsDirectoryTemplate.php?PEWSerialInt=3572 (March 23, 2006).

"Scientific Innovations Help Developing Nations," *Earth & Sky Radio Series,* www.earthsky.com/humanworld/shows.php?date=20050519 (March 23, 2006).

—Margaret Alic

Erika J. Kendrick

1974—

Entertainment and marketing executive, event planner, producer, author

Erika Kendrick is president of the New York network of the National Association of Black Female Executives in Music and Entertainment (NABFEME), a non-profit group whose mission is to support women of color in the entertainment industry through various alliances and support programs. Realizing how much the group did for her own life and career, Kendrick is dedicated to its principles. She is a remarkable woman with a career that is already worthy of a memoir, as one literary agent told her. Kendrick is a marketing executive and event planner in the entertainment industry and has worked for some of the most successful entertainment and pubic relations firms in the industry. Creating marketing campaigns for some of the biggest celebrities, Kendrick's work is featured in national publications like *Ebony* magazine. Kendrick also writes and produces for television. In 2007 she will publish her first novel, despite having no prior experience in publishing. A second novel is slated to publish in 2008.

Kendrick had a wonderful upbringing in a loving home on Chicago's south side. Her arrival had been a long-anticipated blessing for her parents, Benjamin and Estaleta Kendrick. The couple had tried for years to start a family, so when their baby girl was born on May 19, 1974, they believed that she was indeed special. With all the attention her parents lavished on her, it's curious that Kendrick would spend most of her youth worried that the world wouldn't notice her. "As I got older, I even became afraid of not being recognized professionally," Kendrick said in an interview with *Contemporary Black Biography (CBB)*. "I needed to know my purpose...my passion." Kendrick spent her

early years in an anxious and painful search for whatever that was. It was a dark time in her life that lasted until her late twenties. "At the time, I believed that if I could get a ray of hope, I would grab it and hold on to it," Kendrick told *CBB*.

After high school, Kendrick went off to Stanford University and completed an undergraduate degree in psychology, a field that had always piqued her interest, in 1996. Later she completed an M.B.A. in marketing and international business at the University of Illinois in 2002. That year Kendrick found an opportunity to do promotional and marketing work for Clive Davis at J Records, one of the hottest labels in the business. Spending several months at the label, Kendrick learned about the music business and developed a "thick skin." The music industry isn't an easy one, especially for a woman, Kendrick noted. "It was an 'ole boy network,'" she told *CBB*, "and I had gone into it blindly." Her next job, a sales job with Island Def Jam Records, offered her greater opportunities, and so excited her that she didn't even mind the office they gave her: the supply room. At Island Def Jam Records, she danced backup for several groups and performed in a few music and cable access videos. In 2003, Kendrick left Island Def Jam Records.

Kendrick had grown tired of the dog-eat-dog music business and turned her sights elsewhere. It was during this time that Kendrick realized that marketing was what she was "born to do." She has since worked in marketing and production for such companies as the Apollo Theater in Harlem and Way Out World Productions in New York. She enjoys the psychology behind

At a Glance . . .

Born on May 19, 1974, in Chicago, IL. *Education:* Stanford University, BA, psychology, 1996; University of Illinois, MBA, marketing and international business, 2002.

Career: Chicago Bulls *Luva*-bulls/ NBA Chicago Bulls, Chicago, IL, cheerleader/dancer, 1998-99; Ogilvy Public Relations Worldwide, intern, Chicago, IL, 2001; J Records, promotions and marketing, 2002; Island Def Jam, New York, NY, marketing and sales, 2002-03; Apollo Theater, Harlem, NY, marketing and production, 2004; Way Out World Productions, New York, NY, pilot producer, 2004; Random House, New York, NY, author, 2006–.

Memberships: National Association of Black Female Executives in Music and Entertainment, New York Chapter, president; National Association of Black Journalists; Delta Sigma Theta, Inc.; Stanford Alumni Association; National Black MBA Association.

Awards: Exceptional Women in Business, 2004; Who's Who Among Graduate Students, 2002.

Addresses: *Office*—Erika Benjamin, Inc., 561 10th Avenue, Suite 42F, New York, NY 10036.

marketing. "I like how it relates to what drives the consumer, and the fact that it allows a degree of creativity." The work often involves aggressive marketing to increase brand awareness and visibility in the "trendsetter's segment of the urban market." Kendrick also produces for television and independent film out of New York City. Even though Kendrick discovered how to employ her talents, she also credited another factor for her success. "I think fear motivates me also," she told *CBB.* "I've always been driven by it to do well. It has made me push to be good at things that I may not have been good at initially."

Kendrick attributes much of her success to the National Association of Black Female Executives in Music and Entertainment (NABFEME) and its founder, Johnnie Walker. When Kendrick became involved with NABFEME in 2002, she was going through a particularly rough time in her life. She said they saved her life. Walker, who was senior vice president of promotions at Island Def Jam Records at the time, had started the organization to assist women of color who were filling the ranks of the music business in greater numbers. Kendrick met Walker at one of NABFEME's mixers and bared her soul to Walker about what she was feeling about her life and career. Kendrick wanted to make it in the entertainment world but could not get the break she needed. She was extremely and dangerously depressed and she knew it. Walker took her under her wing, invited her to a conference in Toronto, and then to the company's New York offices for several weeks. While there, Kendrick received a job offer from another executive who had also heard what Kendrick was going through. She's been sailing ever since.

Building on this success, Kendrick found good fortune in another arena in 2006: publishing. Random House will publish Kendrick's first novel in 2007 and a second novel in 2008. Her first novel, about a rookie cheerleader, grabbed the attention of an interested agent immediately after she sent it out. The agent loved Kendrick's characters and shopped the book around until she found the Random House deal. Kendrick had never published before. In fact, although she always loved to write, she had never let anyone read any of her writing. But she sensed that this work was good enough to publish. The idea for the novel had come from a series of small pieces Kendrick had written while writing screenplays for television. She had looked over her collection one day and realized that she might have enough material for a novel. Her writing career—launched with *Confessions of a Rookie Cheerleader,* which she described as a "sweet love story"—was just waiting to be discovered.

Sources

On-line

"Erika Kendrick," *NABFEME,* www.nabfeme.org/html/Kendrick-erika2.htm (July 20, 2006).

Other

Additional information for this profile was obtained through an interview with Erika J. Kendrick on August 10, 2006.

—Sharon Melson Fletcher

Debra Killings

196(?)—

Vocalist, bassist, songwriter

With the big acoustic bass guitar she held in publicity photos, Debra Killings stood out in the world of gospel music after the release of her debut solo album, *Surrender,* on the Verity label in 2003. Killings was a multifaceted talent: she sang, wrote songs, and played many of the instruments heard on the album. Brandon A. Perry of the Indianapolis *Recorder* compared Killings with a musician famed for lyrical content that was far from gospel: "Like the secular music maestro Prince," he wrote, "Killings can play several instruments, especially bass guitar, rhythm guitar, keyboards, and drums." Before the release of *Surrender,* Killings's various talents had brought her a busy career as a session musician in Atlanta's vital urban music scene.

Born in the late 1960s, Killings was inspired in her unusual choice of instrument by an artist who held strong romantic attraction for girls of her generation. "It all started the first time I saw the Jackson 5," she told the *Miami Times.* "When I saw Jermaine [Jackson] playing the bass, I was hooked. Besides, I had a crush on him back then, too. I thought that, if I could play the bass, maybe I could meet Jermaine." That fantasy didn't pan out, but it did lead to a live appearance in front of a big crowd: Killings's older brother James was in a band that was scheduled to play at her high school prom, and Killings filled in when the band's bassist had to miss the gig due to an emergency.

Hooked, Killings began to work harder on her bass playing, and her brother James gave her some tips on technique. She became a member of the band, which took the name Modest Fok (pronounced "folk") and gained a following around the Atlanta area. The

group's sound was influenced by that of the chart-topping Earth, Wind and Fire. Over 11 years, they rose to the top of the Atlanta club scene and opened for national touring acts such as Zapp, the O'Jays, and the Bar-Kays. Part of the attraction was the tall, elegant Killings on bass—the only other prominent female bassist in the R&B genre at the time was Joyce "Fenderella" Irby of the all-woman group Klymaxx.

Killings learned other instruments and began writing songs. She contributed nine songs to Modest Fok's debut album, *Love or the Single Life,* which was released on Eastwest, an imprint of the major Atco label, in 1992. It was Joyce Irby who recommended the group to Atco executive Sylvia Rhone. Killings had already begun to stretch out her talents with session work by then; she received background vocal, production, and instrumental credits on the dance-pop album *The House That Glass Built,* by the group Glasswurk, in 1988. The title track of *Love or the Single Life* cracked *Billboard* magazine's hip-hop/R&B top 40.

As Atlanta evolved into a more and more important music center, Killings found herself in demand as a session musician. Performing both on bass and as a background vocalist, she notched between five and ten album credits almost every year between 1992 and 2005. On occasion, Killings also played guitar, drums, and keyboards, and did production and arranging work. Her slowest year was 1994, but one of her two credits that year was for backup vocals on an early Atlanta hip-hop classic—OutKast's *Southernplayalis-*

ticadillacmuzik. Killings continued to appear on Out-Kast albums up to the 2003 double-CD smash *Speakerboxxx/The Love Below,* and she was heard on some of the top-selling hip-hop and R&B releases of the late 1990s: discs like Monica's *The Boy Is Mine* and TLC's *FanMail* and *3D.* She played bass on both of the TLC discs. Killings was a favorite of producers and rappers for her adaptable bass style. On one OutKast album, she told Greg Olwell of *Bass Player* magazine, "I rolled up a paper towel and threaded it through the strings for a muted, heavy sound."

A committed Christian, Killings experienced no difficulty working in the secular hip-hop environment. "It's just living an everyday life to me," she explained to a *GospelFlava* interviewer. "Some people wake up and go to Wal-Mart. There's a lot of people who aren't born again in those situations also. So it was basically a job for me. I try to walk right, talk right, and carry myself right so that I could be a light to them." A bigger problem for Killings was discrimination against women in the music industry. "It affects you because as a woman, you seem to not get as much respect," she said in a Kay3Music interview. "You are pooled into a basket of mediocre and not adequate. But I'm not the show-off type that needs to go in and bust doors down."

As Killings looked for the opportunity to launch a solo career, gospel seemed to be the right direction for her next move. She had made music in churches since her childhood, and as she began playing in an Atlanta church band her songwriting went in a gospel direction. Killings made two demo recordings that passed through the hands of music executive Ian Burke and ended up with new Verity Records president Max Siegel in 2002. Even though Verity was a major force

in the gospel field and Killings had no track record in gospel, Siegel made Killings the first artist he signed to a contract at Verity.

His judgment proved accurate. Killings contributed several songs of her own to her debut album *Surrender,* and she turned to hip-hop producer Dallas Austin and former Xscape member Kandi Burress for "Message in the Music," an appealing song about the importance of music in drawing young people to religious services. "We were down in Miami, and Dallas just said, 'Debra, we have to come up with a song that talks about just growing up in the church,'" Killings recalled to *GospelFlava.* "When the preacher starts, I start yawning; I was tired and ready to go. I couldn't wait to leave," Killings sang. But then "The choir sang. They were off the chain. I started feeling differently." Most of the other songs on the album featured Killings prominently on the bass. *Surrender* brought Killings a nomination for best new artist at the gospel industry's Stellar Awards, held in Houston in January of 2004.

The album also raised Killings's profile as a session musician still higher. She played bass on rock legend Santana's *All That I Am* album in 2005 (with OutKast member Big Boi), and her schedule in 2005 and 2006 was packed with church appearances and a guest appearance on the album *Breathe Again* by the single-named New York-to-Atlanta transplant Jones and his new vocal group, the RITW Worshippers. Anticipation for the next manifestation of Debra Killings and her distinctive talents ran high.

Selected works

Albums

(With Modest Fok) *Love or the Single Life,* 1992.
Surrender, Verity, 2003.

Selected album credits (background vocals, unless otherwise noted)

Glasswurk, *House That Glass Built,* 1988 (background vocals, producer, instrumentation).
Bobby Brown, *Bobby,* 1992.
Toni Braxton, *Toni Braxton,* 2003.
OutKast, *Southernplayalisticadillacmuzik,* 1993.
Deion Sanders, *Prime Time,* 1995.
OutKast, *ATLiens,* 1996.
OutKast, *Aquemini,* 1998.
Monica, *The Boy Is Mine,* 1998.
TLC, *FanMail,* 1999 (bass, vocals).
TLC, *3D,* 2002 (bass, background vocals).
OutKast, *Speakerboxxx/The Love Below,* 2003 (bass, vocals).
Nelly, *Suit,* 2004 (bass).
Nelly, *Sweatsuit,* 2005 (bass).
Santana, *All That I Am,* 2005 (bass).

Sources

Periodicals

Atlanta Journal-Constitution, January 10, 2004, p. B2.
Bass Player, October 1, 2003, p. 24.
Billboard, November 5, 2005, p. 57.
Chicago Defender, August 14, 2003, p. 13.
Miami Times, June 25, 1992, p. D2.
Recorder (Indianapolis, IN), July 4, 1992, p. B1; February 27, 2004, p. B1.
State (Columbia, SC), August 15, 2003, p. E10.

On-line

"Bio," *Debra Killings,* www.debrakillings.com (March 29, 2006).

"Debra Killings," *All Music Guide,* www.allmusic.com (March 29, 2006).
"Debra Killings, *Surrender,*" *Christianity Today,* www.christianitytoday.com/music/reviews/2003/surrender.html (March 29, 2006).
"Debra Killings, *Surrender,*" *GospelFlava,* www.gospelflava.com.reviews/debrakillings.html (March 29, 2006).
"An Interview with Debra Killings," *Kay3Music,* www.kay3music.com/intervue/interviews.asp?id=33 (March 29, 2006).
"Interview with Debra Killings: There is a Message in Her Music," *GospelFlava,* www.gospelflava.com/articles/debrakillings2.html (March 29, 2006).

—James M. Manheim

Coretta Scott King

1927-2006

Civil rights activist, writer, singer

King, Coretta Scott, photograph. © Flip Schulke/Corbis.

On April 8, 1968, four days after her husband, civil rights leader Dr. Martin Luther King, Jr., was brutally gunned down by assassin James Earl Ray on the balcony of a Memphis motel, Coretta Scott King flew to that city to take her husband's place at the head of the march for nonviolent social change. After the march, King rose and addressed the crowd, urging them to join with her in pursuing her husband's dream: "And those of you who believe in what Martin Luther King, Jr., stood for, I would challenge you today to see that his spirit never dies.... From this moment on we are going to go forward. We are going to continue his work to make all people truly free and to make every person feel that he is a human being."

That day King began her emergence as one of the most charismatic and forceful civil rights leaders in the United States. She founded and served as president of the $10 million Martin Luther King, Jr., Center for Nonviolent Social Change in Atlanta, the first institution to honor an African American civil rights leader. She also gave hundreds of speeches everywhere from churches to college campuses, traveled the world over to meet with international, national, and local leaders to discuss race relations and human rights, wrote her autobiography, and edited a book of Dr. King's quotations. At the time of her death in 2006, she was widely revered as a symbol of dignity and perseverance in the face of great personal loss, as well as a champion of equal rights for all.

Raised in Racist South

Coretta Scott was born on April 27, 1927, into an America where—simply because of the color of their skin—black people were often taught in impoverished, segregated schools, denied access to hotels and restaurants and hospitals, and beaten and imprisoned at the slightest real or imagined offense. Coretta was the second of three children born to Obadiah and Bernice Scott of Heiberger, Alabama, nine miles outside of Marion. The Scotts raised their children on a farm that had been in their family since the Civil War. Though it was rare for black people to own land in the South at that time, the Scotts were not affluent. They were especially hard hit economically during the Depression years of the late 1920s and early 1930s. Coretta herself hoed and picked cotton to earn money for the family. Obie Scott raised garden veg-

At a Glance . . .

Born Coretta Scott on April 27, 1927, in Marion, AL; died January 31, 2006, in Baja California, Mexico; daughter of Obadiah and Bernice (McMurray) Scott; married Martin Luther King, Jr. (a Baptist minister and civil rights leader), June 18, 1953 (died April 4, 1968); children: Yolanda Denise, Martin Luther III, Dexter Scott, Bernice Albertine. *Education*: Antioch College, AB, 1951; New England Conservatory of Music, MusB, 1954.

Career: Concert singer, activist, lecturer, author. Debuted as singer in Springfield, OH, 1948; delegate to White House Conference on Children and Youth, 1960; Women's Strike for Peace delegate to disarmament conference, Geneva, Switzerland, 1962; Morris Brown College, Atlanta, GA, voice instructor, 1962; Martin Luther King, Jr., Center for Nonviolent Social Change, Inc., Atlanta, founding president and chief executive officer, 1969-2006; Cable News Network, Atlanta, commentator, 1980-2000s.

Memberships: Southern Christian Leadership Conference, board member; National Council of Negro Women; Women's Strike for Peace; Women's International League for Peace and Freedom; NAACP; Martin Luther King, Jr. Foundation, president.

Awards: National Council on Negro Women Annual Brotherhood Award, 1957; Louise Waterman Wise Award, 1963; Myrtle Wreath Award, Cleveland Hadassah, 1965; Wateler Peace Prize, 1968; Dag Hammerskjoeld Award, 1969; Pacem in Terris award, International Overseas Service Foundation, 1969; Premi Antonio Feltrinelli, 1969, for exceptional display of high moral valor; Leadership for Freedom Award, Roosevelt University, 1971; Martin Luther King Memorial Medal, College of the City of New York, 1971; Eugene V. Debs Award, 1982; Freedom Award, National Civil Rights Museum, 1991; Frontrunner Award, Sara Lee Corporation, 1996; humanitarian award, Martin Luther King Jr. State Holiday Commission, 1999; numerous honorary degrees.

etables, hogs, cows, and chickens on the farm and drove a taxi to supplement the family income. When he invested his savings in a sawmill of his own, it mysteriously burned to the ground after just two weeks.

Disillusioned but undefeated, Mr. Scott then became the first black man in his community to own a truck. He hauled lumber, an occupation which brought him into direct competition with white men, who grew more and more threatened by him as the availability of jobs declined. He was frequently stopped on the highway and harassed at gunpoint. Nonetheless, he eventually opened a country store. Mr. Scott had a sixth-grade education, which was considerable for a black man of his generation, and according to her friend and biographer Octavia Vivian, Coretta wondered later how much he might have achieved if he had the opportunity to earn a high school diploma.

Coretta's mother, Bernice, was the person from whom Coretta inherited both her musical talent and her desire for an education. Though she had only a fourth-grade education herself, Mrs. Scott insisted that her daughters attend college even if each had only one dress to wear. Thanks to her dedication and to some scholarship assistance, the Scotts were able to send all three of their children to college. Coretta's older sister Edythe was the first full-time black student ever to live on the campus of Antioch College. (After two years there, however, Edythe transferred to Ohio State University, which had a more racially diverse student body.) Obie Leonard, Coretta's younger brother, became a minister after attending Central State College in Wilberforce, Ohio, for two years.

An unusually sensitive and intelligent child, Coretta learned early on to recognize discrimination. Her first six years of education were spent at the Crossroads School, a one-room frame schoolhouse where just two teachers taught all six grades. Each day during the five-mile walk from their home to Crossroads, Coretta and her sister and brother were passed on the road by the school bus carrying the white children to their school in Marion. This experience, among others, awakened in Coretta an awareness of racial injustices and a sense of mission to end discrimination. She firmly believed herself destined to some sort of work that would help to improve the condition of oppressed people, especially those "black and deprived" as she had been, she told *Ebony*.

Pursued Education in the North

For a long time King thought that she would make her contribution through music. After graduating from Crossroads at the top of her classes, King went on to Lincoln High School in Marion, a private missionary school where, for the first time, she encountered college-educated teachers, both black and white. At Lincoln she began to develop her musical talent. She played the trumpet and piano and sang in the chorus, appearing as a soloist in a number of school recitals and musicals. Her high school music teacher, Olive J. Williams, is credited with inspiring her to consider music as a career.

Because Lincoln was ten miles away, Coretta and the other black students from her area had to leave home early Monday morning and could not return until the weekend. Coretta's mother, displaying the same calm determination that stood King herself in such good stead throughout her public life, decided that the children should not have to be away from home for such long stretches of time. She secured a bus and every school day drove all of the children herself the ten miles each way to and from school, an unheard-of activity for a woman in those days.

In 1945, King graduated first in her high school class and enrolled at Antioch College in Yellow Springs, Ohio. She had been granted a partial scholarship by the college's Race Relations Committee. Though she was at first anxious about adjusting to the alien environment of the northern school and about competing with the white students, she also realized the advantages of attending college in the North: northern schools were generally considered academically superior to those in the South. King decided to major in elementary education and in music.

While at Antioch, King participated in the college's challenging cooperative work-study program, in which students alternated a period of work with a period of study. As a work-study student she served the community in various roles, including that of nursery school attendant, camp counselor, and library assistant. Despite her earlier fears, she found most of her many opportunities at Antioch rewarding and challenging. She apparently did not encounter overt racial prejudice at the college until it came time for her to student teach.

Took a Stand on Racial Issues

Customarily, Antioch's education students were placed in the Yellow Springs, Ohio, public school district to practice teach, but those schools had no black teachers at that time. The supervisor of the program asked King to agree either to travel nine miles away to an all-black school to teach or to teach at the Antioch Demonstration School. Frustrated, King decided to take a stand about her right to teach in the public schools, regardless of her race.

She took her complaint all the way to the president of the college, but to no avail. Even her fellow students refused to support her, fearing that to do so would cost all of them their practice-teaching positions and ultimately their degrees. Bitterly disappointed to discover the shallowness of Antioch's commitment to integration, King decided to accept the compromise position at the Antioch Demonstration School and strengthened her resolve to quietly but firmly resist racial injustices.

Meanwhile, King's interest in music was growing. She added violin to her repertoire of musical instruments and sang in the choir at the Second Baptist Church in Springfield, Ohio, where she gave her first solo concert in 1948. Concerts in Pennsylvania and Alabama followed, and she began to consider continuing her musical education after college. The chairman of the music department at Antioch encouraged her to apply to Boston's New England Conservatory of Music and to the Smith Noyes Foundation for fellowship support.

By the time she graduated in June of 1951, King had been accepted at the conservatory. She decided to give up her plans to become a teacher and to pursue a career on the concert stage. Although her tuition was fully covered by the fellowship, King still had to earn her room and board. She had already arranged to rent a room in the home of a wealthy Massachusetts family. When she arrived in Boston, she further arranged to clean the fifth floor of the house, which she shared with two other students, and two stairways, in exchange for her bed and breakfast. Without money for dinner, though, she was forced to survive on the foods she could afford, like crackers, peanut butter, and fruit. As biographer Vivian put it, King "was in the unique position of living at one of the wealthiest addresses in America and starving."

Later her financial situation began to improve. The Urban League found her a job as a file clerk at a mail-order firm, and after her first year, she began receiving out-of-state aid from her home state of Alabama. This aid was provided for black students barred by segregation from attending white institutions in-state. King studied voice with retired opera star Marie Sundelius at the conservatory and also sang with the chorus and the Old South Choir.

Met and Married Martin Luther King, Jr.

While King was studying at the conservatory, another voice student introduced her to a young minister from Atlanta who was studying for a doctorate in theology at Boston University. Coretta Scott's first meeting with Martin Luther King, Jr., went badly; he overwhelmed the rather reserved young woman by hinting at marriage on that very first date. Nonetheless, they continued to see each other. Coretta was impressed with King's drive and his concern for the underprivileged. His feelings seemed so similar to her own. But she wondered if—with his solidly middle-class background—he could ever really understand the poverty he hoped to help alleviate. Moreover, as he continued to press her about marriage, she was forced to wrestle with the thought of giving up her dream of becoming a concert singer.

In the end, King and Scott's many similarities won out over their differences. Both had been precocious children, voracious readers, and excellent students. Both had fathers whose willingness to stand up for justice for blacks in the South had impressed their children deeply. Scott and King were married on the lawn of Coretta's parents' home in Heiberger by the Reverend King, Sr., on June 18, 1953. After the wedding, the couple returned to Boston to complete their educations. King was then offered positions at two Northern churches, two Southern churches, and three schools. They chose to accept the pastorate of the Dexter Avenue Baptist Church in Montgomery, Alabama, and moved there in September of 1954.

On December 1, 1955, a black seamstress named Rosa Parks sat down in the first row reserved for black people at the back of a public bus in Montgomery. She had worked all day and was tired. When the bus pulled up to the Empire Theater stop, a crowd of white people boarded. Following the laws and customs of the segregated South, the bus driver stood up and asked the black people to move further toward the back of the bus. Three other people moved immediately, but Rosa Parks remained in her seat. When she refused once again to move, a policeman was summoned, and she was arrested for defying segregation laws. Martin Luther King, Jr., organized the Montgomery bus boycott in protest, and the civil rights movement was born. A year later, as a result of the phenomenally successful boycott, the Supreme Court declared Alabama's bus segregation laws unconstitutional.

The Kings' first child, Yolanda Denise, fondly nicknamed "Yoki" by her father, had been born just two weeks before the beginning of the boycott in 1955. The couple went on to have two sons and another daughter. As Dr. King became more and more deeply involved in his nonviolent civil rights crusade, the burden of raising the children as well as a great deal of administrative work for the movement fell to Coretta. She handled the mail and phone calls from his office in their home, including the increasing number of threats on her husband's life.

Robert Johnson, in a 1991 article for *Jet*, recalled an anecdote once related by Martin Luther King, Jr. about his wife. Their phone had rung in the middle of the night. A sleepy Coretta picked it up to hear an angry voice on the other end of the line snarl: "I want to speak to that nigger who's running the bus boycott!" Calmly she replied, "My husband is asleep and does not wish to be disturbed. He told me to write the name and number of anyone who called to threaten his life so that he could return the call in the morning when he wakes up fresh." Indeed, King remained outwardly calm even when her husband was actually stabbed at a book signing in New York City by a black woman who was later institutionalized for mental incompetence. Splitting her time in the city between his hospital room and a temporary office that was set up for her there, King maintained the smooth operation of the civil rights movement.

Offered Steadying Presence in Civil Rights Movement

King's grace under pressure did not desert her even when the family's home in Montgomery was bombed. She, a friend from church, and Yolanda, then an infant, were the only ones home at the time of the incident, and no one was hurt. But from that moment on, King was acutely aware of the constant danger they faced. The harassment, the jailings, the bombings, and the threats terrified all of them. King realized that she could never find a way to live with such terror; she could either turn her back on their life's work, or banish the fear. She claimed in her autobiography that from then on she lived without fear but held onto the knowledge that death could come to any one of them because of their work to end racial injustice.

During this time King also pursued a number of activities independent of her husband's work. Aside from fulfilling the speaking engagements that he could not keep, she taught voice in the music department of Morris Brown College in Atlanta, where they had moved in 1960, when Martin assumed the co-pastorate of the Ebenezer Baptist Church alongside his father. In addition, King was a Women's Strike for Peace delegate at the Disarmament Conference attended by representatives of seventeen nations and held in Geneva, Switzerland, in 1962. Moreover, she made use of her artistic talents by developing and performing in the Freedom Concert, which featured readings, music, and poetry narrating the history of the civil rights movement. Proceeds from the very successful program were contributed to the Southern Christian Leadership Conference, of which Dr. King was then head.

When Martin Luther King, Jr., was assassinated in April of 1968, his wife's commitment to civil rights faced its most severe trial yet. She was, however, better prepared for such a loss than most people would be, both because of her strong religious faith and because she had long ago confronted the dangers inherent in her husband's work. In the days and weeks that followed his death, she calmed the anger and despair of King followers and urged recommitment to the philosophy of nonviolence. She walked in his place at marches and spoke at civil rights and anti-Vietnam War rallies. Gradually she came to be seen as the worthy successor to Dr. King and a leader and symbol of the civil rights struggle.

Became Leader in Her Own Right

Before the end of her first year without her husband, King announced plans for the creation of the Martin Luther King, Jr., Center for Nonviolent Social Change in King's hometown of Atlanta. Begun in the basement of her home in Atlanta, the King Center would grow to cover three full blocks near the Ebenezer Baptist

Church. The center houses offices, Dr. King's elevated marble crypt surrounded by a 100-foot long reflecting pool, and the Freedom Hall meeting facility, containing a 3000-seat auditorium, conference rooms, a cultural center, and the King Library and Archives. More than one and a half million visitors stroll down the arch-covered Freedom Walk each year. The center has an annual budget of $3.2 million and employs more than 60 people. Its library serves five thousand scholars annually, who come to peruse the more than one million documents of the civil rights movement held there, including the personal papers of Dr. Martin Luther King, Jr. By 1995, King had stepped down as chairman and CEO of the King Center, passing the job to her youngest son, Dexter King.

The King Center also sponsors programs in voter education and registration, literacy, the performing arts, early childhood education, and internships for college students from around the world who come to learn effective means of nonviolent social protest. A Federal Bureau of Prisons Project, which is a conflict-resolution training program for prison personnel; a Single Parents Program providing job training, housing assistance, and counseling services; and a Black Family Project, which studies the crises facing black families and coordinates resources to alleviate them, are among the innovative programs the center offers.

In addition, the center launched the petition campaign in favor of making Dr. King's birthday a national holiday. The drive for a holiday began soon after his death and was led by a coalition of black leaders, legislators, and entertainers. Six million signatures were collected and presented to U.S. Congress. After a decade and a half of demonstrations, lobbying, letter-writing campaigns, speeches, and marches—including one attended by several hundred thousand people commemorating the twentieth anniversary of Dr. King's March on Washington—the holiday proponents finally won out. On November 2, 1983, under pressure from black politicians in his own party, then-President Ronald Reagan finally signed the bill designating the third Monday in January as the King Holiday, beginning in 1986.

Even as she aged, King remained a spokesperson for issues affecting justice and civil rights. In 1983, King coordinated the Coalition of Conscience, which sponsored the 20th Anniversary March on Washington. In 1985, she was arrested along with three of her children at the South African embassy in Washington, D.C., in a protest against apartheid. In 1987, she was one of the leaders in the "Mobilization Against Fear and Intimidation" in Forsyth County, Ga. In 1988, she re-convened the Coalition of Conscience for the 25th Anniversary March on Washington. She was in the news again in 1997, calling for a new trial for her husband's convicted killer, James Earl Ray, who died the following year in prison without receiving a new trial. King was among those who believed that Ray was not the true killer, instead adhering to the conspiracy theory that a government intelligence agency committed the crime and used him as a patsy to cover it up.

As evidenced by her support for reform in South Africa, King has supported civil rights and freedom for people the world over. In March 2004, while speaking at the Richard Stockton College of New Jersey, King spoke out in support of the right of same-sex couples to marry. The issue had come to a head in the early months of 2004, with same-sex couples lining up outside courthouses across the country asking to be legally married in civil ceremonies. She called it a civil rights issue.

In the mid-to late-1990s, the King family drew sharp criticism for their handling of the center and King's legacy, at the core of which was a feud with the National Park Service over a proposed visitors center across the street from the King center. The King family planned to open an interactive museum and felt the Park Service plan would interfere. The two sides came to an agreement, and the Park Service opened their facility in 1996, but the King family did not go forward with their ideas. By 1999, the King family was again under fire for maintaining tight control over the Martin Luther King, Jr., image and his works, as well as for reaping generous profits off of the rights. But neither King nor her son would comment on any such controversy.

On January 31, 2006, King passed away in her sleep. She was 78 and had been in failing health since suffering a stroke and heart attack in August of 2005. Her death was widely mourned around the world, and U.S. President George W. Bush took note of her passing during his annual State of the Union address, noting that "Today our nation lost a beloved, graceful, courageous woman, who called America to its founding ideals and carried on a noble dream," according to *U.S. News & World Report*. Her funeral, held at the New Birth Missionary Baptist Church in Atlanta, was attended by more than 10,000 people, including four U.S. presidents and a who's who of African American figures from the worlds of politics, entertainment, and the continuing movement for civil rights for all people. Former President Bill Clinton, recalling the way that King carried on her work after the death of her husband, implored those in the audience, according to *Jet,* "If you want to treat our friend Coretta like a role model, then model her behavior. We can follow in her steps."

Selected writings

My Life with Martin Luther King, Jr., Holt, 1969; revised, 1993.

(Editor) King, Martin Luther, Jr., *The Words of Martin Luther King, Jr.*, Newmarket Press, 1983.

(Compiler) King, Martin Luther, Jr., *The Martin Luther King, Jr., Companion: Quotations from the Speeches, Essays, and Books of Martin Luther King, Jr.,* St. Martin's Press, 1993.

Sources

Books

Gelfand, Dale Evva, *Coretta Scott King: Civil Rights Activist,* Chelsea House, 2006.
King, Coretta Scott, *My Life with Martin Luther King, Jr.,* Holt, 1969.
Press, Petra, *Coretta Scott King: An Unauthorized Biography,* Heinemann, 2000.
Vivian, Octavia, *Coretta: The Story of Mrs. Martin Luther King, Jr.,* Fortress, 1970.

Periodicals

Ebony, January 1980; August 1982; January 1986; January 1987; January 1990; January 1991; April 1, 2006.
Economist, February 4, 2006.
Essence, April 1, 2006.
Jet, February 5, 1981; September 19, 1983; November 7, 1983; November 21, 1983; July 15, 1985; January 20, 1986; May 8, 1989; January 21, 1991; February 20, 2006; February 27, 2006.
Newsweek, February 13, 2006.
New York Times, January 31, 2006.
People Weekly, February 13, 2006.
U.S. News & World Report, February 13, 2006.

On-line

"Coretta Scott King, 78, Widow of Dr. Martin Luther King Jr., Dies," *New York Times,* www.nytimes.com/2006/01/31/national/31cnd-coretta.html?ex=1296363600&en=b96d2c2efb2dbbb4&ei=5088&partner=rssnyt&emc (August 2, 2006).
"Mrs. Coretta Scott King, Human Rights Activist and Leader," *The King Center,* www.thekingcenter.org/csk/bio.html (August 2, 2006).
"A Tribute to Coretta Scott King 1927-2006," *Antioch College,* www.antioch-college.edu/news/csk/index.html (August 2, 2006).

—Susan M. Marren and Tom Pendergast

Herbert Lowe

1962—

Journalist, organization executive

Reporter Herbert Lowe has been one of the most visible young African-American journalists in the United States. His journalism career has taken him from small-city newspapers to a court reporting beat at *Newsday* in the nation's largest market, New York City. He earned wide attention for a series of articles about men who had been erroneously convicted of murder. As president of the National Association of Black Journalists (NABJ) from 2003 to 2005, Lowe became a high-profile advocate for increased African-American representation in American newsrooms, and his keen focus on specific issues did much to revitalize an organization that had been losing membership and influence in the years before his presidency.

One of six children born to a single mother, Lowe was a native of Camden, New Jersey, outside of Philadelphia. His journalistic training took place at Marquette University in Milwaukee, Wisconsin, where he completed the requirements for a double major in broadcast journalism and political science, and also found time to serve as president of a group of black journalism students. He graduated from Marquette in 1984. After finishing school he worked for the *Milwaukee Community Journal* and for *Amateur Sports* magazine. Moving on to newspaper news staff jobs, he retained an enthusiasm for the sports teams of his native Philadelphia area.

Landing jobs at the *Press* of Atlantic City, New Jersey, and then the larger Bergen County *Record*, Lowe became president of the Garden State Association of Black Journalists. He moved on to the *Virginian-Pilot* of Norfolk, Virginia, where he received an unusual

honor of a sort: the chairman of the Portsmouth, Virginia, school board, on hearing that Lowe would be leaving for a new job, adjourned a meeting with the statement (as quoted in a letter to the *Virginian-Pilot*) that "Mr. Lowe's coverage of the activities and endeavors of Portsmouth Public Schools has always been fair and accurate. I am sure that we have not heard the last of him or of his successes." While in Virginia, Lowe served as adjunct professor at Norfolk State University.

Lowe moved on to the *Philadelphia Inquirer* in 1993. There he honed his journalistic chops on a variety of stories and assignments, "from the Miss America Pageant to political campaigns, from senseless murders to small-town festivals, from profiling civic advocates to exposing greedy developers," according to his NABJ biography. In 1995 he was elected NABJ secretary, and he won reelection in 1997. Two years later he became the organization's vice president for print publications. His assignments that year included a profile of Philadelphia mayoral candidate Dwight Evans and coverage of a city council meeting in his hometown of Camden that erupted into shouted attacks and shoving matches.

In February of 2000, Lowe took a staff writing position at *Newsday* in Queens, New York. The following year, he ran for the NABJ presidency but lost to Atlanta radio reporter Condace Pressley. His specific assignment at *Newsday* was the Queens court system, but he used that assignment to explore an issue of national significance: while covering a death-penalty trial in 2002, he joined with other reporters on a story, "The

At a Glance . . .

Born in 1962 in Camden, NJ; married, Mira (newspaper editor). *Education:* Marquette University, Milwaukee, WI, BA, political science and broadcast journalism, 1984. *Religion:* Christian.

Career: Reporting posts, *Amateur Sports* magazine, *Milwaukee Community Journal, Press* (Atlantic City, MJ), *Record* (Bergen County, MJ), *Virginian-Pilot* (Norfolk, VA); Philadelphia *Inquirer,* reporter, 1993-2000; *Newsday,* New York, 2000–.

Selected memberships: National Association of Black Journalists, secretary, 1995-99; vice president, print publications, 1999-2001; president, 2003-05; UNITY Journalists of Color, board member; Garden State Association of Black Journalists, past president; Alpha Phi Alpha fraternity; New York Association of Black Journalists.

Selected awards: Griot award, New York Association of Black Journalists, for series "The Wronged Men."

Addresses: *Office*—Newsday, Inc., 235 Pinelawn Rd, Melville, NY 11747-4250.

Wronged Men," that dealt with the situations of prisoners wrongfully convicted of murder. The story won a Griot award from the New York Association of Black Journalists (the organization's highest award) and became a finalist for a Deadline Club Award, presented by the New York chapters of the Society for Professional Journalists.

Supporters urged Lowe to run again for the NABJ presidency, and in 2003 he was elected. The organization he took over had a $2 million budget, but it had been mired in financial problems and losing membership for several years. "Someone once told me that NABJ has steadfastly refused to live up to its potential," Lowe observed ruefully to Errin Haines of the *NABJ Journal.* "I want to prove them wrong. We're not going to be able to do everything, but we're going to try to make a difference." Among the goals he articulated to Haines were these: "I want it to be said that during this administration we relieved ourselves of the perception that we are a one-week-a-year association and became a year-round association. That we once again began fighting for black journalists and shining a light on black journalists."

Lowe worked to address both specific and systemic issues related to newsroom diversity. A study of the Washington, D.C. press corps carried out during his presidency revealed that minority journalists (Americans of Asian, African, Hispanic, or Native American descent) made up less than 12 percent of Washington reporters, a poor showing compared with the more than 30 percent of the nation's population these groups represented. "The numbers generated by this survey," Lowe was quoted as saying in the *Washington Post,* "quantify what black journalists have always known—that we don't get to cover some of the most coveted beats in our profession, the ones that involve coverage of the most pressing issues affecting our country overall and our communities." Lowe also stepped up recruitment efforts directed at promising high school and college black journalists, and he tried to address a trend that saw black journalists leave the profession for better-paying academic or public relations jobs after becoming frustrated about their prospects for advancement.

The issue of professional development was an important one for Lowe. "Yes, they [publishing executives] value diversity, yes they value us, but do they give us an opportunity to lead and achieve?" Lowe asked Martin C. Evans of *Newsday.* "Until we get the offices with the glass windows, we will be dependent on others to do the right thing." Black journalists responded to Lowe's initiatives with a new level of commitment to the NABJ. The organization's membership rose from about 3,100 to more than 4,000 during Lowe's two-year term as president. In 2004 he was named one of *Ebony* magazine's 100+ Most Influential Black Americans, and he maintained his place on the list the following year.

After he stepped down from the NABJ presidency in 2005, Lowe remained busy with other organizational posts. In 2003 he had joined the board of UNITY: Journalists of Color, Inc., a pan-ethnic minority journalists' group, and its convention in Washington in August of 2004, drawing 8,100 delegates, was said to be the largest journalistic gathering in American history. His activities for 2006 included a guest speaker slot at a meeting of the World Journalism Institute. Lowe lives in Brooklyn with his wife, Mira, an editor at *Newsday.*

Sources

Periodicals

Ebony, October 2004, p. 28.
NABJ Journal, Winter 2004, p. 10.
Newsday (Melville, NY), August 9, 2004, p. A16.
Philadelphia Inquirer, February 29, 1996, p. A1; March 7, 1999, p. A1.
Sacramento Observer, September 19, 2001, p. G2.
Sun (Baltimore, MD), December 13, 2004, p. C2.

Virginian-Pilot (Norfolk), June 6, 1993, p. 13.
Washington Post, August 5, 2004, p. C4.

On-line

"Biography: Herbert Lowe," *National Association of Black Journalists,* www.nabj.org/pres_corner/story/576p-817c.html (March 29, 2006).

"Herbert Lowe, *Newsday,*" *World Journalism Institute,* www.worldji.com/speakers.asp?speaker_id=16 (March 29, 2006).

—James M. Manheim

Floyd Mayweather, Jr.

1977—

Boxer

Mayweather, Floyd, Jr., photograph. AP Images.

Floyd Mayweather Jr. may be the best boxer in the world, winning four world championships in different weight divisions. Trained by his uncle, former boxing champion Roger Mayweather, Floyd Mayweather Jr's boxing pedigree extends also to his father, contender Floyd Mayweather Sr., and another uncle, Jeff Mayweather, who was also a contender in the lightweight division. Mayweather Jr. emerged as one of the most promising fighters of the 1990s, holding the U.S. amateur championship crown five times and winning the Olympic bronze medal in 1996 in Atlanta, at a weight of 125 pounds. He became World Boxing Council (WBC) super lightweight world champion in 2005, and relinquished his title in 2006 to compete for and win the International Boxing Council (IBC) welterweight championship that year. He was also a WBC super featherweight champion in 1998 and lightweight champion in 2002 . Known as "Pretty Boy" Floyd Mayweather in boxing circles because of his rare ability to leave a fight without damage to his face, in 2005 *The Ring* magazine rated him the top pound-for-pound boxer in the world.

Floyd Mayweather Jr. was born in Grand Rapids, Michigan, on February 24, 1977. His father, Floyd Mayweather Sr., was a contender for the welterweight title in the late 1970s and 1980s. Mayweather Jr. became known for his defensive ability, a skill he often attributed to his father, who was his first trainer. After a dispute with his father, Mayweather Jr. began training with his uncle, Roger Mayweather, a former super featherweight (130lb) and super lightweight world champion known for his aggression and offensive strengths.

Mayweather Jr. began boxing at the age of seven and won his first national Golden Gloves championship in 1993 at a weight of 106 pounds. He won the Golden Gloves again in 1994 (at 112 pounds) and in 1996 (at 125 pounds). He was U.S. national champion in 1995 and took a bronze medal at the 1996 Atlanta Olympics, beating Lorenzo Aragon of Cuba 16-3. He lost his fight for the silver medal place to Serafim Todorov of Bulgaria, but the split decision of 10-9 against Mayweather was highly controversial. Many commentators and spectators thought Mayweather had won the fight and the decision was contested unsuccessfully by the

At a Glance . . .

Born Floyd Mayweather Jr. on February 24, 1977, in Grand Rapids, MI; children: four.

Career: Professional boxer, 1996–.

Awards: Michigan State Golden Gloves champion, 106 pounds, 1993; National Golden Gloves champion, 106 pounds, 1993; Michigan State Golden Gloves champion, 112 pounds, 1994; National Golden Gloves champion, 112 pounds, 1994; Outstanding Boxer Award, 1994; National PAL champion, 125 pounds, 1995; Outstanding Boxer Award, 1995; U.S. National champion, 125 pounds, 1995; Michigan State Golden Gloves champion, 125 pounds, 1996; National Golden Gloves champion, 125 pounds, 1996; Olympic bronze medalist, 125 pounds, 1996; WBC super featherweight champion, 1998-2002; WBC lightweight champion, 2002-04; WBC super lightweight champion, 2005; IBC welterweight champion, 2006; WBC Boxer of the Year, 2006.

U.S. team. In all Mayweather fought in 90 amateur bouts, winning all but 6 of them.

Mayweather turned professional in October 1996 at the age of 19 and won 17 professional fights before taking the WBC super featherweight world title from Genaro Hernandez in 1998. Hernandez, who at the time had an admirable record of 38 fights, one draw and one defeat, was worn down by the newcomer's pace and strength. After being knocked down Hernandez withdrew in the eighth round. Mayweather's first of eight defenses of the title came in December 1998, when he stopped Angel Manfredy in a technical knockout (TKO) in the second round. Between then and March 2000 he defended the title a further four times, using his orthodox defensive posture and sharp jab to wear down opponents. By then still unbeaten Mayweather had been noted as one of the most promising fighters of his generation.

Mayweather fought the eighth and final defense of his title on November 10, 2001 against Jesus Chavez, an experienced fighter then ranked number one in the world. Chavez proved to be a tough opponent, but the fight was stopped by his corner in the ninth round; Mayweather had led the points in all of them. Not long after the fight Mayweather moved up from the super featherweight division and contested the WBC Lightweight (135 pounds) title in April 2002 against defending champion Jose Luis Castillo. Beating Castillo was not easy—Mayweather had an injured shoulder—but

he took the title on points over 12 rounds and defended it three times. The third time, against Philip N'dou in November 2003 ranks as one of his most brilliant performances. Commenting on the fight for *East Side Boxing* Frank Lotierzo wrote: "he led off with a lead right uppercut to start one exchange and ended the fight in the seventh round with a flurry of three straight right hand leads. Please make sure you contact me first, the next time you see a fight ended with that sequence of punches. Not only was it beautiful and unique, it was devastating!" The victory set the scene for another change of division to super lightweight in 2004. He took the WBC super lightweight title from Arturo Gatti on June 25, 2005, in a contest that was also his first lucrative pay-per-view experience. Franz Lidz of *Sports Illustrated* said of the fight: "Pretty Boy Floyd…made easy work of boxing's foremost crowd-pleaser—outpunching the puncher by more than four to one—to win his third world title in as many weight classes."

Mayweather's success as an athlete has at times been overshadowed by his desire to live "the life": the home in Vegas, the rapper friends, the large entourage. His feud with his father has also cast a shadow. Mayweather Sr. was in jail for drug trafficking while his son was competing in the Atlanta Olympics and Mayweather Jr. faced a jail term of his own in 2005 when former girlfriend Josie Harris accused him of battery. He was acquitted after Harris herself testified for the defense. Mayweather has a reputation for a quick temper and rapidly changing moods; as a result he is not a popular boxer, but despite his family feuds and public bust-ups he is a stunning fighter. Richard Hoffer, writing in *Sports Illustrated,* said of Mayweather: "He drives us crazy with his various feuds and civil disturbances. Yet he remains stubbornly dedicated to his sport, the one guy taking on all comers, winning always."

With a strong claim to be the best boxer in the world pound-for-pound in the first decade of the twenty-first century, Mayweather fought and beat Sharmba Mitchell on November 19, 2005 to make his welterweight debut at 147 pounds. In his second welterweight match, Mayweather snagged his fourth championship, taking the IBF welterweight title from Zab Judah after a 12-round bout in April 2006.

Mayweather remained unbeaten in 36 professional contests in 2006. His formidable power, speed, defensive skill, and self-described "chin of granite" combine to make him one of the most complete boxers of his era. Two matches in which he fought and won with injured hands hint at the possibility of a physical weakness, but also highlight his courage, determination, and the extent of his talent. As he said after winning the WBC Lightweight title in 2002 "Other champions, when they get hurt, they don't even show up to the fight. I get hurt, I keep fighting." "I'm not in this game to lose," Mayweather told the *Washington Post*, "I'm in it to win. I'm not in it for the money, but to be a living legend. I am a living legend." With his drive and skill, it seems likely that when he retires Mayweather will rank among the all-time boxing greats.

Sources

Periodicals

Jet, March 8, 1999, p. 50; May 12, 2003, p. 50; November 17, 2003, p. 52; June 14, 2004, p. 51; August 8, 2005, p. 50.
Los Angeles Times, April 8, 2006, p. D6.
New York Times, April 9, 2006, p. 8.3.
Sports Illustrated, January 29, 2001, p. 97; June 27, 2005, p. 62; July 4, 2005, p. 74.
Washington Post, November 19, 2005, p. E3.

On-line

"Floyd Mayweather Column," *USA Today,* www.usa-today.com/sports/columnist/saraceno/2005-06-26-mayweather-column_x.htm (February 28, 2006).
"Floyd Mayweather Interview Transcript," *East Side Boxing* www.eastsideboxing.com/news.php?p= 3114&more=1 (February 28, 2006).
"Floyd Mayweather Jr.: All Questions Answered," *East Side Boxing* www.eastsideboxing.com/news.php? p=95&more=1 (February 28, 2006).
"HBO Fighters: Floyd Mayweather," *HBO,* www.hbo. com/boxing/fighters/mayweather/index.shtml (February 28, 2006).

—Chris Routledge

Raymond J. McGuire

1957(?)—

Investment banker

Raymond J. McGuire, who became global co-head of investment banking at Citigroup Corporate and Investment Banking in 2005, has been recognized as one of the most talented African Americans in this highly competitive field. Before moving to Citigroup, he held positions at First Boston Corporation, Merrill Lynch & Co., and Morgan Stanley, advising corporate clients on strategies regarding multi-billion dollar business mergers. McGuire has also been noted for his work on the boards of several nonprofit organizations, with a particular focus on education and the arts.

Unlike many Wall Street professionals who were trained from an early age to think about managing wealth because their families had inherited assets, McGuire came from a humble background. "I've got a lot of silver now," McGuire told Lynn Norment of *Ebony*, "but I wasn't born with a silver spoon." In fact, he had never heard of investment banking before going to college. He was raised by his mother—a social worker—in inner city Dayton, Ohio. As a teenager, he worked every summer. His first job was making boxes for Field's dress shop in Dayton. Later, he worked construction at a local Air Force base and as a hospital orderly. Though money was not plentiful, the family emphasized education. "My mother did everything she could," McGuire explained in *Ebony*, "to be sure that I received the best education that money could buy, even though we couldn't afford it."

In high school, McGuire excelled in both sports and academics, serving as school president and captain of the basketball team. After his junior year, he transferred to the Hotchkiss School, a prep school in Connecticut, where he had been offered a scholarship. The change, he admitted to *New York Times*, writer Andrew Ross Sorkin, was a bit of a culture shock. But he excelled academically and went on to attend Harvard, where he earned his BA in 1979. In 1980, McGuire attended the University of Nice, France, on a Rotary Fellowship. He then returned to Massachusetts to earn a law degree from Harvard Law School and an MBA from Harvard Business School in 1984.

While still in graduate school, McGuire began his association with the First Boston Corporation. As he recalled to Sorkin, he received an interview for a summer job with the firm in 1982 and was told he had five minutes to make his case. Realizing that modesty would not impress his interviewer, McGuire answered that "Harvard Law School, Harvard Business School and Harvard College pride themselves on taking the cream of the crop. I pride myself on being the film off the top of the cream." He got the job.

McGuire remained with First Boston, which later became Credit Suisse First Boston, until 1988. That year, he joined two mentors from First Boston, Joseph Perella and Bruce Wasserstein, as a partner in their newly-established advisory firm, Wasserstein & Perella. In 1993 he left Wasserstein & Perella to become managing director in Merrill Lynch's Mergers & Acquisitions Group. There he served as a strategic advisor to clients interested in buying or selling companies or subsidiaries; he specialized in consumer products and paper and forest products industries. Among the major

At a Glance . . .

Born in 1957(?) in Dayton, OH. *Education:* Harvard College, AB, cum laude, 1979; Harvard Business School, MBA, 1984; Harvard Law School, JD, 1984.

Career: First Boston Corporation, Boston, MA, associate, 1984-88; Wasserstein Perella & Co., Inc., partner, 1988-93; Merrill Lynch & Co., Inc., Mergers and Acquisitions Group, managing director, 1993-2000; Morgan Stanley, Mergers and Acquisitions global co-head, 2000-05; Citigroup, global co-head of investment banking, 2005–.

Memberships: De La Salle Academy board of directors, chair; International Center of Photography board of directors, executive committee; Lincoln Center board of trustees; New York-Presbyterian Hospital board of trustees; Mayor's Cultural Affairs Advisory Committee for the City of New York board of directors; San Remo Tenants' Corporation board of directors, president; Studio Museum in Harlem board of directors, chair; Alex Hillman Family Foundation board of trustees; Whitney Museum of American Art board of directors, vice chair and investment committee chair; Enterprise Foundation board of directors; Joseph and Claire Flom Foundation board of directors.

Awards: Alumni Professional Achievement Award, Harvard Business School; Distinguished Patron of the Arts, Pratt Institute; named one of the Top 50 African Americans on Wall Street, *Black Enterprise,* 2002.

Addresses: *Office*—Citigroup, 399 Park Ave., New York, NY 10043.

transactions in which he played a leading role were the merger of the James River and the Fort Howard companies, which created a new company in 1997 with expected annual sales worth more than $7 billion; and Jefferson-Smurfit's 1998 purchase of Stone Container Corporation, a deal worth $6.5 billion that created one of the world's largest manufacturers of paperboard and paperboard packaging products. According to a *Black Enterprise* article by Nicole Marie Richardson, Merrill Lynch attained top ranking as a handler of mergers and acquisitions during McGuire's

tenure at the company, with $220 billion in deals in 2001.

In 2000 McGuire moved to Morgan Stanley, where he became co-head of Mergers and Acquisitions. He played a key role in the $14.9 billion sale of Nabisco Holdings to the Philip Morris Company in 2000, and in Pfizer's sale of its Schick Wilkinson Sword business to Energizer for $930 million in 2003. Among his major achievements as senior banker on the company's General Electric account was his advice relating to the Unilever Group's sale of its fragrance division to Coty, Inc. The terms of the deal, completed in late 2005, included $800 million in cash for Unilever, as well as possible additional payments dependent on future sales. McGuire's other clients have included Dial Corporation and Kimberly-Clark.

The Wall Street world was startled when McGuire announced his resignation from Morgan Stanley in 2005 to take a position as co-head of investment banking at Citigroup Corporate and Investment Banking. As Sorkin observed in the *New York Times*, Citigroup "has not historically had the elite cachet in mergers-and-acquisitions advising," making McGuire's move there all the more surprising. McGuire, Sorkin wrote, hopes to play a major role in improving Citigroup's status as a provider of sound investment advice.

McGuire, who lives in New York City, is a prominent supporter of several nonprofit organizations. An avid collector of art, including works by Harlem Renaissance painter Romare Bearden, McGuire is chairman of the board of the Studio Museum in Harlem and vice chairman of the board and investment committee chairman of the Whitney Museum of American Art. He also serves on the executive committee of the International Center of Photography, is a trustee of the Lincoln Center and chairman of the board of the De La Salle Academy, and is a membership of the board of the Mayor's Cultural Affairs Advisory Committee for the City of New York. In addition, he serves as a trustee of New York-Presbyterian Hospital. For Harvard University, he has served as a member of the Overseers/Directors Nominating Committee.

In 2002, *Black Enterprise* named McGuire one of the Top 50 African Americans on Wall Street. He has also received the Alumni Professional Achievement Award from the Harvard Business School, and was named a Distinguished Patron of the Arts by the Pratt Institute.

Discussing his accomplishments with Lynn Norment of *Ebony*, McGuire commented that the world of investment banking is highly competitive and requires excellence and commitment. "This job is not for everybody," he said. "It is exacting and there really is no room for error.... When you are less than the best, you're just no part of the equation; you're not part of the game."

Sources

Periodicals

Black Enterprise, October 2002, p. 88; July 2005, p. 32.

Ebony, February 1999.

New York Times, June 10, 2005.

On-line

"Profile: Raymond J. McGuire," *Citigroup*, www.citi-group.com, (January 15. 2006).

—E. M. Shostak

Nellie Yvonne McKay

19(??)-2006

Educator, writer

Nellie Yvonne McKay "was the central figure in the establishing of black women's studies as a presence in academic and intellectual life," declared Craig Werner, her colleague at the University of Wisconsin at Madison, to the *New York Times*. Known among her colleagues for her intellect, she did not focus on winning personal accolades, although she garnered many during her career. "She could have been an academic superstar," Werner told Barbara Wolff reporting for the *University of Wisconsin-Madison* Web site at the time of McKay's death. "She chose instead to build a community."

Used Education to Escape Poverty

Nellie Yvonne Reynolds was born to Jamaican parents and raised in the Harlem district of New York City. She kept the details of her age private, but her friends and colleagues estimated she was most likely born in the late 1930s or early 1940s. She and her two sisters grew up knowing poverty and racial discrimination. McKay explained to *Contemporary Black Biography* (*CBB*) that "education was their religion"—their way out of difficulty, their way to dignity. While her two sisters chose to go into banking and teaching in a public school, McKay chose to become a part of academic life.

"Mom taught us all to read before ever going to school. Our only job as kids was to go to school," McKay told *CBB*. "Mom and Dad provided enough so that that was all we had to do. We never got caught up in other distractions, not even TV. We stayed home and read

books aloud to each other, and on our own. To this day we all collect books." While her entire family were avid readers and collectors of books, it was McKay who went on to major in English literature and make a career of it.

From the time she was a little girl, Nellie McKay had always wanted to teach. But she had imagined herself teaching at the kindergarten level, not in college. Her ability to teach higher education was confirmed by two college professors, Michael Cooper (in English, a Shakespeare scholar) and John McDermott (in Philosophy, a William James scholar). Both men took her under their wing and encouraged her to give wings to others. "I could have come out a Philosophy major," she told *CBB*, "but then I couldn't teach English. I declared my major when I figured an English major could always teach philosophy." She earned her master's degree at Harvard in 1971 and a doctorate in 1977. She majored in English and American Literature, and spent the rest of her life immersed in teaching at the college and university level.

Inspired by Civil Rights Movement

McKay might not have ended up specializing in African American literature and women's studies if it were not for two traumatic events in her formative years in college. A race riot during her junior year at Queens College opened her eyes to the problem of racial injustice. She came to better understand the struggle for equality when 100 Blacks from the Bronx came on campus in the fall of 1967 to stir things up and mobilize student support for the civil rights movement. McKay started out as a Shakespearean English major, but the civil rights movement jolted her out of her apathy about race. "Before then I never quite understood how terrible and serious the race problem was, how it penetrated all of society, not just individual hearts," McKay recalled to *CBB*.

The other consciousness-raising, career-shifting experience happened to McKay while studying at Harvard University in the early 1970s. As she told the story, "Back then, Harvard was not a very hospitable place

for the handful of women or minorities who were allowed in. Admitting a few Blacks was a self-protective and self-congratulatory gesture. Others, especially white males, didn't think we really belonged there. Harvard took the cream of the crop but did not want too many Blacks, which would upset the institution." McKay kept her eyes open and learned a lot at Harvard.

McKay outlasted her white peers at the university. As she shared with *CBB*, "The attrition rate, once you got in, was much higher for whites than for Blacks. The rich white folk could just go home and find someplace else to go or something else to do; their family would still support them, no matter what. But we had no choice. How do you go home and tell your grandma, who knew the value of hard work and had just spent her life savings to get you into college, that you found college life 'hard'? You can't! You just stuck it out." Thanks to her parents' abiding belief in her unlimited potential, McKay was able to persevere beyond these racial underpinnings at Harvard, earning her Ph.D. in English and American literature. Her doctoral thesis, on the Black male and modernist writer Eugene Toomer, was published in 1984 as her first book, *Jean Toomer, Artist: A Study of His Literary Life and Work, 1894-1936*.

Found Life's Work in Teaching

Simmons, a small, all-women's college in the Boston area, gave McKay her first full-time, long-term teaching position in 1973. Simmons was, and still is, noted for educating working class women committed to earning a living in traditionally female professions (nursing, grade school teaching, etc.). The school stood in contrast with rest of the "Seven Sister Schools" in New England, (Barnard, Mount Holyoke, Pembroke, Radcliffe, Smith, Wellesley), which were largely dedicated to teaching the "daughters of the rich and the intelligentsia," according to McKay. Always committed to helping others, McKay chose to dedicate herself to giving wings to working class women who shared her roots and aspirations during her five years at Simmons.

McKay found herself in a very different world when she joined the faculty of the University of Wisconsin-Madison on a joint appointment to teach in both the African American studies and English departments in 1978; later this position was expanded into a partial third appointment to the women's studies department. The African American studies and women's studies departments were ten years old at the time and were struggling to hold their own. However, with McKay championing both departments, the UW-Madison quickly started growing national reputations in both areas. McKay belonged to a galvanizing feminist movement and a burgeoning generation of women scholars who were struggling against male domination; this domination extended to the field of African American literature, where women authors had only recently been considered as worthy of sharing the literary spotlight with their male peers.

Co-Edited "Bible" of African American Literary Tradition

McKay's most significant academic contribution was the *Norton Anthology of African American Literature*, which she co-edited with Henry Louis Gates Jr. with the intent of redressing "the fragmented history of African American writing." Ten years of research resulted in what one reviewer in *Booklist* magazine called "a magisterial volume," not only for its formidable size, but also for the wide scope of its included works. This authoritative canon provides illuminating historical commentary, spanning 250 years of 118 poets and writers–including the oral roots of African American letters, a grand selection of spirituals, gospel, sermons, folktales, and blues, jazz, and rap lyrics. Most of these Black writers, male and female, write about the Black experience, which used to be mostly about being good and rebutting negative stereotypes. But by the end of the 20th-century, Black writers convey much more complicated images. In their aggregate, these works are considered to be "often pioneering, always exceptional" and "richly diverse," according to the *Booklist* reviewer. As such, McKay and Gates' work lives up to what *Booklist* called "the golden reputation of all of Norton's literary anthologies," which the *New York Times* noted "define the accepted norms for great literature." "Never again will anybody anywhere not be able to know about the existence of the African-American literature tradition," McKay said, as quoted in her obituary in the *Milwaukee Journal Sentinel*. "This is a bible, as far as I'm concerned."

In addition to her many literary contributions, Nellie McKay distinguished herself in academe as a passionate teacher and "cultural custodian." "Nellie was always in her office from sunrise to well past dusk, every day, with her door open, nurturing students and colleagues, building the models that will shape her disciplines for decades to come," Werner remembered to Wolff. McKay related in a 1998 interview with *Contemporary Black Biography* that the most satisfying part of her teaching career was the chance to help her students to "succeed in whatever field of endeavor they choose." She opened her students' minds to new possibilities by teaching African American studies. "They use it as a way of learning about people and cultures different than themselves, which helps them live useful lives in social work, political science, and the like." Her faculty peers elected her to Phi Kappa Phi in 1989; the UW-Madison Chancellor gave her the Distinguished Teaching award in 1992; and she received the Outstanding Contributions to the System award in 1996. For her work on the *Norton Anthology*, her colleagues around the country gave her the MELUS award, acknowledging in 1996 her tremendous contributions to

multi-ethnic literature in the U.S. She was inducted into the Wisconsin Academy of Sciences, Arts and Letters in 2001, and presented with an honorary degree from the University of Michigan in 2002.

McKay never lost enthusiasm for her life's work. She stopped only when she succumbed to cancer on January 22, 2006. She is survived by her two grown children and the thriving intellectual community she nurtured.

Selected works

Books

Jean Toomer, Artist: A Study of His Literary Life and Work—1894-1936, University of North Carolina Press, 1984.
Compiler, *Critical Essays on Toni Morrison,* G.K. Hall, 1988.
Contributor, *Black Studies in the United States: Three Essays,* Ford Foundation, 1990.
Co-editor with Henry Gates Jr., *Norton Anthology of African American Literature,* W.W. Norton, 1996.
Co-editor with Kathryn Earle, *Approaches to Teaching the Novels of Toni Morrison,* 1997.
Co-editor with Frances Smith Foster, *Incidents in the Life of a Slave Girl: Contexts, Criticism, Harriet Jacobs,* W.W. Norton, 2001.

Sources

Periodicals

Booklist, January 1, 1997, p. 809.
The Nation, May 12, 1997, pp. 42-46.
Milwaukee Journal Sentinel, January 24, 2006.
National Review, March 10, 1997, pp. 50-53.
New York Times, December 12, 1996; January 28, 2006.

On-line

"Online Newshour: African American Literary Anthology—March 7, 1997," *PBS,* www.pbs.org/newshour/gergen/march97/african_lit_3-7.html (July 11, 2006).
"Online Newshour Forum: Nellie McKay—Norton Anthology of African American Literature—March 18, 1997," *PBS,* www.pbs.org/newshour/forum/march97/mckay_3-18.html (July 10, 2006).

Other

Additional information for this profile was obtained from a personal interview with Nellie McKay in January of 1998.

—Dietrich Gruen and Sara Pendergast

C. Ray Nagin

1956—

Mayor, media executive

Nagin, Ray, photograph. Roger L. Wollenberg/UPI/Landov.

Politics in New Orleans have long been as murky as the bayou waters that circle the Southern city. Backroom deals, bribery, and corruption have caused many political commentators to change the city's nickname from the Big Easy to the Big Sleazy. Whether the accusations were true or not, the rumors were enough to stifle the city and by 2002 New Orleans was sinking under massive debt and rampant crime. Businesses were reluctant to build in the city and young people were making mass exoduses in search of better places to work and raise families. Into this grim picture entered C. Ray Nagin, a New Orleans cable executive and visionary. With no political experience and little campaign money, Nagin came out of nowhere to win the 2002 mayoral election on a platform of anti-corruption and economic development. Leaving behind a well-paid executive position to take on the challenges of revitalizing the city that care truly had forgotten, Nagin said during his inaugural speech, "The winds of change are blowing, and they are fanning the flames of a renaissance in our great city," according to *Jet*. New Orleanians hoped he was right. Just when Nagin's popularity was soaring and his aggressive attack on the city's corruption was showing signs of success, Hurri-cane Katrina brought in winds of change that devastated the city. Winning re-election in 2006, Nagin set out to restart New Orleans' renaissance from the ground up.

Gained Responsibility Early

Clarence Ray Nagin, Jr., was born on June 11, 1956, in New Orleans's Charity Hospital and raised in the scruffy neighborhoods of 7th Ward, Treme, and Algiers. To support Nagin and his two sisters, Nagin's mother ran a K-Mart lunch counter and his father held down several jobs: cutting fabric at a clothing factory during the day, cleaning up at City Hall at night, and working as a mechanic in between.

At O. Perry Walker High School, Nagin excelled in sports and scored a baseball scholarship to Alabama's Tuskegee University where he earned a degree in accounting in 1978. Following graduation, Nagin moved to Detroit, Michigan, to work at General Motors. In 1981 he transferred to Dallas, Texas, and took a position with Associates Corporation. The following year he married Seletha Smith whose parents lived across the street from his parents in New Orleans.

At a Glance . . .

Born on June 11, 1956, in New Orleans, LA; married Seletha Smith Nagin, 1982; children: Jeremy, Jarin, Tianna. *Education*: Tuskegee University, BS, accounting, 1978; Tulane University, MBA, 1994. *Politics*: Democrat.

Career: General Motors, Detroit, MI, late 1978-81; Associates Corp, Dallas, TX, 1981-85; Cox Communications, vice president and general manager, 1985-2002; City of New Orleans, mayor, 2002–.

Memberships: Orleans and Jefferson Parish Business Councils; Greater New Orleans Education Foundation; Covenant House and United Way, past board member;United Negro College Fund Walkathon, past chairman; Louisiana Cable Television Association, past president; 100 Black Men of Metro New Orleans, past president.

Awards: Better Business Bureau, Excellent Customer Service Award, 1993; Louisiana State Board of Education, Distinguished Business Partner Award, 1994; Young Leadership Council, Diversity and Role Model, 1995; Spirit of Greatness Award, 1997; *Gambit Weekly*, New Orleanian of the Year, 1998; National Telly Award (for Tiger Woods exclusive interview), 2001.

Addresses: *Office*—New Orleans City Hall, 1300 Perdido Street, New Orleans, LA 70112.

In 1985 Nagin moved back to Louisiana and became controller of Cox Communications, the cable television franchise serving Southeast Louisiana. Four years later he was transferred to Cox New Orleans, which at the time was the poorest performer in the Cox network. According to the *Tulanian*, "Profits were down, complaints were up and customer growth was stagnant." Nagin revitalized the ailing division with a combination of technology and customer service including a $500 million upgrade of the system's fiber-optic cable and introduction of digital cable television. He launched a popular 24-hour news service—the first in the country—with the local CBS affiliate. He also began hosting his own twice-a-week cable call-in show to address customer concerns. His actions are credited with increasing Cox's subscribers by 180,000 and creating over 800 new jobs. By 2002 85% of customers reported being satisfied with Cox—up from less than

40% when Nagin joined the company. By that time Nagin had been promoted to vice president and general manager.

During his tenure at Cox, Nagin kept busy doing more than turning around the company. In 1993 he enrolled in Tulane University's executive Master's of Business Administration (MBA) program, an intensive part-time program geared toward busy professionals. "I was in the process of taking on much more responsibility than I had had at the time at Cox and said, basically, 'What do you need that will better prepare you for this?'" Nagin told the *Tulanian*. "I looked around and saw the executive MBA program as being a great way for me to add a couple of tools to my toolbox. It's been invaluable."

Sought Opportunities for New Orleans

In 1998 Nagin used some of those business tools to bring hockey to New Orleans. He served as the spokesperson for a group of 12 investors that bought a franchise from the East Coast Hockey League. The New Orleans Brass debuted to unexpected popularity, helping Nagin and his group land a coveted lease deal at the city's state-of-the-art New Orleans Arena. The deal was typical of Nagin's style. "Ray is not afraid to take risks, and that was quite a risk," a Brass partner told the *Tulanian*. "You start talking about black folks owning a hockey team? In New Orleans? That's a pretty strange situation, but that's what sets Ray apart. He thinks outside traditional boxes." Nagin became one of the principal owners of the team and, until his run for mayor, also served as president of the franchise.

Nagin was also very active in civic and community issues. He served on the boards of Covenant House, a center for runaway teens, as well as the United Way. He was also a three-time chairman for the United Negro College Fund Walkathon and president of the group 100 Black Men of Metro New Orleans. In a professional capacity he served as president of the Louisiana Cable Television Association. Nagin's activities brought him recognition. In 1995 he earned the Diversity and Role Model Award from the Young Leadership Council of New Orleans. In 1998 *Gambit Weekly*, the city's alternative paper, named him New Orleanian of the Year. Meanwhile he and wife, Seletha, raised two sons, Jeremy and Jarin, and late in the 1990s had daughter Tianna.

In October of 2001 two-time New Orleans mayor Marc Morial—son of the city's first black mayor—lost a bid that would have allowed him to run for a third term. The race for the city's next mayor was suddenly wide open. Several long time Louisiana politicos emerged as early leaders in the race including a state senator, two city council members, and the police superintendent. However, none of them seemed to capture the interest of the city. "I was looking at the candidates and paying attention and I just didn't see, uh, a spark, a different kind of candidate who was focusing on the things that were necessary to make this a better environment for my kids and my grandkids," Nagin told the *Tulanian*. However he still had no plans to run himself. "Running for mayor had been something that people had suggested to me," he told the *Tulanian*. "I was always resistant, saying there's no way I would get into politics. I'd rather play on the sidelines and be a king maker rather than be the king himself." Yet the subject of his running kept coming up. Beth James, a colleague who later became Nagin's director of economic development, suggested he run during a luncheon. Then his favorite shoeshine guy suggested it again. "We were talking about politics. I was giving him my opinion, he was giving me his, and he looked up and said, 'Man, you really ought to run for mayor,'" Nagin told *The Tulanian*. "That's how it started." What cinched the deal was a conversation with his teenaged son. "I was talking to him and some of his friends one day, and they told me they didn't see a future for themselves in New Orleans," he recalled to *New Orleans Magazine*. "At that point, I kind of decided I was either going to be part of the problem or part of the solution, so I jumped in."

Entered Politics, Gained Experience

After commissioning a poll to gauge the public's feelings about the race, Nagin learned that voters were as unimpressed by the candidates as he was. They were tired of politics as usual and ready to support an outsider. Nagin, with no political experience and little notoriety outside of business circles, was just the type of candidate they wanted. Largely self-funded, Nagin joined the mayoral race just two months shy of the primary. "If we hope to rise above petty politics and bickering, we've got to elect someone who won't bring a lot of baggage and political infighting to the office of mayor," *The Tulanian* quoted Nagin as saying during his announcement to run. "I suggest to you that I'm the candidate with the best opportunity to achieve that goal because I've operated outside the political mud-wrestling pit."

With natural charisma, camera-ready good looks, and a grassroots campaign that focused on beating crime, ending corruption, and fostering economic development, Nagin quickly gained ground. He soon won endorsements from the city's two largest papers. His name was suddenly everywhere and New Orleanians were newly enthused about the race. To the shock of political observers nationwide, Nagin finished first in the primary. He would face police chief Richard Pennington in the run off to office.

Despite Pennington's popularity as the man who cleaned up New Orleans's notoriously corrupt police department, Nagin coasted easily to victory with 59% of the vote. He had promised change and the city entrusted him with it. However, during his victory speech Nagin acknowledged it would not be easy. "I don't have a Superman undershirt under my suit," *Jet* quoted him as saying. "It didn't take us one year to get into this shape, and it won't take a year to get out."

The New Orleans Nagin inherited was indeed in bad shape. Analysts predicted a possible $50 million shortfall in the budget. Businesses were closing up or moving out of the city. Murder and violent crime were at vicious highs with at least one homicide occurring every night. Above all of it was the hulking ghost of corruption— New Orleans's reputation for bribery and nepotism. "Corruption had gone on in the open for so long that there was really a feeling of hopelessness," the president of New Orleans crime commission told the *Los Angeles Times*. "There was a sense that it was so embedded in the culture of the community, there was no way to change it." Nagin made fighting corruption one of his priorities. "Before we can grow the economy, we need to make sure that everybody understands what the rules of engagement are," Nagin told the *Tulanian*. "You need to have a level playing field where people can compete. Then you can create an environment for business growth and job creation."

Nagin began his term in office by peopling his staff with business leaders, not political insiders. "I surrounded myself with people who think outside the normal box of government, with a few governmental people sprinkled in to kind of make sure we have the experience levels we need. That's basically how we've approached it—as new thinkers, as change agents, as a group trying to make the city better," he told the *Tulanian*. With his administration set, Nagin quickly turned to corruption. On a steamy July morning in 2002 police fanned out across the city and arrested dozens of people straight from their beds. Arrestees included low-level city bureaucrats, brake-tag inspectors, and illegally licensed cab drivers. The sweep also resulted in the arrests of the city's utilities director and head of the taxicab bureau. Though some dismissed the sting operation as an attack on petty officials—one Louisiana political commentator told the *Los Angeles Times*, "There was a sense that, God, all we're doing is catching little fish"—most New Orleanians welcomed the raid and showered Nagin with gratitude.

Nagin also made other, less dramatic moves soon after taking office. He put tax information and permits and other application processes on-line. He also led the repeal of a 2% entertainment tax that was hurting local and visiting performers. His first operating budget worth $557.2 million won praise from the city council and included a much-needed pay increase for rookie cops. Nagin also brought his business acumen to the city's operations and renegotiated several banking, audit, and collection contracts that were slated to save the city millions of dollars per year.

Despite his many successes, Nagin still faced an uphill battle by the first anniversary of his election. The very environment he created threatened to hurt his popularity. *Gambit Weekly* noted, "voters are more optimistic than ever about the future of New Orleans, but that optimism has produced expectations that may outstrip anyone's ability to deliver." In the same article Nagin acknowledged, "The burden is huge. I will not discount that at all. There are lots of expectations in this city…. We have unleashed this tremendous optimism in this city that people have been thirsting for a long time. I don't know what to do about that other than to stay consistent and to stay focused on the key issues."

Nagin did, and Susan Howell of University of New Orleans reported in the *Washington Post* that Nagin enjoyed popularity ratings of approximately 80 percent by 2003, saying "He's very, very popular…. The key thing is the corruption sweep. He's actually aggressively dismantling a system of grants and contracting that's benefited mayors and their contributors for decades. All candidates say they're going to do that, but he has been aggressive about it, and people are cheering from the sidelines." His continued popularity also helped win the passage of the city's largest bond issue in history in 2004. *Gambit Weekly* praised Nagin in 2005, saying that if he could pull off some of his plans, especially those related to improving public education and race relations, his "tenure will be historic."

Led New Orleans through Katrina

But the cheering stopped when Hurricane Katrina blasted through the city in 2005. Though Nagin had revamped emergency preparedness measures after Hurricane Ivan's near miss of the city in 2004, Katrina brought a devastating blow. As the massive hurricane approached, Nagin took action, ordering the evacuation of nearly half a million New Orleans residents and opening the city's Superdome to residents too poor or otherwise unable to leave. Despite these measures, Katrina proved the city's worst nightmare, smashing protective levees and ripping through the city with forceful winds and flood waters. In its wake, Katrina left unprecedented wreckage. From his post at the Hyatt hotel, Nagin oversaw the cleanup, calling the aftermath "a surreal situation, like a nightmare that I hope we'll wake up from," according to the *Washington Post*.

Nagin sent what he called "a desperate SOS" for national aid, according to the *Miami Times*. But help came slowly, and city residents grew increasingly frustrated as reconstruction planning dragged, city streets remained cluttered with debris, businesses were slow to open, and homes destroyed by the storm left people homeless. Though a steady trickle of residents returned to the city and building projects got underway, the devastation remained prominent into 2006. Speaking about the slowness of reconstruction Nagin said: "It is

kind of like the chicken and the egg. We need people to reopen businesses and we need open businesses to encourage people to return," as quoted in the *Memphis Flyer*.

Efforts to rebuild New Orleans were stressful enough without the added pressure of racial and social injustices so prevalent in the city before the hurricane being brought to the fore in its aftermath. As soon as efforts to plan what to rebuild, where to allocate funding, and who was first in line for relief began, the racial and social disparities of New Orleans residents came into focus. The city had a population of nearly half a million before Katrina, but afterwards estimates suggested that less than half that would return and that the racial balance of those returning may be more white than black. For his attempts to help drive a vision of the city being reshaped in its former image, Nagin drew criticism for emphasizing his preference in keeping the racial balance in the city tipped in favor of blacks.

Discussions about race fueled debate about the 2006 mayoral elections, because Nagin had been elected to his first term by a majority of whites, with the black vote going to his opponent. Despite being challenged by 22 opponents and losing support from many of his former corporate supporters, Nagin emerged victorious in May 2006. With Congressional funding and new plans for reconstruction, Nagin entered his second term with a fresh mandate: to rebuild, and in part, reinvent the city. The blueprint for the rebuilding came in July 2006. Announcing the plan, Nagin praised those who had already taken matters into their own hands, saying "it's democracy in action," but he added that "Now it's time to get everyone up to the same place and pull all of the pieces together so we can keep the recovery and rebuilding process going in the right direction," according to the *New York Times*. Only time will tell if Nagin is up to the task.

Sources

Periodicals

Gambit Weekly, May 17, 2005, p. 14.
Jet, March 18, 2002, p. 8; May 27, 2002, p. 33.
Los Angeles Times, September 29, 2002 p. A24.
Memphis Flyer, December 8-14, 2005, p. 8.
Miami Times, September 7-13, 2005, p. A1.
New Orleans CityBusiness, December 23, 2002; December 30, 2002; March 24, 2003.
New Orleans Magazine, January 2003, p. 11.
New York Times, May 22, 2006, p. A1; July 6, 2006, p. A14.
Seattle Times, August 29, 2005, p. A1.
Washington Post, July 20, 2003; September 2, 2005, p. C1.

On-line

"About Ray," *Ray Nagin For Mayor,* www.raynagin-formayor.com/about_ray.html (July 8, 2003).

"Biography of Mayor C. Ray Nagin," *The City of New Orleans Official Website*, www.new-orleans.la.us/home/mayorsOffice/biography.php (July 8, 2003).

"Nagin Apologized for Saying on Martin Luther King Day that New Orleans Would Be a 'Chocolate' City Again and that 'God Was Mad at America.'" *Chicago Tribune*, www.chicagotribune.com/news/nation world/chi-0601180052jan18,1,1331355.story?coll=chi-newsnationworld-hed (January 18, 2006).

"Nagin Blasted What He Called a Lack of Coordination in Relief Efforts in New Orleans in the Aftermath of Hurricane Katrina," *CNN.com*, www.cnn.com/2005/WEATHER/08/31/katrina.levees/index.html, (September 4, 2005).

"Nagin Declared a State of Emergency and Ordered an Evacuation of New Orleans as Hurricane Katrina Approached," *CNN.com*, www.cnn.com/2005/WEATHER/08/28/hurricane.katrina/index.html (August 28, 2005).

"Nagin Unveiled a Panel of Civic Leaders Charged with Developing a Plan for the Rebirth of New Orleans by the End of the Year," *CNN.com*, www.cnn.com/2005/US/09/30/nagin.plan/index.html (September 30, 2005).

"Ray Nagin," *Tulanian*, https://aurora.tcs.tulane.edu/article_news_details.cfm?ArticleID=4713 (July 8, 2003).

"Ray Nagin Wins Mayoral Election," *WWL TV*, www.wwltv.com/local/Election_Day.45a8854.html (July 8, 2003).

"Ray of Hope," *Gambit Weekly*, www.bestofneworleans.com/dispatch/2002-05-07/news_feat2.html (July 8, 2003).

—Ashyia Henderson, Candace LaBalle, and Sara Pendergast

Fayard Nicholas

1914-2006

Dancer

Nicholas, Fayard, photograph. © Reuters/Corbis.

The fabulous dancing of brothers Fayard and Harold Nicholas amazed and delighted audiences the world over during the 1930s and 1940s, and they are remembered today as perhaps the greatest dance team ever to appear on film. Combining tap, jazz, and ballet moves with gravity-defying acrobatics, the Nicholas Brothers created a unique style of dance that they exhibited on Vaudeville, Broadway, on international stages and in Hollywood films. "They were confident, dapper, and gifted and always appeared to be relaxing, playing themselves, whether extending the limits of human flight in dance or resting within its myriad rhythms and stops, in top hat and tails and tuxedos, in boaters and spats," wrote Emory Holmes II in the *Los Angeles Times*. Jennifer Dunning of the *New York Times* wrote that "the Nicholas Brothers epitomized flashy acrobatic brilliance during their long career as a star nightclub, film and Broadway dance duo. They sailed through 10-foot jumps, danced up walls and flipped off into full ballet splits.... In a time of graceless racial stereotyping, they, like [Lena] Horne, never lost their dignity."

Followed Family into Theater Career

Fayard Antonio Nicholas was born in Mobile, Alabama, in 1914. His unusual first name was suggested by a family friend who had traveled to France and encountered the name there. Fayard's younger brother, Harold Lloyd Nicholas, was born in New York City in 1921, and named after the famous silent film comedian. Their parents, Ulysses and Viola Nicholas, were musicians at Black Vaudeville theaters. The Nicholas family, which included a sister, Dorothy, moved frequently. While living in Philadelphia in the early 1930s, Fayard, a teenager, began to carefully observe the dancers at the Standard Theater, where his parents managed the orchestra. "The main dancer of the day was Bill Robinson, and his personality just knocked me out. His taps were so very clear. He used wooden soles on the toe and on the heel, which made him unique. And, man, he had personality. He could do a little step like dah-dah, dah-dah-dah, and get a big hand for it. And when somebody else did exactly the same step, it didn't mean anything," Fayard recalled to Howard Reich of the *Chicago Tribune*.

At a Glance . . .

Born Fayard Antonio Nicholas in Mobile, AL, in 1914; son of Ulysses Domonick Nicholas (a drummer) and Viola Harden Nicholas (a pianist); married Barbara, January, 1967 (deceased 1997); married Katherine Hopkins, 2000; children: Anthony, Paul, Nina.

Career: Dancer on stage and in films. Began career in vaudeville in early 1930s. Performed regularly at the Cotton Club, NY, 1932-34; made Broadway debut in *The Ziegfeld Follies,* 1936; also appeared in nightclubs and variety shows around the world, 1950s through 1970s; performed at the White House in 1942, 1955, and 1987; Royal Command performance, London, 1948.

Awards: Inducted into Black Filmmakers Hall of Fame, 1978; *Ebony* magazine, Lifetime Achievement Award, 1987; Antoinette Perry Award, Best Choreography, 1989, for *Black and Blue*; Kennedy Center Honors, 1991; National Black Media Coalition Lifetime Achivement Award, 1992; *Dance Magazine* award, 1995; inducted into the National Museum of Dance, 2001.

By imitating the performers he saw on stage, Fayard taught himself to dance. He then passed along his newfound skill to his younger siblings. Dorothy did not take to dance but Harold, like Fayard, showed a remarkable natural ability. This raw talent, combined with hours of practicing in the living room of the family's apartment, made the Nicholas Brothers a dance team of professional quality. "We never had teachers, Fayard could watch and pick up things.... He was a natural," Harold told Robert Blau of the *Chicago Tribune*. The brothers were soon featured at the Standard and Pearl theaters in Philadelphia and also made an appearance on the Horn and Hardart Children's Hour radio show. Recognizing their sons' gift for dance, Ulysses and Viola Nicholas relocated the family to the Harlem section of New York City, where the boys appeared at the Lafayette Theatre and made their screen debut in *Pie, Pie Blackbird*, a musical short starring the Eubie Blake Orchestra. Their work in the short film won them a long-running job at the prestigious Cotton Club, performing on the same bill with such legendary entertainers as Cab Calloway, Ethel Waters, and Duke Ellington. Reflecting the racial standards of the time, all the performers in Cotton Club shows were black, but only whites were allowed into Cotton Club audiences. But those among these restricted audiences were often top names in show business. Broadway star Tallulah Bankhead was so charmed by young Harold she bought him a bicycle. "I rode that bicycle for years around Harlem. It was an English one with brakes on the handlebars, the first one we'd ever seen there," Harold Nicholas recalled to Dunning. Harold appeared without Fayard in some films produced in New York, most notably *The Emperor Jones* (1933), a screen adaptation of the Eugene O'Neill drama starring Paul Robeson.

Danced in Hollywood Films

In 1934, film producer Samuel Goldwyn saw the Nicholas Brothers perform at the Cotton Club and invited them to appear in their first Hollywood movie, *Kid Millions*, with Eddie Cantor and Ethel Merman. After appearing in a few other Hollywood films, including *The Big Broadcast* of 1936, the brothers returned to New York to make their Broadway debut in *The Ziegfeld Follies* of 1936. Their act preceded that of the show's head liner, famed comedienne Fanny Brice. The applause Fayard and Harold received was so tumultuous that Brice routinely asked "Is it all right to speak now?" before starting her comedy skit. In 1936, the Nicholas Brothers went across the Atlantic for the first time to appear in the London revue Lew Leslie's Blackbirds and in the film *Calling All Stars*. The following year they were back on Broadway in the musical *Babes in Arms*, featuring songs by Rodgers and Hart and choreography by George Balanchine. In *Babes in Arms*, Fayard did a flip across eight bent-over chorus girls and Harold did a split slide underneath the chorus's spread legs, finishing standing up. Despite athletic moves such as these, the Nicholas Brothers objected to their style being characterized as acrobatically oriented "flash." "We call our style of dancing classical tap. Some people think we're a flash act. But we're not. At the end of the act, we'd put those splits in, but we'd do them gracefully. You don't just hit, bam and jump up. We tried to make it look easy. It's not easy. But we tried to make it look that way—come up and smile," Fayard explained to Carla Hall of the *Washington Post*.

In 1940, the Nicholas Brothers returned to Hollywood to appear in *Down Argentine Way* with Don Ameche and a young newcomer, Betty Grable. Fayard recalled to Hall that "when they first released this film and showed it in all the theaters all over the world, right after our number, the audience in the theater started clapping their hands and whistling and stomping their feet. The operator in the projection room had to rewind the film and show it over again." On the basis of this film's success, Twentieth Century-Fox Pictures gave the Nicholas Brothers a five-year contract. Their movies for Twentieth Century-Fox include *Sun Valley Serenade* (1941), in which they danced their high-flying "Chattanooga Choo-Choo" number; *Orchestra Wives* (1942), in which they bounced off walls in backflips; and *Stormy Weather* (1943), which showcased an all-African American cast including Lena Horne (whose rendition of the title song became a classic recording), Fats Waller, Bill "Bojangles" Robinson, Cab Calloway, Eddie Anderson, and Dooley Wilson. In *Stormy Weather*, the brothers, clad in tails, danced up a gleaming white staircase, then came down in a fabulous display of leapfrogging.

Deeply impressed by the Nicholas Brothers' ability, Twentieth Century-Fox studio choreographer Nick Castle challenged them to take their talent to the limit. "He thought of all the crazy, impossible things for us to do," Harold said of Castle to Blau. When performing their dance numbers on film the Nicholas Brothers did not wear taps on their shoes since the sound would not be picked up clearly. Instead, the brothers would go into a studio to record the right tapping sounds, which would then be inserted into the soundtrack.

Racism Limited Success

Despite their popularity with audiences and obvious talent, the Nicholas Brothers remained a specialty act. In Hollywood of the 1940s, stardom for black performers was out of the question. "We never got a chance to do Gene Kelly and Fred Astaire routines and have songs written for us and be in the movies throughout. We would do one number and steal the show. The [white] actors would come on and do a whole script, talking and singing. And then the Nicholas Brothers would come on and do one number and the picture was ours…they weren't writing dialogue for blacks unless they were chauffeurs, maids…or something like that," Harold told Aldore Collier of *Ebony*.

Fayard and Harold Nicholas objected to the notion that in lending their talents to Hollywood they were self-serving "sell-outs" to a racist system, however. A sequence in the 1996 Tony Award winning musical *Bring in 'da Noise, Bring in 'da Funk,* directed and co-created by George C. Wolfe, featured a tap dance team called "Grin & Flash," clearly based on the Nicholas Brothers. They were portrayed as smiling pawns without any concern for the condition of other African Americans. Also slammed in the show was Bill "Bojangles" Robinson, who was dubbed "Uncle Huck-a-Buck." Fayard and Harold argued that criticism of this kind mischaracterizes the racist climate of Hollywood and America in the 1930s and 1940s. "We were never written into the script. They just didn't know how. They couldn't put us up there with Betty Grable, so…there was no need to talk about it," Harold explained to Pamela Sommers of the *Washington Post*. Fayard agrees that efforts to diminish their screen legacy are unfair. "Why should they try to bring down the pioneers who made it possible to do what they're doing today? They should say, 'Thank you,'" Fayard told Sommers.

As the popularity of the Hollywood musical and of tap dancing began to decline after World War II, so did the career of the Nicholas Brothers. Though both brothers possessed vocal and dramatic talent, it was difficult for others to see them as anything but tap dancers. "They never thought about giving us other things to do. When tap dancing faded, people weren't all that enthusiastic about hiring us," Harold told Collier. In 1946, the brothers returned to Broadway to co-star with Pearl Bailey in the all-black musical *St. Louis Woman,* with music by Harold Arlen and lyrics by Johnny Mercer. In the show, which received mixed reviews and lasted for only a few months, Harold introduced the song "Come Rain or Come Shine," later to become a standard recorded by countless singers. In 1948, the Nicholas Brothers made their last joint appearance in a Hollywood film in the Metro-Goldwyn-Mayer production *The Pirate,* starring Gene Kelly and Judy Garland. In the film, Fayard and Harold danced with Kelly in the "Be a Clown" number.

The Nicholas Brothers spent most of the 1950s working in Europe. Late in the decade Fayard returned to North America to tour the United States and Mexico as a solo act. Harold remained in Europe until 1964, performing in theaters and casinos. Adjusting to not being part of a brother act was not easy. "I was always looking for him. But eventually I got used to it," Harold told Hall. An appearance with Fayard on the television variety show *The Hollywood Palace* brought Harold back to the United States. The Nicholas Brothers worked as a team in engagements around the world until age limited Fayard's ability to perform in the 1980s. Harold continued as a solo, with an increased emphasis on singing. "I never got the opportunity to sing as much as I wanted to. We made such a thing with the dancing," Harold told Dunning. Harold also appeared in the touring company of the play *The Tap Dance Kid* in the mid-1980s and performed in a nine-month show as the lead in the Las Vegas production of *Sophisticated Ladies,* a musical featuring the songs of Duke Ellington. On screen Harold has had acting roles in several films, including *Uptown Saturday Night* (1974), with Bill Cosby and Sidney Poitier; *Tap* (1989), with Gregory Hines and Savion Glover; *The Five Heartbeats* (1991), directed by and starring Robert Townsend; and *Funny Bones* (1995), with Jerry Lewis and Leslie Caron. Fayard appeared in a dramatic role in the drama *The Liberation of L.B. Jones* (1970), a drama about Southern racism with Roscoe Lee Browne and Lee J. Cobb, and in 1989 won a Tony Award for his choreography of the Broadway revue *Black and Blue*.

Grand Old Men of Dance

A revival of interest in African-American participation in early films brought renewed attention and recognition to the work of the Nicholas Brothers beginning in the 1990s. They were celebrated at the prestigious Kennedy Center Honors in 1991 and won a *Dance Magazine* award in 1995. "The Nicholas Brothers' film performances helped to further develop and to preserve a form of dancing that grew out of a vernacular tradition and was amplified and refined in vaudeville and variety theaters. Like Fred Astaire and Charles 'Honi' Coles, Fayard and Harold Nicholas enriched and polished a specifically American dance style and transformed it into theatrical art," wrote Joseph H. Mazo in *Dance Magazine*. In April 1998, a tribute to the Nicholas Brothers was held at Carnegie Hall in New York City. The star-filled event, entitled "From Harlem to Hollywood," was hosted by Bill Cosby and offered a line up that included Lena Horne, Bobby Short, Ben Vereen, Maurice Hines, and Savion Glover. Seated in a position of honor on stage, neither Fayard nor Harold got up to dance but Harold did add a few side steps to his rendition of the song "Mister Bojangles." Fayard joked to Caroline Palmer in an article on the *Theatre-Dance* Web site: "I'll do a little shim sham shimmy, but I can't do what I used to do. I'd be crazy if I tried to do a split now. My mind says I can do it, but my body says no way!" In 2001, the brothers were also inducted into the National Museum of Dance.

Both brothers remained active and engaged until late in their lives. Harold lived on the Upper West Side of New York City until his death on July 3, 2000. Fayard—widowed in 1997 after a thirty-year marriage to his second wife, Barbara—remarried in July 2000 to dancer and yoga instructor Katherine Hopkins. The couple made their home in a cottage at the Motion Picture and Television Village in Woodland Hills, California, and Fayard occasionally appeared at dance events and had a bit part in the 2002 film *Night at the Golden Eagle*. Looking back on his long career in a 2005 interview with *People Weekly*, Nicholas said "If my brother and I were doing our thing in this time, there's no telling what we would have accomplished. But we got along pretty well in this prejudiced world. We had such wonderful times. And I'm still having a wonderful time." That wonderful time continued until January 24, 2006, when Nicholas succumbed to pneumonia following an earlier stroke. The Nicholas Brothers will be remembered as some of the greatest dancers ever to appear on stage and screen.

Selected works

Films

Kid Millions, Samuel Goldwyn, 1934.
The Big Broadcast of 1936, Paramount, 1935.
My American Wife, MGM, 1936..
Down Argentine Way, Twentieth Century-Fox, 1940.
Sun Valley Serenade, Twentieth Century-Fox, 1941.
Orchestra Wives, Twentieth Century-Fox, 1942.
Stormy Weather, Twentieth Century-Fox, 1943.

The Pirate, MGM, 1948.
The Liberation of L.B. Jones, Columbia, 1970.
Night at the Golden Eagle, 2002.

Plays

The Ziegfeld Follies, New York, 1936.
Lew Leslie's Blackbird, London, 1936.
Babes in Arms, New York, 1937.
St. Louis Woman, New York, 1946.
Sammy on Broadway, New York, 1974.
(Choreographer) *Black and Blue*, New York, 1989.

Sources

Books

Bogle, Donald, *Blacks in American Films and Television*, Garland, 1988.
Hill, Constance Valis, *Brotherhood in Rhythm: The Jazz Tap Dancing of the Nicholas Brothers*, Oxford University Press, 2000.

Periodicals

Chicago Tribune, May 11, 1986, sect. 13, p. 10; December 22, 1991, sect. 13, p. 10.
Dance Magazine, April 1995, p. 40; July 1998, p. 62; April 2006, p. 96.
Ebony, May 1983, p. 103-106; May 1991, p.88-90.
Independent (London), July 5, 2000.
Jet, July 24, 2000, p. 53; February 13, 2006, p. 64.
Los Angeles Times, April 26, 1998, magazine sect., p. 18-20, 36.
Michigan Chronicle, June 17, 1998.
New Yorker, February 15, 1988, p. 25.
New York Times, March 28, 1998, p. C18; April 8, 1998, p. E8.
People Weekly, February 21, 2005, p. 102.
Variety, January 30, 2006, p. 72.
Washington Post, December 8, 1991, p. G1; June 9, 1996, p. G4.

On-line

"Fayard and Harold Nicholas," *Tap Dance*, www.tapdance.org/tap/people/nichbros.htm (July 12, 2006).
The Official Fayard Nicholas Website, www.nicholas-brothers.com/index.htm (July 12, 2006).
Palmer, Caroline, "Amazing Feet: The Nicholas Brothers," *TheatreDance*, www.theatredance.com/nicholas01.html (July 12, 2006).

—Mary Kalfatovic and Tom Pendergast

Donald M. Payne

1934—

Politician

In November of 1988 Donald M. Payne made history when he became the first black from New Jersey elected to the U.S. Congress. A former city councilman and Democratic leader from Newark, Payne won a nearly 80,000-vote victory over his Republican challenger in New Jersey's 10th Congressional District, which encompasses Newark and several surrounding cities in Essex and Union County. Payne's victory, virtually assured when he was a winner in the earlier Democratic primary, marked his third try at becoming a congressional representative. On two previous attempts, he was defeated by longtime Democratic incumbent Peter Rodino, former chairman of the House Judiciary Committee and one of Congress's leading advocates of civil rights legislation. Rodino's 1989 retirement cleared the way for Payne's election, and as in previous campaigns, Payne emphasized the importance of black representation for the predominantly black district. "When Congress was established, it was designed to have all segments of the population represented," Payne commented to Joseph F. Sullivan in the *New York Times*. The election of his state's first black congressman, he predicted, would "make the country stronger and make New Jersey stronger." Payne's prediction certainly started his own strong career. By 2004 he had won nine consecutive terms in office by wide margins, and had risen to wield great influence in Congress.

Formed Early Interest in Politics

Payne was born in 1934 in an Italian-American section of Newark known as Doodletown. The son of a dock worker and one-time chauffeur, Payne grew up in a working-class area where, as he told Sullivan, "everyone, whites and blacks, worked for low wages, although we didn't think of it as living in poverty, and there was a real sense of neighborhood, of depending on one another." Eventually, however, Payne became aware of the limited economic opportunities available to minorities; "I didn't have a black teacher all through elementary and high school until my senior year," he recalled to Sullivan.

His early experiences fueled Payne's interest in politics. His first political experience came in 1954, when he ran his brother William's successful campaign to be elected Newark's first black district leader. William Payne, who first became involved in politics as an organizer for a Rodino reelection campaign in the 1950s, went on to manage his brother Donald's successful 1988 congressional campaign. Payne's own political career evolved from his work as a schoolteacher and subsequent service with the Young Men's Christian Association (YMCA). After receiving his undergraduate degree from Seton Hall University in 1957, Payne taught English and social studies for seven years in the Newark public school system. In the early 1960s he began doing community work with the YMCA, organizing self-help projects that brought together local street gang members and adult volunteers. Also during this time, the death of his wife from cancer left him solely in charge of his two preschool-age children, Donald, Jr., and Wanda. Payne eventually left teaching and joined the Prudential Insurance Company in Newark as a manager, keeping a full schedule that

Born Donald Milford Payne, July 16, 1934, in Newark, NJ; son of William Evander (a dock worker) and Norma (Garrett) Payne; married Hazel Johnson, June 18, 1958 (died, 1963); children: three. *Education*: Seton Hall University, BA, 1957; Springfield College, MA, 1963.

Career: South Side High School, Newark, NJ, teacher, 1957; Robert Treat Junior High School, Newark, teacher, 1957-59; Pulaski Elementary School, Passaic, NJ, teacher, 1959-64; Prudential Insurance Company, Newark, manager, 1964-75, National Council of Young Men's Christian Associations (YMCA), national president, 1970-?, chairman of Refugee and Rehabilitation Committee, 1973-81; South Ward Democratic organization, Newark, chairman, 1970-88; Essex County (New Jersey) Board of Chosen Freeholders, member, 1972-78; Urban Data Systems, Newark, vice-president, 1976-?; Newark Municipal City Council, member, 1982-1988; U.S. House of Representatives, Washington, DC, Democratic congressman from New Jersey, 1988–.

Awards: Bishop John T. Walker Distinguished Humanitarian Service Award, 2004; honorary doctorates, Chicago State University, Drew University, Essex County College and William Paterson University.

Addresses: *Office*—2209 Rayburn House Office Building, Washington, D.C. 20515-3010; *Web*—www.house.gov/payne/links/index.html.

mixed family, career, and volunteer work with the YMCA. Payne rose high enough within the YMCA ranks to be named its national president in 1970—the first black ever to hold the position. Three years later he was elected chairman of the YMCA's World Refugee and Rehabilitation Committee, a position which took him to more than eighty countries.

By the end of the 1960s and into the early 1970s, Payne also made his mark as a prominent member of the local Newark political scene. In the late 1960s he moved to Newark's South Ward and helped to revamp—along with future New Jersey State minority assembly leader Willie Brown—the district's Democratic Party organization. Led by Payne, who served as its president for eighteen years, the organization went on to produce a number of prominent Newark politi-

cians, including Mayor Sharpe James, State Senator Wynona Lipman, and councilmen Donald Tucker and Ralph T. Grant. Payne made further political moves in the early 1970s with his election to the Essex County Board of Freeholders, a county-level body of legislators. Payne served as the board's director from 1978 until 1982, during which time he made his first unsuccessful bid at a seat in the U.S. Congress.

In 1982, Payne was elected to the Newark City Council, a position from which he would launch his successful 1988 congressional campaign. Rebounding from a second primary defeat to Rodino in 1986, Payne persevered to make himself the leading candidate to fill Rodino's 10th Congressional District seat when the representative announced his 1989 retirement after forty years of service. Payne ran his successful campaign on a message that the district, which had become predominantly black during the 1970s, should have a black congressman as its representative. Combined with his pledge to be a positive role model and active worker on behalf of young people, Payne won the June 1988 Democratic nomination over fellow black politician Ralph T. Grant, a prelude to his landslide victory five months later over Republican challenger Michael Webb. Upon winning the election, Payne commented to Sullivan on his persistence in capturing the congressional seat he had long aspired to. "Nothing is as powerful as a dream whose time has come," Payne stated. "Sometimes a political leader is marching a little in front or a little behind the people, but once in a while the marcher and the drumbeat are in exactly the same cadence, and then, finally, good things happen."

Payne also had words of praise for Rodino, the Italian-American congressman who ably served as the district's representative for more than forty years. "When Congressman Rodino defeated incumbent Republican Fred Hartley in 1948, Italian-Americans were being discriminated against in employment and housing, and his election made them very proud.... He was loved and revered." Aspiring to be a similar type of representative, Payne described a major objective as being the assessment of the needs of his constituents with regard to the omnibus drug bill and legislation surrounding catastrophic health insurance. He summed up in *Ebony* his feelings on being the first black congressman from his home state: "It means a dream fulfilled. It means you've got to be qualified. It means pride. It means thinking about Dr. Martin Luther King and Medgar Evers.... It means New Jersey has taken its rightful place with other areas of this country that have finally put a member of its own race in Congress."

Formed Solid Political Reputation

Payne established himself as a career politician, working to support his constituents by securing seniority in Congress. Throughout each of the nine terms he has served in office, Payne gained access to some of the most powerful committees. Among his many appointments, he held the position of chairman of the Congressional Black Caucus. Payne was also one of five congressional representatives selected by President Clinton to represent the country on a six-nation African tour in 1998. In 2003 President Bush appointed Payne to serve as a Congressional delegate to the United Nations. In 2006 Payne served on the Democratic Steering Committee, a group that assigns Democrats to congressional committees and is influential in shaping the legislative agenda. In addition, he served on the House Committee on Education and the Workforce and the International Relations Committee, in which he held a ranking member position in the Subcommittee on the Western Hemisphere and Subcommittee on Africa, Global Human Rights and International Operations.

Payne's efforts were recognized in the bills he helped pass, including the school improvement initiative Goals 2000; the School-to-Work Opportunities Act; the National Service Act and the Student Loan Bill, the millions of dollars in economic support he has secured for his constituent counties, and the international efforts he spearheaded to send aid to Sudan, Rwanda, Liberia, and other war-torn or impoverished countries. Colin Powell praised Payne in 2004 at the Bishop John T. Walker Memorial Dinner, saying according to Political Transcript Wire, that Payne brings to his job "a passion that we need to get our bureaucracy to work, to make sure the government does what it should be doing." Into his ninth term in office, Payne seemed to have only just begun his work, and continued to cast his net wide in order to use his senior influence in Congress to good ends.

Sources

Periodicals

Africa Analysis, December 14, 2001.
CQ Weekly, October 27, 2001.
Ebony, May 1989.
Newsweek, June 9, 1986.
New York Beacon, July 1-7, 2004.
New York Times, June 8, 1988; June 9, 1988; November 5, 1988; November 9, 1988; November 10, 1988, January 5, 2005.
Political Transcript Wire, November 5, 2004.

On-line

"Ambassador Andrew Young Lecture Series on Africa, Remarks by Congressman Donald M. Payne," *The Africa Society of the National Summit on Africa,* www.africasummit.org/news/payneremarks.html (July 12, 2006).
Congressman Donald M. Payne, 10th District New Jersey, www.house.gov/payne/links/index.html (July 12, 2006).

—Michael E. Mueller and Sara Pendergast

Charles E. Phillips, Jr.

1959—

Executive

Phillips, Charles E., Jr., photograph. Daniel Acker/Bloomberg News/Landov.

As co-president and director, Charles E. Phillips Jr. took the helm of Oracle Corporation—one of the largest technology providers to business and governments around the world—in 2004. Oracle is a pioneer in relational database management systems, developing systems software, relational databases, and middleware that enable organizations to manage information. Phillips oversaw all global field operations and corporate strategy for the company. His prior work as a technology stock analyst for Morgan Stanley Dean Witter earned him status as an industry expert. Phillips' work philosophy, as he explained it to *Black Enterprise,* neatly summed up how he blazed a path for himself to become a leader at one of America's most powerful companies. He committed himself to: "having a passion for what you do, being technically prepared all the time, and having a willingness to take risks." His continued commitment to his work boded well for Oracle.

Phillips was born in June of 1959 in Little Rock, Arkansas. A self-professed "gadget guy" all his life, Phillips was fascinated by computers and technology from an early age. He spent his spare time during high school building computers for his friends and family. Phillips was lucky enough to figure out early on what he wanted to do with his life. He knew his career would involve computers, so after high school he joined the Air Force Academy to study computer science and to follow in his father's footsteps. His father had made it clear that he expected one of his four sons to be an Air Force man. Phillips had entered the academy with high hopes, but disappointment came in the form of declining eyesight, forcing Phillips to take a different path. He stayed in the military but switched to the Marine Corps, a difficult transition for Phillips as he found himself in the midst of a starkly new culture. It didn't take long for him to receive an unwelcome chill from the predominately Southern, middle-aged marines he outranked upon arrival on base as a second lieutenant. Phillips was assigned to the data processing and logistics area, managing computer systems, and eventually earning promotion to captain.

Phillips navigated another transition when he left the Marine Corps and went to work on Wall Street. Phillips knew nothing about business stock. The subject had not circulated in the predominantly military neighbor-

At a Glance . . .

Born Charles E. Phillips Jr. in June, 1959, Little Rock, AR. *Education:* United States Air Force Academy, BS, computer science; Hampton University, MBA; New York Law School, JD, 1993. *Military service:* U.S. Marine Corps, captain.

Career: Wall Street firms, information technology analyst, 1986-94; Morgan Stanley, principal, 1994-5; managing director, 1995-2003; Oracle Corporation, Redwood Shores, CA, executive vice president, Strategy, Partnerships, and Business Development, 2003-4; president, director, 2004–.

Memberships: Viacom Corporation Board of Directors; Jazz at Lincoln Center in New York City Board of Directors; New York Law School Board of Directors; Morgan Stanley, Board of Directors.

Awards: *Institutional Investor* magazine, Number One Enterprise Software Industry Analyst, 1994-2003; *Black Enterprise* magazine, Top 50 African Americans on Wall Street, 2002.

Addresses: *Office*—Oracle Corporation, 500 Oracle Parkway, Redwood Shores, CA 94065.

hoods of his youth; not a soul he knew even owned stock. But possessing an innate sense for the requirements of the work, Phillips had done his homework and felt he would be good at it. After receiving plenty of rejection he finally landed a job with Morgan Stanley Dean Witter's Institutional Securities Division. Phillips spent nine years with the company, becoming well known for his acumen in the technology sector. Investors came to rely on his recommendations when making investments in technology stocks. Phillips eventually worked his way to principal, then managing director at the firm.

Phillips had become one of the stars of Wall Street. *Institutional Investor* magazine named him the number one software analyst for nine years running. *Black Enterprise Magazine* placed him on their list of "Top 50 African Americans on Wall Street" in 2002. Many in the industry read his articles on the purchasing plans

of top CIOs. He had earned the respect of his peers. So, when Oracle CEO Larry Ellison offered Phillips the position of co-president he knew the type of relationships Phillips had nurtured with business and financial leaders. With the company's focus on improved customer interactions and Phillips' track record and experience as a tech analyst, Ellison saw Phillips as the perfect choice. Ellison's choice was grounded in first-hand knowledge. Ellison and Phillips had formed an excellent working relationship over the years. And the *New York Times* called Phillips one of Oracle's "biggest fans," for his decade of recommendations for the corporation's stock.

Not long after Phillips' arrival at the Silicon Valley Headquarters he scored a big win, receiving credit for wooing investors during Oracle's takeover of its rival, PeopleSoft. The takeover had been a hostile one, starting just a couple of weeks after Phillips joined Oracle. Despite a legal tangle that lasted until 2004, Oracle and Phillips emerged victorious. Though the phenomenal growth experienced by Oracle in the 1990s may have slowed, Phillips' career seemed to have just gotten started.

Sources

Periodicals

Black Enterprise, January 2004, p.41; April 2004, p.26.
Business Week Online, June 25, 2003 p. 1.
New York Times, May 17, 2003, p. C3.
Wall Street Journal, June 16, 2003, p. C1.

On-line

"Charles E. Phillips Jr," *Forbes*, www.forbes.com/ finance/mktguideapps/personinfo/FromPersonId-PersonTearsheet.jhtml?passedPersonId=880818 (March 01, 2006).
"Oracle Executive Biographies," *Oracle*, www.oracle. com/corporate/pressroom/html/pressportal/exec/ cphillips.html (March 01, 2006).
"Why Oracle Loves a Fight," *Business Week Online*, http://infotrac.galegroup.com/itw/infomark/835/ 87/111557961w3/purl=rc1_BCPM_0_ A130058133&dyn=6!nxt_2_0_A130058133?sw_ aep=itsbtrial (March 10, 2005).

Other

Additional information for this profile was obtained from Oracle Corporation.

—Sharon Melson Fletcher

Kyla A. Pratt

1986—

Actor

Kyla Pratt carved out a niche for herself in Hollywood as the likable teen in a long list of film and television projects. Working steadily since the age of ten, Pratt has been the voice of Penny Proud in the kids' hit series, *The Proud Family,* on ABC, and played the younger daughter of comedy veteran Eddie Murphy in the three *Doctor Dolittle* movies. Her popular appeal was confirmed in 2005 when producers for the UPN sitcom retooled the focus of *One on One,* one of the highest rated sitcoms among African-American viewers, to focus more on her character, Breanna Barnes.

Born on September 16, 1986, in Los Angeles, Pratt was the first of five children in her family. Her mother was active in local theater, and Pratt's first venture into the performing arts came when she was five years old and served as an extra in a stage production in which her mother was also involved. But acting was not a goal for her, she told Sakina P. Spruell in an interview for *Black Enterprise.* "I didn't really decide to get into this business, it just came up and I started to love it." she explained to Spruell. "My grandma showed off my pictures on an airplane and another passenger asked for me to be in a fashion show. Then an agent

Pratt, Kyla, photograph. © Vaughn Youtz/Zuma/Corbis.

approached us and we signed with them."

Pratt's first paying job came in a 1995 television commercial for an interactive computer game. She worked steadily after that, beginning with an appearance in *The Baby-Sitters Club* television series and a stint as one of the playmate kids in the *Barney* television series. That job led to her feature-film debut in *Barney's Great Adventure,* the 1998 movie that starred the lovable purple dinosaur. Over the next few years, Pratt worked steadily in sitcoms and television dramas. Her credits include *Living Single, The Parent 'Hood, ER, Moesha, The Hughleys, The Parkers, Lizzie McGuire,* and even an episode of *Friends.* She also made some memorable television commercials for the Women's National Basketball League, including one in which she upbraided Houston Comets guard Cynthia Cooper.

Pratt was cast as one of the two daughters in *Doctor Dolittle,* the 1998 feature film, with Eddie Murphy in the title role, about a man with a secret talent for conversing with animals. This modern adaptation of a long-ago children's story proved one of the surprise box-office hits of the summer, and Pratt appeared in its

At a Glance . . .

Born on September 16, 1986, in Los Angeles, CA.

Career: Actor, 1995–.

Addresses: *Office*—c/o UPN, 11800 Wilshire Blvd., Los Angeles, CA 90025.

two sequels as the increasingly grown-up Maya Dolittle. Other film roles from this time included *Love & Basketball* in 2000, in which she played the younger version of the film's star, Sanaa Lathan, and *The Seat Filler,* a romance featuring heartthrob Shemar Moore and executive-produced by Hollywood heavyweights Will Smith and wife Jada Pinkett Smith.

One of Pratt's first regularly recurring television roles came with *One on One,* the UPN sitcom that debuted in 2001. She played Breanna, the fourteen-year-old daughter of divorced parents. When her mother's new job disrupts their Atlanta household schedule, Breanna goes to live with her father, a popular sports broadcaster played by Flex Alexander, in Baltimore. The series' storylines originally focused on her bachelor father's often-comic difficulties in adjusting to life as a single parent, and of a headstrong daughter unused to his suddenly strict rules with her. The show began to revolve more around Pratt's character starting with its fifth season in 2005, with plotlines centered on her new life as a college student in California. Breanna's off-again, on-again relationship with her longtime best friend, Arnaz (Robert Ri'chard), provided much of the series' drama that season.

One on One grew to become one of the top-rated sitcoms among African-American viewers. Pratt was also involved in another popular show, *The Proud Family,* as the voice of Penny Proud in the animated series. Her increasingly busy work schedule forced her to give up a regular school schedule—for a time, she was a student at the Hamilton High School Academy of Music, a magnet school for the performing arts and part of the Los Angeles United School District—and work with a tutor instead. But by the time she turned 16 in 2002, she had saved enough to buy herself a car when she received her driver's license.

Pratt's first starring role in a feature film came in 2004 with *Fat Albert,* the big-screen version of a popular

1970s television cartoon series based on characters created by Bill Cosby. Pratt was cast in one of the leads as Doris, an unhappy teen who watches a rerun of the show, cries, and a teardrop that leaks into the remote suddenly brings the characters to life inside her house. "From there, the movie, alas, just lies down and dies, despite the capable efforts of the young cast," declared *New York Times* reviewer Manohla Dargis.

In 2006, Pratt appeared in the third *Doctor Dolittle* movie, and kept up with her *One on One* role. After having landed what many ten-year-olds would call their dream job, and then working steadily into adulthood, there are a few drawbacks to her career, she admitted to Spruell in *Black Enterprise.* "At first, I didn't like all the heat, hair spray, or tugging on my hair," she confessed. "For the weeks that I don't have to work, I don't wear makeup at all." Having one's own tutor on the set is not the easiest route to earning a high-school diploma, either. She still had to maintain a C average despite working on the set up to nine hours a day. When *Buffalo News* journalist Angela Stefano asked her if she had any advice to aspiring actors, Pratt cautioned them to "get into it because you love acting, not just for the money involved. If you don't love it, the whole process will get boring after a while."

Selected works

Films

Barney's Great Adventure, 1998.
Doctor Dolittle, 1998.
Love & Basketball, 2000.
Doctor Dolittle 2, 2001.
The Seat Filler, 2004.
Fat Albert, 2004.
Doctor Dolittle 3, 2006.

Television

One on One, 2001—.
The Proud Family, 2001—.

Sources

Periodicals

Black Enterprise, March 2003, p. S10.
Buffalo News, May 14, 2003, p. N3.
New York Times, December 24, 2004.
Variety, December 27, 2004, p. 16.
WWD, December 23, 2004, p. 4.

—Carol Brennan

Lou Rawls

1936-2006

Singer, humanitarian

Upon his death from cancer in 2006, Lou Rawls was remembered by a star-studded list of celebrities not only for his memorable singing career—Rawls issued more than 60 albums over the course of his 40-year career, and he won three Grammy Awards—but also for his lengthy career as a humanitarian. Explaining his musical durability to the *American Business Review* in 1997, Rawls explained: "I didn't try to change every time the music changed. I just stayed in that pocket where I was 'cause it was comfortable and the people liked it." The

Rawls, Lou, photograph. CBS/Landov.

same could be said for his humanitarian efforts, because for more than 25 years Rawls hosted the United Negro College Fund (UNCF) annual telethon, earning that charity more than $200 million. Over the course of time Rawls became something of an American institution, instantly recognizable by his comfortable crooner's baritone voice and several of his trademark tunes, including "You'll Never Find Another Love Like Mine," "Lady Love," and "Love Is a Hurtin' Thing."

Despite his claims to music stability, Rawls' early years were marked by sometimes dramatic changes in style. Rawls had been by turns streetwise and sophisticated. Beginning his career, as did so many other African

American singers, in the gospel field, he was groomed as a pop/jazz singer after signing with the Capitol label in the early 1960s. He first found mass success with a series of rootsy, heavily blues-tinged monologue-song combinations recorded later in that decade. In the 1970s his career was reborn in the area of middle-of-the-road black pop that sometimes pointed in the direction of disco. Although he was never identified with the cutting edge of black music, he nevertheless resisted recording-company efforts to push his style in a certain direction, insisting on his own instincts regarding his musical development. In so doing, he created a body of music that reflected the experiences of a wide cross-section of African Americans and Americans of other backgrounds.

Rooted in Gospel

Louis Allen Rawls was born on December 1, 1936, in Chicago. He was raised largely by his grandmother, both his parents having left the household during Rawls's childhood. Rawls grew up on Chicago's south side, at a time when the area was in the process of

At a Glance . . .

Born Louis Allen Rawls, December 1, 1936, in Chicago; died January 6, 2006, of cancer; son of Virgil (a Baptist minister) and Evelyn Rawls; raised mostly by grandmother Eliza Rawls; married to wife Lana Jean, 1961 (divorced, 1973); married Ceci, 1989 (divorced, 2003); married Nina Inman, 2004; children: Louanna, Kendra Smith, Lou Jr., and Aiden Allen. *Religion:* Baptist. *Military service:* U.S. Army, 1956-58.

Career: Vocalist, mid-1950s-2006. Sang gospel music in church from age of seven; joined gospel group Pilgrim Travelers (other members included Sam Cooke), mid-1950s; signed by Capitol Records, 1962; signed by Philadelphia International label, 1975; launched United Negro College Fund "Parade of Stars" television fundraiser, 1979.

Awards: Grammy awards for single "Dead End Street," 1967; LP *A Natural Man,* 1971; LP *Unmistakably Lou,* 1977.

ascending to its place at the top of the blues world. Rawls's south-side neighborhood was a hotbed of musical talent, eventually producing such successful acts as Curtis Mayfield, the Dells, and Sam Cooke. He saw concerts by such acts as Arthur Prysock and the legendary Louis Armstrong at the south side's Regal Theater, but Rawls's instincts were more rooted in Gospel music, having sung in his grandmother's Baptist church choir from the age of seven.

After singing with gospel groups as a teenager, Rawls joined with Cooke and two other vocalists to form the Pilgrim Travelers. After completing a stint in the U.S. Army, Rawls toured extensively with the Pilgrim Travelers, but in 1958 the group's car collided with a truck. While Cooke escaped with minor injuries, Rawls was near death on the way to the hospital, remained in a coma for most of the next week, and suffered memory loss lasting a year. The terrible accident proved to be a life-changing experience for the singer. "I had plenty of time to think," he later told the *Arizona Republic.* "I didn't want to just go someday; I really wanted to do something good, to make a mark."

Rawls began making appearances wherever he could build his skills—on the blues-oriented "chitlin' circuit" and in small clubs and coffeehouses around Los Angeles. His finances were strained, but he did land a small part in the *77 Sunset Strip* television series. While performing at a Hollywood club called Pandora's Box, located close to the headquarters of Capitol Records,

Rawls was spotted by a Capitol producer and signed to the label in 1962. Another success that year was singing backup vocal to Cooke on Cooke's hit "Bring It on Home to Me." That classic recording harkened back to the days when Cooke and Rawls had sung gospel music together.

Rawls's first big success came when he began to introduce blues stage devices, such as monologues about poverty, into his music. A 1964 recording of the powerful country classic "Tobacco Road" gained some notice, and the song remained a fixture of Rawls's live shows for years afterward. The 1966 LP *Lou Rawls Live* effectively showcased the monologue technique and gave Rawls his first gold record. From then until his departure from Capitol in 1971, Rawls's recordings were reliably successful; he recorded a total of 28 albums for the label during this period.

Rawls moved briefly to the MGM label in 1971, and quickly notched one of the biggest hits of his career with "Natural Man," originally the B-side of another song released as a single. But the singer clashed with MGM executives over the lightweight musical fare that they wanted him to record and he soon left the label, signing briefly with the independent Bell Records, where he collaborated with the songwriting pair of Darryl Hall and John Oates. In 1975 Rawls found success when he embarked on a collaboration with another hit-making pair, the Philadelphia producers and songwriters Kenny Gamble and Leon Huff. Signing with the duo's Philadelphia International label, he released such singles as "You'll Never Find Another Love Like Mine," which became a million-seller in 1976 and garnered substantial play in the dance clubs that incubated the emerging style known as disco.

Seventies Hits Launch Humanitarian Career

With this music Rawls found himself a long way from his chitlin'-circuit roots. The style pioneered by Gamble and Huff was heavily produced, aimed at sharp-dressed urban crowds. Yet Rawls adapted seamlessly and showed staying power in his new incarnation as a hit-maker. The 1977 LP *Undeniably Lou* won a Grammy award for Best R&B Performance, and Rawls continued to record for Philadelphia International well into the 1980s.

Rawls parlayed his celebrity into a lucrative position as advertising spokesman for the giant Anheuser-Busch brewery, makers of Budweiser beer. In 1979 the brewery backed the singer in what would became the most recognizable and important activity of his later career: his establishment and nurturing of the annual Parade of Stars telethon, conducted for the benefit of the United Negro College Fund.

Rawls served for 26 years the host of the television program, which varied between three and seven hours in length and which has showcased leading performers in a variety of musical styles. In 2004, the United Negro College Fund honored Rawls's longstanding connection to the charity by holding a 25th anniversary tribute to him featuring performances by Stevie Wonder, Yolanda Adams, Ashanti, Beyonce, and many others. At that time, it was estimated that Rawls had helped raise over $200 million for the charity. The money benefited a group of small, historically black colleges and universities, all of which opened their doors to students of limited economic means. Tens of thousands of African American students quite simply owed their college educations to Lou Rawls.

By the 1990s Rawls was an institution. He kept busy over the years giving live musical performances, and he also appeared in several television programs and movies, including the 1995 film *Leaving Las Vegas.* Yet he never lost his commitment to the UNCF, and his work on the telethon continued to consume much of his energy. As he told the *Arizona Republic,* "It is, by far, my proudest achievement."

Rawls died on January 6, 2006, from complications from lung and liver cancer. Aretha Franklin remember Rawls fondly in *Jet*: "Lou was a great guy—with a great sense of humor. He was a man's man. A dear and old treasured friend who made a serious impact in the interest of historically Black colleges and Black folks. We should always remember and salute Lou Rawls. He will be missed." Rawls's longtime commitment to the United Negro College Fund was commemorated beginning in 2006 by the creation of the Lou Rawls Lifetime Achievement Award, given each year to a popular artist "whose career reflects the quality of commitment to UNCF and its mission that was Rawls' hallmark." His will be big shoes to fill.

Selected discography

Tobacco Road, Capitol, 1963.
Lou Rawls Live, Capitol, 1966.
Best from Lou Rawls, Capitol, 1968.
A Natural Man, MGM, 1971.
All Things in Time, Philadelphia International, 1976.
Unmistakably Lou, Philadelphia International, 1977.
When the Night Comes, Epic, 1983.
It's Supposed to Be Fun, Blue Note, 1990.
Portrait of the Blues, Manhattan, 1993.
Christmas Is the Time, Manhattan, 1993.
Ballads, Capitol, 1997 (reissue).
Love Is a Hurtin' Thing, Capitol, 1997 (reissue).
Rawls Sings Sinatra, Savoy Jazz, 2003.
Lou Rawls: Love Songs, The Right Stuff/EMI, 2005.

Sources

Books

Stambler, Irwin, *The Encyclopedia of Pop, Rock & Soul,* rev. ed., St. Martin's, 1989.
Larkin, Colin, editor, *The Guinness Encyclopedia of Popular Music,* Guinness, 1992.
Romanowski, Patricia, editor, *The New Rolling Stone Encyclopedia of Rock & Roll,* Fireside, 1995.
Contemporary Musicians, Vol. 19, Gale, 1997.

Periodicals

American Business Review, July 12, 1997, p. 5.
Arizona Republic, April 25, 1997, p. D13.
Ebony, October 1978, p. 112; March 2006, p. 178.
Jet, November 17, 1997, p. 64; January 12, 2004, p. 105; January 9, 2006, p. 53.
New York Times, January 6, 2006.
St. Louis Post-Dispatch, October 3, 1997, p. E4.
Stereo Review, July 1993, p. 91.
USA Today, October 16, 1997, p. D4; January 18, 1998, p. D3.
Variety, January 16, 2006, p. 47.

On-line

In Memoriam: Lou Rawls, www.lourawls.com (July 10, 2006).

—James M. Manheim and Tom Pendergast

Michael V. Roberts

1948—

Businessman

Michael V. Roberts has been turning the business world on its head since he began making deals in the 1970s. With his brother Steve, he started Roberts-Roberts & Associates, a consulting firm. This led to opportunities in politics, real estate, broadcasting, wireless communication and construction, just to name a few. Roberts' perseverance and vision have also made him a popular speaker at colleges and conventions.

Roberts, Michael, photograph. Photo courtesy of Michael Gregory Photography. Reproduced by permission.

graduation, he attended Forest Park Community College, and then transferred to Lindenwood University, where he earned a Bachelor of Science degree. Throughout his matriculation, Roberts also sold African dashikis (shirts) and other African imports to stores. He graduated, and with a grant from the Danforth Foundation and money he earned from his sales, Roberts enrolled at St. Louis University to study law. He earned his JD and began Roberts-Roberts & Associates while his brother studied law at Washington University.

Sold Dashikis and Studied Law

Michael V. Roberts was born in St. Louis, Missouri, on October 24, 1948. He was the eldest of four children, born to Victor, a postal worker, and Delores Roberts, a homemaker who became a teacher after her children had grown. The family lived in a two-family flat with their grandmother for the first years of Roberts' childhood. Growing up, Roberts was very close to his brother Steve, who was three and a half years his junior.

When another sibling was born, the Roberts family moved to an all-white neighborhood. Roberts attended the newly integrated Northwest High School. After

Roberts-Roberts & Associates' main focus was to help companies figure out ways to increase minority business participation in government contracts. Though he had little experience as a consultant, Roberts used his natural skills as a businessman to help the business thrive. He told *Forbes,* "We grab at a chance and then figure out how we're going to do it and how we're going to pay for it." His tactics worked, and the business grew.

Roberts had his sights set on more than just business success. He also wanted to make a difference in his community through politics. In the late 1970s, he

At a Glance . . .

Born on October 24, 1948, in St. Louis, MO; son of Victor (U.S. postal worker) and Delores (homemaker, teacher); married Jeanne, children: four. *Education:* Attended Forest Park Community College; Lindenwood University, BS; The Hague Academy of International Law, Netherlands, 1972; International Institute of Human Rights, Strasbourg, France, 1973; St. Louis University Law School, JD, 1974. *Politics:* Democrat.

Career: Roberts-Roberts & Associates (now The Roberts Companies), founder, 1974–; founded more than 30 other companies, including Roberts Brothers Properties, 1982–; Roberts Broadcasting Company, 1989–; Roberts Wireless Communications, 1998–; Roberts Isle, 1998–; Roberts Tower Company, 2001–; Roberts Custom Cabinetry and Woodworking, 2005–.

Memberships: Kappa Alpha Psi Fraternity; Alamosa PCS Holdings, board of directors, 2001—; St Louis Arts & Education Council; Better Family Life, board of directors; Home Shopping Network, board of directors.

Awards: *Black Enterprise* Top 100 Industrial/Service companies list, 2000, 2003, 2005; Spirit of St. Louis award, Mayoral Office, St. Louis, MO, 2003; Gateway Classic Sports Foundation, honoree, 2004.

Addresses: *Office*—The Roberts Companies, 1408 N. Kings Hwy, St Louis, MO 63113; *Web*—www. michaelvroberts.com.

accomplished his dream of becoming involved in politics. Roberts was chosen as Jimmy Carter's St. Louis campaign manager in his presidential bid. When Carter became president, Roberts was a frequent guest at the White House. Roberts was elected as an alderman on the St. Louis City Council. He was the youngest person ever elected at the age of 28. His brother continued the tradition by being elected at age 26, a year after the elder entered office. He, his brother, and three other council members would work together to help revitalize the city's downtown area. The city took on several ambitious construction projects that, in turn, bolstered the city's economy.

Purchased Real Estate to Save Neighborhood

When Roberts noticed that his childhood neighborhood was suffering from decline, he determined that he would stop the decay. Together with his brother, Roberts began Roberts Brothers Properties (RBP), and purchased a 200,000-square foot building from retailer Sears. They renovated the building, and began to lease out portions to various businesses to help the neighborhood stay afloat. Roberts stated to St. Louis's *Riverfront Times*, "We've put our money, our experience, our expertise, our life into this neighborhood. We have to be a [part] of this renaissance of inner-city hard-core areas. If we don't, then who will?" In addition to leasing out to 50 businesses, RBP and Robert-Roberts & Associates moved into the top floor. Roberts also rechristened the building, naming it after his father, who had retired from the U.S. Post Office after 39 years. RBP would continue to purchase old buildings and land, then would either renovate or construct new buildings. Their tenants ranged from Blockbuster Video, State Farm Insurance, and the leading grocery store chain in St. Louis, Schnucks, to various governmental agencies. With the success of rebuilding their childhood neighborhood, Roberts and his brother looked beyond their hometown, expanding their efforts to Denver, Colorado, where they began purchasing land and building strip malls.

After eight years as an alderman, Roberts left his position to run for city council president. He lost, but filed a lawsuit for a recount, arguing that the punch-card system was faulty and that the minority voters in St. Louis did not understand how the system worked. His case was dismissed by the 8th U.S. Circuit Court of Appeals. He was also chastised by the court for using the Voting Rights Act for his own gain. He would later send the papers from his court case to Vice President Al Gore to help him during his fight for the presidency in 2000.

Roberts was introduced to someone who was looking for minority businessmen interested in broadcasting. He and his brother formed Roberts Broadcasting Company, and joined the fray of minority businesses vying for broadcasting licenses. After six years, Roberts Broadcasting won a license. They searched for programming, and entered talks with the Home Shopping Network (HSN). Roberts persuaded HSN to pay his company $3.8 million to build a television station to receive their satellite signal, and another $1.6 million to air their programming. HSN agreed, and WRBU-TV Channel 46 debuted. The television station was the first station built in St. Louis in more than 20 years. It was also one of the few in the country that was fully automated, needing only a technician to come in and change tapes. Roberts Broadcasting Company would later add 11 more stations to its list in locations throughout the country, including Denver, Colorado, Nashville, Tennessee, Salt Lake City, Utah, and Colombia, South Carolina. Roberts would sell or merge eight of the stations in later years. He also changed networks, switching from HSN to the United Paramount Network (UPN).

Hopped on Wireless Communication Bandwagon

In the late 1990s, wireless communication was an emerging business, and Roberts wanted in on the action. Meetings between the brothers and Sprint led to the formation of Roberts Wireless Communications. Roberts was able to persuade Sprint to allow them to build a wireless network in Missouri, and parts of Kansas and Illinois. This new venture would cost $78 million. Roberts approached several companies, but only Lucent Technologies would give $56 million, while Roberts Wireless would take care of the remaining $22 million, and then, only if the Roberts brothers would use their company as collateral. Roberts and his company began building towers throughout the state, and also opened the first Sprint store in St. Louis. Roberts then merged with Alamosa Communications, who bought out his company for $300 million, and assumed the $56 million debt to Lucent.

Building towers in three states brought about the formation of Roberts Towers Company in 2001. Roberts built towers for cellular phones, and also broadcasting towers. The company also expanded into Oklahoma (cell phone towers) and Utah, New Mexico, and Tennessee (broadcasting). After expanding into several new territories, Roberts Wireless Communications became the United States eighth largest tower company, leasing to all of the major wireless communication giants.

Though a large amount of attention was given to his growing broadcasting and wireless communication companies, Roberts continued to expand his empire by making several major building purchases. Roberts Brothers Properties purchased the St. Louis Board of Education building in downtown St. Louis. Roberts renovated the inside of the office building and turned it into residential lofts and retail stores. Roberts Lofts opened to much fanfare, offering up lofts as small as 784 square feet, up to 2,200 square feet penthouses. Roberts also purchased the building across the street and built a garage.

Purchased Hotels and Airplanes, Wrote Memoir

Roberts approached Wyndham Hotels, LLC to purchase the Mayfair Hotel, located in the middle of the downtown area. He also bought the old Orpheum Vaudeville Theatre that was adjacent to the Mayfair Hotel, and renovated it. He and his brother needed a tax write-off, and the two purchased a Gulfstream III, a 12-passenger luxury business jet, and a Hawker jet, which sits eight passengers. With Million Air managing operations out of Dallas, Texas, Roberts Aviation was formed. Roberts also acquired another hotel in Atlanta, Georgia, and christened it The Roberts Mayfair Hotel-Atlanta. He bought land in the Bahamas, one of his favorite vacation destinations, and built a 50-unit condominium and apartment gated community.

Not one to rest on his laurels, Roberts began speaking to several businesses, schools, and organizations about his success and ways for others to become successful. He also wrote a book, *Action Has No Season, Secrets to Gaining Wealth and Authority*. He stated in his foreword that he wrote his book for his children, because "[i]n order to ensure their success in this ever-changing global business world, they would need the advice and counsel of a visionary capitalist such as me."

Roberts and his brother began 34 businesses. He told *Commerce* magazine, "We are diversified. I always felt that was important. If you limit yourself to one sector of business opportunities in this economy, you die." They continued to use the office in the first building they acquired, but the company name was now The Roberts Companies. In addition to Roberts being the chairman and chief executive officer, his brother Steve was president and chief operations officer. Their father came out of retirement to become chief financial officer of the company. Their siblings and two of Roberts' own children also work for the brothers' companies.

In addition to becoming a major player in St. Louis, Roberts gave back to his community through donations and time. He was a member of Kappa Alpha Psi, St. Louis Council on World Affairs, and on the board of directors for various organizations, including Better Family Life. He devoted as much time to his business as he did to his family, which included his wife, Jeanne, and four children.

Selected writings

Action Has No Season, Secrets to Gaining Wealth and Authority, Authorhouse, 2005.

Sources

Books

Action Has No Season, Secrets to Gaining Wealth and Authority, Authorhouse, 2005.
Who's Who Among African Americans, 18th Edition, Thomson Gale, 2005.

Periodicals

Black Enterprise, December 2001; June 2003; June 2005.
Business Wire, July 24, 2003.

Commerce, May 2003.
Forbes, October 16, 2000, pp. 170-173.
Jet, August 11, 2003, p. 12.
Riverfront Times (St. Louis, MO), March 17, 2004.

On-line

"About the Roberts Companies," *Roberts Tower Company,* www.robertstower.com/about_us.asp (March 1, 2005).
"Action Has No Season, Secrets to Gaining Wealth and Authority," *Authorhouse,* www.authorhouse.com/bookstore/itemdetail.aspx?bookid=24359 (March 1, 2005).

Michael V. Roberts, www.michaelvroberts.com (March 1, 2005).
"Mike's Newsroom," *Michael V. Roberts,* www.michaelvroberts.com (March 1, 2005).
"Roberts Lofts on the Plaza Revitalizes Historic St. Louis Board of Education Building," *St. Louis Front Page,* www.slfp.com/CNews030405.htm (March 1, 2005).
"Walk of Fame Recognizes Local African Americans," *Newsgram City of St. Louis,* http://stlouis.missouri.org/citygov/newsgram/volumes/volume10/gatewayawards.htm (March 1, 2005).

—Ashyia N. Henderson

David Satcher

1941—

Physician, educator, administrator

Satcher, David, photograph. AP Images.

Dr. David Satcher attained distinction for his leadership at the highest levels of American health care. The first African-American director of the Centers for Disease Control and Prevention (CDC), Satcher increased the agency's attention on disease prevention and promoted such protective measures as cancer screening and increased physical activity. In 1998 President Clinton appointed Satcher the 16th surgeon general, as well as Assistant Secretary for Health. Satcher was the second person in American history to hold both positions at once. As surgeon general, Satcher led the charge to focus national attention on the racial and ethnic disparities in health care, and he was the first surgeon general to report on mental health issues. In 2002 Satcher assumed the directorship of the National Primary Care Center at Morehouse School of Medicine, the first nationally funded center with a mission to enhance community-oriented primary care, where he continued his focus on disparities in access to health care especially among minority and poor populations. Combined, Satcher's commitment to making health care accessible to all Americans and his effectiveness as a leader, kept him in the limelight as what USA Today had once called him: "one of the nation's most influential physicians."

According to Peter Applebome in the New York Times, what makes Satcher a physician of note "is less what he says than what he has done. In a nation where it's almost impossible to flip across a radio dial without hearing the standard talk show litany of what government and society can't do, his life has been an exercise in walking up to locked doors and somehow finding a key." Indeed, Satcher placed a premium on focusing his efforts on the needs of his community.

Inspired by Overcoming Childhood Illness

Satcher's desire to become a doctor may have been planted in his earliest years, when he himself almost succumbed to a deadly disease. At the tender age of two, he contracted whooping cough–an illness for which immunizations exist today–and he nearly died. Satcher told the Los Angeles Times that he can remember the painful and desperate struggle to draw each breath, and the valiant efforts his mother and a

At a Glance . . .

Born on March 2, 1941, in Anniston, AL; son of Wilmer (a foundry worker) and Anna Satcher; married Callie (died of breast cancer); married Nola Richardson (a poet); children: Gretchen, David, Daraka, Daryl. *Education*: Morehouse College, BS (honors), 1963; Case Western Reserve School of Medicine, MD, PhD, 1970.

Career: King-Drew Sickle Cell Center, Los Angeles, CA, director, 1971-79; Second Baptist Free Clinic, Los Angeles, medical director, 1974-79; Charles R. Drew Postgraduate Medical School, Los Angeles, interim dean, c.1975; Morehouse College School of Medicine, Atlanta, GA, chairman of Department of Community Medicine and Family Practice, 1979-82; Meharry Medical College, Nashville, TN, college president and chief executive officer of Hubbard Hospital, both 1982-93; Centers for Disease Control and Prevention (CDC), Atlanta, director, 1994-98; 16th Surgeon General of the United States, 1998-2002; Assistant Secretary for Health, 1998-2001; Henry J. Kaiser Family Foundation, senior visiting fellow, 2002; National Primary Care Center, director, 2002–; Morehouse School of Medicine, Interim President, 2003-06; The Poussaint-Satcher-Cosby Chair, Satcher Health Leadership Institute, Morehouse School of Medicine, 2006–.

Memberships: Institute of Medicine, National Academy of Sciences, Alpha Omega Alpha.

Awards: American Black Achievement Award, business and professions category, 1994; Didi Hirsch "Erasing the Stigma" Mental Health Leadership Award, 2000; National Association of Mental Illness Distinguished Service Award, 2000; National Foundation for Infectious Disease, Jimmy and Rosalynn Carter Award for Humanitarian Contributions to the Health of Humankind, 2001; Institute of Medicine, Rhoda and Bernard Sarnat International Prize in Mental Health, 2002; *American Journal of Health Promotion*, Robert F. Allen Symbol of H.O.P.E. (Helping Other People Through Empowerment) Award, 2003.

Addresses: *Office*—National Center for Primary Care at Morehouse School of Medicine, 720 Westview Drive, SW, Atlanta, Georgia 30310.

black physician went to in order to preserve his life. At one point he was given just a week to live, but he managed to survive. As he grew up, his mother often reminisced about the ordeal, and he began to dream of becoming a doctor. As Marlene Cimons put it in the *Los Angeles Times*, this unforgettable childhood experience "inspired Satcher's decision, at age 8, to make medicine his calling. Like the doctor who helped save him, Satcher would help others without adequate medical care. Moreover, his near-death from a disease that today is preventable by immunization only heightened that commitment."

Satcher's background might have seemed an unlikely one to produce a prominent national physician. He was born and raised in Anniston, Alabama, one of ten children of self-taught farmers who did not attend school beyond the elementary level. "I may have come from a poor family economically, but they were not poor in spirit," Satcher told the *Los Angeles Times*. "We had a rich environment from the spirit of my parents, both of whom had a vision for their children. They didn't keep us out of school working in the fields. They made it clear that school came first, and that teachers were heroes." Satcher's parents were also deeply religious. His father perfected his reading by studying scripture and encouraged Satcher to develop leadership techniques through church programs.

Satcher recalled in *USA Today* that he began talking about becoming a doctor when he was in the third grade. "I grew up saying I was going to go back to Anniston and be a family physician," he said. "And that was during the time when no one in Anniston was going to college, much less anyone black." In 1959 Satcher's persistence was rewarded. He received a full scholarship to Morehouse College in Atlanta, and he moved there to study biology. Supporting himself with odd jobs and earning honors grades, he graduated Phi Beta Kappa in 1963. The idea of returning to Anniston began to dim when he was accepted at the prestigious Case Western Reserve School of Medicine in Cleveland, Ohio.

At Case Western, Satcher studied cytogenetics—a discipline having to do with inherited irregularities in cells—earning a Ph.D. in the field in 1970. Simultaneously, he acquired his general medical degree. After completing his residency at the University of Rochester, he moved to Los Angeles, California, and began to use his education in practical ways. He took a position as director of the King-Drew Sickle Cell Center, a research laboratory devoted to finding a cure for sickle cell anemia.

Realized His Potential to Help

At the same time, Satcher taught at the University of California, Los Angeles, served as an interim dean at the Charles R. Drew Postgraduate Medical School, and helped to open and direct a free clinic at the Second

Baptist Church in Watts, a poor section of Los Angeles. Longtime Satcher friend Ben Haimowitz told the *Washington Post* that the gifted doctor "could have gone anywhere he wanted in academic medicine.... He could have picked where he wanted to go, and where he wanted to go was Watts." Satcher himself put it more succinctly in *USA Today*: "I discovered that there were a lot of Anniston, Alabamas in this country and that I had the ability to help them."

In 1979 Satcher moved to Atlanta, Georgia, to become the chairman of the Morehouse College School of Medicine's Department of Community Medicine and Family Practice. There he was able to fulfill his dream of preparing young men and women to practice medicine in poor and urban areas where qualified physicians were often in short supply. Morehouse was the newest of three historically black four-year medical colleges in the United States. Another older institution was Meharry Medical College in Nashville. By the early 1980s, Meharry had fallen upon hard times. The school was in danger of losing its accreditation: massive debts had accumulated and the ratio of students to teachers was too high. In 1982, Meharry's board of trustees appointed Satcher president of the college and chief executive officer of the associated Hubbard Hospital. Satcher moved to Nashville and began the process of addressing Meharry's many dilemmas.

A 1986 *Ebony* magazine profile of Meharry Medical College revealed that the institution had undergone a dramatic turnaround in its fortunes after Satcher's arrival. Both the medical school and Hubbard Hospital had balanced their budgets, and a capital campaign had raised more than $25 million in gifts and pledges. More than 40 new faculty members had been hired, and as many as 94 percent of the students who enrolled were graduating after passing national examinations for health professionals. "Meharry today is on a sounder footing than possibly at any other time in its long history," wrote *Ebony* contributor Thad Martin. "Much of the credit for the school's turnaround, faculty and administration agree, has to go to Dr. Satcher."

Satcher himself preferred to consider Meharry's success a team effort, rather than a single-handed coup on his part. He was nevertheless proud of the institution's improving outlook, as well as its dedication to educating young, committed black health professionals. "At any level, most black students score lower on all standardized tests," Satcher told the *Los Angeles Times*. "Meharry tried to work with that knowledge. We took students no other medical schools would take, students that others had given up on. We said: No student will be allowed to graduate without passing both parts of the national boards.... That meant we had to get them ready.... Meharry took them, believing there was nothing more important we could do than develop people. Many of those students are now full professors at those medical schools where they were turned down."

One problem remained at Meharry: finding a large enough hospital system to serve as a hands-on educational tool for the students. In a controversial move in 1988, Satcher proposed the merger of Hubbard Hospital with the larger but struggling Nashville General Hospital. The merger would mean that Nashville General–a hospital serving mostly white patients–would become a principal teaching center for Meharry's black students. According to Marlene Cimons, the proposal was controversial "because black doctors would be caring for mostly white patients. But the plan–which Satcher says evoked a 'community debate that spanned several years and resulted in a coalition of support which cut across all racial, ethnic and economic levels'– worked, saving both the hospital and the school." The merger was in process when Satcher was approached about the job at the Centers for Disease Control and Prevention.

Directed CDC

Satcher was a primary candidate for the post at the CDC because of his long-standing commitment to preventive health care, as well as his demonstrated knowledge of urban and poverty-related public health problems. He was chosen by Health and Human Services secretary Donna Shalala in the summer of 1993 to head the CDC–an organization troubled with proposed budget cuts and charges of improprieties and discrimination in hiring and promotions. Shalala told the *Los Angeles Times* that Satcher is "one of the great catches of [President Bill] Clinton's administration." She added: "We consider CDC one of the jewels in our crown, and he's the right person at the right time. We were very anxious to get him. He's got first-class credentials. He is a physician and a leader in health, and he has particular concerns about prevention and minority health, which is of great concern to this department."

Satcher began to work with the agency in the autumn of 1993. Officially he took over as director on January 1, 1994. During his four-year tenure, Satcher emphasized community outreach programs on healthy lifestyles and enlisted the aid of public schools and churches in order to spread positive messages about diet, exercise, and avoidance of drugs and alcohol among the younger generation of Americans especially. "As early as you can get to people in terms of diet, exercise and avoidance of toxics, you do it," he told the *New York Times*.

Education, even about controversial issues, was a cornerstone of his tenure. Satcher spoke openly about the need to provide condoms and information about their use to sexually active people in order to decrease their risk of infection with AIDS. He told the *New York Times* that he was comfortable with the idea of condom distribution in schools. "My attitude is that we really have to provide people in this country with the information they need to protect themselves from this virus," he said. "And we can't let political, cultural or religious differences interfere with that." Satcher also continued the CDC's growing role in addressing violence as a public health issue. The physician told the *New York Times*: "If you look at the major cause of death today, it's not smallpox or polio or even infectious diseases. Violence is the leading cause of lost life in this country today. If it's not a public health problem, why are all those people dying from it?" Satcher emphasized, however, that in becoming involved in the fight against violence, the CDC will not neglect its traditional role of identifying and seeking to curb infectious diseases, researching cures for a variety of ailments, and urging immunizations not only for children but for adults as well.

Satcher's distinctive view of leadership helped him rally the country to better health and propelled his national career. Asked by *Ebony* magazine how he planned to run the CDC, the new director said: "I have no illusions of grandeur of what I as an individual can do without the help of other people. So I don't have any problems with high expectations as long as people say we're going to work together. I'm a team player. I function best when I can get the team going. That's how I view leadership." Indeed, his leadership skills were so impressive that the President soon came calling.

Became 16th U.S. Surgeon General

Appointed U.S. Surgeon General in 1998 by President Clinton, Satcher put his leadership skills to even greater use. He focused the Department on racial and ethnic disparities in health and spoke out in promotion of the national health agenda called Healthy People 2010. Speaking at the Library of Congress during African American History Month in 2000 about the surgeon general's report, Satcher was the first surgeon general to declare that "mental illness is just like any other disease, only it happens to involve the brain." And about the areas of personal health, including tobacco and other substance abuses, physical inactivity, obesity, and sexual behavior, Satcher added: "It is not just a matter of taking individual responsibility. It is also the responsibility of the community." During his tenure as surgeon general, Satcher released reports on tobacco and health; mental health; developed strategies to prevent suicide; to promote oral health; to increase sexual health and responsible sexual behavior; to prevent youth violence; and to address the national occurrence of obesity. In speeches promoting the national health agenda, Satcher spoke persuasively about how to reach the goals.

Perhaps the most telling reason for his success as surgeon general can be seen in his own description of his legacy. About his approach to the position, Satcher told *CWRU Magazine*: "They call the surgeon general the nation's doctor. If you're the nation's doctor, the nation is like your patient. So I had this idea that if I listened carefully and tried to implement good strate-

gies to respond, then I could do a good job." When leaving the post, Satcher told *CWRU Magazine* that "I hope that my legacy will be that I did, in fact, listen to the American people and responded with effective programs in areas that people had shied away from." While his actions certainly supported that legacy, Satcher did not quietly retire from the public eye. Instead, he continued his emphasis on community responsibility when he took the directorship of the National Primary Care Center at Morehouse School of Medicine in 2002. The center is the first nationally funded center with a mission to enhance community-oriented primary care.

Kept Focus on National Issues

He directed the school's National Primary Care Center, and even served as interim president for the college from 2003 to 2006, but his involvement with the school grew deeper in 2006 when Satcher accepted the first Poussaint-Satcher-Cosby Chair, a position named in his honor as well as noted psychiatrist Dr. Alvin F. Poussaint and entertainer and philanthropist Bill Cosby. As chair, Satcher would start up Morehouse School of Medicine's Satcher Health Leadership Institute to focus on mental and sexual health, as well as such community health issues as those that face the health of the black family.

Satcher's work to change the nation's attitudes toward health, personal and community responsibility, and to influence future medical school curricula to support those efforts relied heavily on his skills as an effective and compassionate leader. And Satcher left no doubt as to his aspirations for his work. "If we can do a good job, I think it will impact health and healthcare throughout this country and perhaps the world," according to *CWRU*. With Satcher's dedication and vision, it seems very likely that he will reach his goal.

Sources

Atlanta Constitution, August 21, 1993, p. A-4.
Case Western Reserve University Magazine, Fall 2002, pp. 24-27.
Ebony, March 1986, p. 44-50; January 1994, p. 80-82.
Journal of the American Medical Association, August 19, 1998, pp. 590-1; May 1, 2002, pp. 2199-200.
Los Angeles Times, March 1, 1994, p. E-1.
New York Times, September 12, 1993, p. A-8; September 26, 1993, p. E-7.
USA Today, December 7, 1993, p. D-8.
Washington Post, August 24, 1993, p. Health-6.

On-line

"First Poussant-Satcher-Cosby Chair Awarded at Morehouse," *Morehouse School of Medicine*, www.msm.edu/OIA/index.htm (July 25, 2006).

"National Primary Care Center Opens," *American Academy of Family Physicians,* www.aafp.org/fpr/20021200/1.html (August 10, 2006).

"Surgeon General's Keynote Address African American Month," *Library of Congress,* www.loc.gov/loc/lcib/0003/healthy.html (August 10, 2006).

—Anne Janette Johnson and Sara Pendergast

Albertina Sisulu

1918—

Political activist

Albertina Sisulu lived under nearly unimaginable circumstances for much of her adult life as one of the most harassed opponents of apartheid in South Africa. This was a widely reviled system of segregation laws that restricted nearly every aspect of life, including their political rights, for the country's majority black population. Arrested on several occasions for her activism, Sisulu also spent 26 years waiting for the unlikely release of her husband Walter, one of the leaders of the African National Congress. Unlike her counterpart Winnie Mandela, wife of the country's first post-apartheid president, Sisulu forged a reputation for quiet strength and moral leadership, and is often called the Mother of the Nation.

Born in 1918, Sisulu was from South Africa's native Xhosa ethnic group, whose home was the fertile Transkei district in the Eastern Cape Province. She was named Nontsikelelo, which means "blessings." During her childhood, blacks in this part of South Africa—a country governed entirely by white Europeans of British and Dutch descent—were taxed heavily, and most males paid the fees by migrant labor work in the country's gold mines that took them far away from their families. Sisulu's father did this, and fell victim to the terrible working conditions in the mines, as many did. "One day he started coughing, the next week he began losing weight and soon he could hardly breathe," she recalled in an interview with *Times* of London writer Alice Thomson. "It was very painful to watch."

Trained as a Nurse

By the time she was 15 years old, Sisulu had lost both of her parents, and vowed never to marry because she now had several brothers and sisters to support. She attended a Roman Catholic school, and from there went on to a nursing program for blacks at what was called the Johannesburg Non-European Hospital. She met Walter Sisulu in Johannesburg after being introduced by his cousin, a nursing classmate of hers. Also a Xhosa from the Transkei, Walter Sisulu had been a gold miner and factory worker before becoming active in the African National Congress (ANC), the leading political organization for South African blacks since 1912. Her future husband, along with Nelson Mandela and Oliver Tambo, founded the ANC's Youth League, which took a much more militant stance against their homeland's whites-only regime.

Sisulu had not been politically active before she met Walter, but took up the black nationalist cause eagerly. They married in July of 1944, and began their family in a house in the Soweto, the Johannesburg slum where blacks were confined. She joined the ANC Women's League in 1948, the same year a newly dominant South African government began enacting a much stricter series of segregation laws for blacks, mixed-race residents, and the class of shopkeepers of Indian heritage. A year later, her husband became general secretary of the ANC, while she still worked full-time as a nurse to support them. Both were targeted by South Africa's dreaded internal police for their political activities and arrested and jailed several times each.

In 1954 Sisulu became one of the co-founders of the Federation of South African Women (FSAW), a group that sought to forge alliances with liberal-leaning white women who were also uneasy with apartheid's human-rights abuses. One of the most blatant examples of this was the "pass" law. This required South Africa's blacks to carry a government-issued document with all their personal information whenever they ventured outside an all-black area like Soweto. Police could stop any black person and demand to see their pass, and blacks could not even venture into white neighborhoods without specific permission. When the apartheid government extended the scope of the pass laws, the FSAW responded with organized protests, including one that numbered 20,000 women on a march to the prime minister's office. Sisulu spent two weeks in jail for her role in the demonstration, while her husband and other ANC leaders were in the midst of a five-year trial for treason.

Husband Jailed for Life

ANC leaders like Mandela and Walter Sisulu were eventually forced to go underground. Meanwhile, Albertina Sisulu remained politically active and in 1963 was jailed again; this time she spent nearly 90 days in solitary confinement without a trial. Her treatment in jail was entirely permissible thanks to a new detention law aimed at eliminating opposition to apartheid. Her husband and Mandela were captured that same year, tried again for treason, and sentenced to life in prison, along with six other ANC leaders, in 1964. They were held at the notorious Robben Island facility, a coastal prison from which escape alive was deemed impossible. Sisulu and Winnie Mandela were allowed to visit

their husbands twice a year, for 30 minutes each visit. "Walter was a prophet, he told me everything," she told Thomson in the *Times* of London interview. "He briefed me about life so that when he left I knew what to do."

Sisulu and her husband had five children by then, and adopted two of her sister's children when her sister died. A sympathetic Roman Catholic organization paid for the children to attend a boarding school in Swaziland, which was safer than Johannesburg. By then, all mission-run schools for blacks, like the one Sisulu herself had attended, had been outlawed by the South African government. The ANC was also outlawed, but protests against the apartheid regime continued unabated.

The couple's children grew to be committed to their parents' cause, and several suffered for their efforts. For a number of years the whereabouts of the Sisulus' journalist son, Zwelakhe, was not known. He had been taken into custody, and human-rights abuses in South Africa were so immense that it was common for family members to be given absolutely no information on his incarceration. The couple's daughter Lindiwe was arrested in the mid-1970s and survived torture.

Between 1964 and 1981, Sisulu was under near-continuous banning orders, meaning she was effectively silenced. She could not speak to journalists, be quoted in print, or speak in the presence of more than three persons. She also endured a ten-year period of dusk-to-dawn house arrest. In 1981, the banning orders were finally lifted, and her husband and Mandela were transferred to a Cape Town prison.

Granted Hard-to-Get Passport

Sisulu was arrested again in 1983, and charged with leading ANC songs, distributing literature, and displaying the ANC flag at a funeral of another activist. She was given a four-year sentence, which was suspended on appeal. That same year, she co-founded the United Democratic Front (UDF), a coalition of anti-apartheid groups. Two years later, after government forces destroyed a black squatters' township near Cape Town, she was again arrested on charges of inciting the overthrow of the government. The case was dismissed due to lack of evidence.

In 1988, Sisulu was again placed under banning orders, but a new era finally began for South Africa the following year, when the white electorate voted into power a more moderate government. That same year, Sisulu was invited by the governments of the United States and Britain to meet with President George H.W. Bush and Prime Minister Margaret Thatcher, and was granted a passport to travel abroad for the first time in her life. Their informal summit marked the first time an American head of state had met with a representative of a black nationalist group from South Africa.

October 14, 1989, was a historic day in the Sisulu household: all restrictions on her activities and speech were lifted, and on the following day her husband was released. Mandela emerged from prison to worldwide headlines early the next year, the same month that government lifted the ban on the ANC and its activities. A five-year process of negotiation between the two sides began in earnest.

Kept Women's Struggle at Forefront

Despite having entered her seventies by then, Sisulu took an active role in this new era for South Africa as the government moved toward granting full citizenship rights for all. In 1992, she became deputy president of the ANC Women's League, and strongly pushed for full equality for both women and men in the country. "Our women are oppressed three times over," she told Thomson, the *Times* of London writer, that same year on another visit to the country to meet with British political leaders. "They are oppressed by the traditions and customs of our society that expect them to stay at home as carers; by the government and by the men folk. All family decisions, however trivial, are made by the men, and yet it is the women who feel desperately responsible for their children's future."

Sisulu cast her first vote in a national election in April of 1994 along with millions of other South African blacks, a historic event that took three days. When the votes were tallied, the Mandela-led ANC ticket won 12 million votes, with 3 million going to the party of apartheid, the National Party. After a long career with the ANC, Walter Sisulu died in 2003.

Sisulu's son Zwelakhe went on to become a key executive with the South African Broadcasting Corporation, while daughter Lindiwe became the Minister of Housing in the ANC cabinet. Daughter-in-law Sheila Sisulu became the South African ambassador to the United States. The ambassador recalled in a 1989 interview with *Ebony* her wedding to Mlungisi Sisulu back in the early 1970s, when her mother-in-law was unable to attend the wedding because of the government restrictions on her. Mlungisi rented the schoolyard across from her house. "He put up a tent and we had the wedding there," Sheila Sisulu told journalist Laura B. Randolph. "My mother-in-law stood at the gate, and we went over to kiss her. She was so strong. She didn't shed a tear, even if under normal circumstances she might have. She was going to maintain her dignity and her strength in the midst of whatever the government tried to throw at her."

Sources

Periodicals

Ebony, October 1999, p. 190.

Independent (London, England), December 2, 1997, p. 16.

New York Times, August 24, 1981; July 12, 1986.

Times (London, England), October 5, 1989; October 2, 1992, p. 4.

—Carol Brennan

Dawn Staley

1970—

Basketball player, coach, organization executive

Dawn Staley made a name for herself as a one of the keenest passers in women's basketball. Once, according to *Sports Illustrated,* she told her high school coach that "I get more pleasure from a pass than from a basket," and she turned into one of the great passers in the women's game. She became a collegiate and professional basketball star, Olympic gold medalist, coach, subject of a seven-story mural, and creator of an after-school program dedicated to improving the lives of girls in her North Philadelphia neighborhood. Put together all the descriptions that might be applied to Dawn Staley, and they add up to a single word: leader.

Staley was born in Philadelphia on May 4, 1970. She grew up in a two-parent household with four older siblings, but the atmosphere of her family's housing project was bleak. "I grew up in a decent environment," she told Douglas S. Looney of *Sports Illustrated.* But then she added, "Well, not decent. Really, it was bad. But you can learn a lot from a bad environment." To stay out of trouble she started spending time on playgrounds with her three older brothers, and she found she could hold her own on the court with bigger, older boys, delivering lightning-quick passes to her teammates. "My advice to girls is to play against the guys," she told Looney. "That gave me the heart to play against anybody. I'm glad they were rough. Guys seem to be born with basketball skills. Girls have to work to develop those skills." At five feet, six inches, Staley had to overcome more than just being a girl. She was considered small, even for a guard, so she worked hard to make her skills on the court make up for anything she lacked in height.

Staley's talent showed when she took the court for the Dobbins Vo-Tech High School Lady Mustangs. She averaged 33.1 points per game over her three-year high school career, during which time the team lost only one game and took three Philadelphia public high school city championships. Staley was named *USA Today*'s national high school player of the year. After receiving hundreds of letters and phone calls from University of Virginia women's basketball coach Debbie Ryan, Staley enrolled at Virginia. By the time she graduated in 1992, she had led the Virginia team to three Atlantic Coast Conference titles and three appearances in the "Final Four" semifinal round of the National Collegiate Athletic Association (NCAA) championship tournament. In 1991 and 1992 she was the NCAA player of the year.

With no women's professional leagues in operation in the United States, Staley joined a team in Segovia, Spain, for the 1992-93 season. She also played in Italy, Brazil, and France before returning to the United States and joining a USA Basketball team that played in the Goodwill Games and in world basketball championships. Her participation on these teams earned her the honor of being named USA Basketball Female Athlete of the Year in 1994. The following year, she opted to take a pay cut to $50,000 in order to stay with USA Basketball and join the 1996 U.S. Olympic basketball team. The decision resulted in the first of three gold medals for Staley (she gave her medal to her mother, whom she called the biggest influence in her life). Her Olympic debut also brought her to the

At a Glance . . .

Born on May 4, 1970, in Philadelphia, PA. *Education:* University of Virginia, BA, rhetoric and communications, 1992.

Career: Professional basketball guard, teams in Segovia, Spain, 1992-93; in Italy, France, Brazil, and Spain, 1993-94; in Tarbes, France, 1994-95; U.S. Olympic team, player, 1996, 2000, 2004; Richmond Rage, American Basketball League, player, 1996-97; Rage, Philadelphia (team moved), player, 1997-98; Charlotte Sting, Women's National Basketball Association, player, 1999-2005; Dawn Staley Foundation, founder, late 1990s; Temple University, head women's basketball coach, 2000–; Houston Comets, player, 2005–.

Selected memberships: USA Basketball Executive Committee.

Selected awards: NCAA National Player of the Year, 1991, 1992; USA Basketball Female Athlete of the Year, 1994, 2004; Olympic gold medals, 1996, 2000, 2004; All-ABL team, 1997-98; American Red Cross Spectrum Award, 1998; Atlantic 10 Coach of the Year, 2001, 2002, 2005; Women's Basketball Coaches Association, Region 1 Coach of the Year, 2005; WNBA All-Star team, three-time member.

Addresses: *Office*—Dawn Staley Foundation, 3502 Scotts Lane, 15-B, Philadelphia, PA 19129. *Web*—www.dawnstaley5.com.

attention of American basketball fans for the first time, and she quickly proved to be a fan favorite. She signed an endorsement contract with Nike athletic shoes, which sponsored a seven-story mural of her in downtown Philadelphia. "I had to go out and sneak a peek the night before [the official unveiling]," Staley told Vicki Michaelis of the *Denver Post*. "I had to take a taxi to go see it."

In the fall after the Olympics, Staley began playing for the Richmond (Virginia) Rage of the new American Basketball League (ABL). The Rage made the finals in the league's championship series in 1997 thanks partly to Staley's double-digit scoring, and she was twice named an ABL all-star. She moved with the Rage to Philadelphia for the 1997-98 season, increasing her popularity in her hometown even more. But the ABL

folded in 1998, and Staley was drafted by the Charlotte Sting of the rival Women's National Basketball Association (WNBA). Joining the Sting in 1999, she averaged 11.5 points per game and ranked third in the league in assists en route to the team's second-place finish in the WNBA Eastern Conference.

Staley was part of the "Dream Team" that won the 2000 Olympic gold medal, and she had another strong season in Charlotte. Other players would have rewarded themselves with vacation time after these accomplishments, but Staley was just getting started. She directed the activities of the Dawn Staley Foundation, which sponsored after-school sports programs at Philadelphia's Hank Gathers Recreation Center—where Staley had gotten her own start. And she made another contribution to athletic life in her hometown when she became head women's basketball coach at Temple University for the 2000-01 season.

The Temple coaching job marked a new maturity in Staley's personality, both on and off the court. As a player at Virginia, she had characterized herself as anti-social and was known for spending time in her room, watching the same movie (*Dirty Dancing* and later *About Last Night*) over and over. Before taking the reins at Temple, Staley had never coached anywhere, at any level. Yet now she talked easily with reporters about plans for the team, and, more importantly, she got results. The Temple squad, which hadn't had a winning season since 1989-90, notched a record of 19 wins and 11 losses in Staley's first season as coach. The team went to the NCAA championship tournament in three of her first five years. Staley won several coaching honors, and as of early 2006 Temple was ranked among the top 20 women's basketball teams in the country.

Staley returned for her third Olympics in Athens, Greece, in 2004. She came home with her third gold medal and a memory of carrying the American flag during the Olympics' opening ceremonies. "The reason I'm here is to help the U.S. win its third straight gold medal and to teach the younger players how to do it again," she told Kelli Anderson of *Sports Illustrated*. Staley's own professional career was winding down, but even as she was traded to the Houston Comets in 2005 she emerged as a leader in the team's stretch drive. She was signed to the Comets for the 2006 season. Continuing to coach at Temple, she was just beginning a new chapter in her remarkable career of basketball leadership: her name came up as a potential coach of the U.S. Olympic women's team in 2008 or 2012.

Sources

Periodicals

Denver Post, July 22, 1996, p. CC1.
Guardian (London, England), July 23, 1996, p. 24.

Houston Chronicle, August 16, 2005, p. 9; February 23, 2006, p. 5.

Philadelphia Inquirer, February 16, 2006.

San Francisco Chronicle, August 13, 2004, p. D11.

Sports Illustrated, November 19, 1990, p. 112; January 29, 2001, p. 104; September 6, 2004, p. 44.

Sports Illustrated for Kids, December 1997, p. 40; January 1, 2005, p. 52.

USA Today, December 7, 2004, p. C1.

On-line

"About Dawn Staley," *Dawn Staley Foundation,* www.dawnstaley5.com/about.htm (April 8, 2006).

"Dawn Staley," *USA Basketball,* www.usabasketball. com/bioswomen/dawn_staley_bio.html (April 8, 2006).

"Dawn Staley," *Women's National Basketball Association,* www.wnba.com/playerfile/dawn_staley/index.html (April 8, 2006).

—James M. Manheim

Kia Steave-Dickerson

1970—

Interior designer

Known for her dramatic use of color and fabrics, interior designer Kia Steave-Dickerson has built a distinguished career in television and film, in addition to running her own design company in Philadelphia, Pennsylvania. She has worked as a set designer and assistant prop manager on several films, and since 2002 has been a member of the design cast on the hit series *Trading Spaces* on cable television.

Born in Philadelphia in 1970, Steave-Dickerson enjoyed an early exposure to the world of design. Her father worked as a theater prop master and costume designer for local drama companies. He was the first African-American member of Local 8 of the International Alliance of Theatrical Stage Employees, and often brought his daughter along while he was on the job. As Steave-Dickerson recalled to Jennifer Baldino Bonett of *Philadelphia Business Journal*, she also used to go "dumpster diving" with her father, helping him salvage discarded furniture that he took home to repair and recover. From her mother, a credit analyst, Steave-Dickerson learned about the practical side of running a business. With her creative and entrepreneurial instincts nurtured from childhood, she knew from an early age that she wanted to go into business for herself. Initially she considered a dry cleaning establishment—the type of business operated by the only African-American entrepreneur she knew from popular culture, George Jefferson of the 1970s sitcom *The Jeffersons*. But, realizing that this field would not provide a creative outlet, she decided to focus on interior design.

After earning a bachelor's degree in textile management and marketing from Philadelphia College of Textiles and Science, now Philadelphia University, Steave-Dickerson worked briefly in retail establishments in the city. Later, she took a job with Maen Line Fabrics in Philadelphia. This position gave her the opportunity to broaden her experience with textiles and also introduced her to valuable future clients. With encouragement from her mentors at Maen Line and seed money she inherited from her father's estate, Steave-Dickerson decided to realize her dream of opening her own business in 1994.

Named K.I.A. Enterprises, her company specialized in fabrics, floor and wall coverings, and window treatments. She soon picked up several prestigious commercial clients, including Loews Hotel Philadelphia, the Inn at Penn, and Lincoln Financial Field. Branching out into the subspecialties of set design and props, Steave-Dickerson began obtaining film and television work. She designed sets for commercials for leading brands such as Betty Crocker, Chrysler, and Bisquick, and also worked on projects for the DuPont Theatre in Delaware.

Film work proved both lucrative and challenging. As assistant to the prop master for the film *Beloved*, for example, which was based on Toni Morrison's novel about a runaway slave who is desperate to protect her children from bondage, Steave-Dickerson was assigned to find and forge an iron slave collar. The designer told *Philadelphia Inquirer* writer Diane Goldsmith that, though the object felt like a "part of history," it also evoked strong feelings for her. After filming was com-

At a Glance . . .

Born in 1970 in Philadelphia, PA. *Education:* Philadelphia College of Textiles and Science (now Philadelphia University), BA.

Career: Set decorator and assistant prop master for films and television commercials; K.I.A. Enterprises, Inc., (interior design company), founder, 1994–; *Trading Spaces,* designer, 2002–.

Addresses: *Office*—K.I.A. Enterprises, Inc., 4601 Market St., Philadelphia, PA 19139.

plete, she kept the collar as a memento. It reminded her of "the black women back then and the strength they needed to persevere," she said. "I do feel it inside." The collar, Goldsmith wrote, was "an important detail in a bid for [the film's] authenticity" and was one of the props that were "key to establishing the movie's mood."

Steave-Dickerson also dressed sets for the film *Men in Black* and served as assistant prop master for M. Night Shyamalan's films *The Sixth Sense, Unbreakable,* and *Signs,* all set in Philadelphia. In addition, she has done sets and props for major stage musicals, including *Grease* and *Cats.* She also appeared as an extra in a scene with Bruce Willis and Samuel L. Jackson in *Unbreakable.* Shyamalan became a particular admirer of her work. According to Bonett, he has called Steave-Dickerson "the funk diva" and noted that her "exotic electricity" makes movie sets "more vibrant."

In 2002 Steave-Dickerson joined the cast of *Trading Spaces,* a cable television program that challenges designers to redecorate a room in two days with only a $1,000 budget. Participants agree to "swap" a designated room with neighbors, and the two teams then compete to create the best redesign in less than 48 hours. Steave-Dickerson quickly established herself as a bold innovator on the show. Among her memorable feats, according to the *Trading Spaces* Web site, were a room in which she suspended the owner's bed from the ceiling, and a room featuring ancient Egyptian motifs such as hieroglyph fabric and a specially-made pyramid fountain. Most dramatic of all, according to the *Trading Spaces* Web site, was Steave-Dickerson's creation of a synthetic grass bedspread accented with silk flowers.

The designer has emphasized her pleasure in being able to feature her home town's specialty shops and

resources on *Trading Spaces.* "I love Philadelphia," she told Bonett. "I feel this is my home, my roots, so I feel that I'm taking everyone who has supported me through the years with me." She also thrives on the pressure involved in her craft. "I like the excitement that comes when you are under deadline," she told a writer for *S2S Magazine.* "And then to stand back [and see] a room that is aesthetically astounding; how wonderful is that when it looked like an absolute mess just a few months ago?"

Steave-Dickerson has also made significant contributions to social programs in the city. In 1997 she established WEK House, a rehab facility in West Philadelphia for men recovering from drug and alcohol abuse or spousal abuse. WEK House receives referrals from local hospitals, and teaches basic life skills to residents to prepare them to reenter mainstream society. Steave-Dickerson hopes to open a similar facility for women. The designer also worked on a Bright Spaces children's room at the Travelers Aid Family Shelter at the Blackwell Human Services Campus in the city. In a press release announcing the Bright Spaces opening, she emphasized her belief that children and adolescents deserve attractive and safe places in which to play and relax after school, adding that she was pleased to be able to serve the neighborhood where she grew up and started her business.

In 1998 and 2003, Steave-Dickerson received honors for entrepreneurship from the minority business community in Philadelphia. The design industry is a particularly demanding one, K.I.A.'s business manager and legal counsel Glenda Gracia noted to Bonett, adding that Steave-Dickerson "continues to meet the standard and raise the bar. Her requirement of herself: Be all that you can be and be the best at that!"

Sources

Periodicals

Philadelphia Business Journal, January 22, 2004.
Philadelphia Inquirer, October 16, 1998, p. E1.

On-line

"Trading Spaces Star Opens Bright Spaces," *Bright Horizons,* www.brighthorizons.com/foundation (March 1, 2004; accessed January 20, 2006).
"Trading Spaces: Meet the Crew: Kia Steave-Dickerson," *TLC Discovery Channel,* http://tlc.discovery.com (January 18, 2006).
"Who Does She Think She Is? She's Kia Steave-Dickerson," *S2S Magazine,* www.s2smagazine.com (September 2004; accessed January 20, 2006).

—E. M. Shostak

Michael Tait

1966—

Singer

Tait, Michael, photograph. Billy Suratt/UPI/Landov.

As part of the phenomenally successful band dc Talk and later as frontman of his own band, Tait, vocalist Michael Tait has been a consistent innovator in the field of contemporary Christian music. A mainstay of Christian rock radio and live music scenes from the late 1980s to the late 1990s, dc Talk pioneered the incorporation of hip-hop and alternative rock sounds into Christian music. After the group went on hiatus, Tait continued to strike out in new directions. His own band was a growing success, and he starred as Jesus Christ in a theatrical presentation, *Hero: The Rock Opera.* Combining a strong devotion to Christ with themes of social justice in his music, Tait was one of Christian music's most admired figures.

Michael Dewayne Tait was born in Washington, DC, on May 18, 1966, and was raised in the northeastern part of the city. His father, Nathel Tait, came to Washington after a grandfather was killed by the Ku Klux Klan and began preaching on the streets, later becoming pastor at Washington's New Bible Church. Michael Tait was the youngest of seven children, and, he told Terry DeBoer of Michigan's *Grand Rapids Press,* he "grew up singing R&B stuff, a little gospel

and some pop stuff, then got into heavy rock. The influences are deep and wide." He and three of his siblings attended a private Christian school, Riverdale Baptist School, in suburban Upper Marlboro, Maryland.

Tait shared a Christian private-school background with two students he befriended at Liberty University in Lynchburg, Virginia, a fundamentalist institution founded by televangelist Jerry Falwell: before they began performing together, Toby McKeehan, Kevin Smith, and Tait were just close college friends. In the late 1980s, McKeehan (who had grown up in suburban Washington) and Tait began performing as dc Talk, taking the name from their mutual hometown. After Smith was added to the group, they were signed to the Forefront label, whose marketing department promoted an alternative "decent Christian" meaning for the dc acronym.

Whatever the name meant, dc Talk was successful from the start. Their 1989 debut, *dc Talk,* and its 1990 successor, *Nu Thang,* each sold over 100,000 copies—impressive for any new Christian act, and even more so because the group's music included hip-hop

At a Glance . . .

Born Michael Dewayne Tait on May 18, 1966, in Washington, DC; son of Nathel Tait, a minister. *Education:* Attended Liberty University, Lynchburg, VA.

Career: dc Talk (band), founding member with Toby McKeehan and Kevin Smith, Lynchburg, VA, late 1980s–; Tait (band), 1996–; E.R.A.C.E. Foundation, founder, 2000s–.

Selected awards: Four Grammy awards for best rock gospel album, 14 Dove Awards, three Billboard Music Awards, three Billboard Music Video Awards (all with dc Talk).

Addresses: *Label*—ForeFront Records, 101 Winners Circle, Brentwood, TN 37207. *Web*—www.taitband.com.

elements, which was almost unheard-of in Christian music at the time. The band members moved to Tennessee, home to a strong branch of the Christian music industry, and their popularity soared after they toured with contemporary Christian superstar Michael W. Smith in 1991. Tait settled in the Nashville suburb of Brentwood.

Along with their innovative sound, dc Talk promoted progressive social themes in their lyrics. "Walls" (co-composed by Tait and McKeehan, and originally included on *Nu Thang*) addressed the issue of racial division, and Tait had the satisfaction of seeing black and white students embrace each other after the band performed the song at a Mississippi high school. The group's insistence on eliminating racism was apparent from the way its individual members crossed musical boundaries: it was one of dc Talk's white members, McKeehan, who had steered the group in the direction of hip-hop, while the dreadlocked Tait favored a monumental rock sound influenced by the Irish supergroup U2. Tait himself downplayed the importance of musical genres. "I don't know how big your god is," he told dc Talk audiences (as quoted by Robert Cherry of the Cleveland *Plain Dealer*), "but my god is bigger than a person's musical format. God works in ways we can't imagine; let's not limit him. The same bricks that build a whorehouse can build a church. It's not the bricks; it's what goes on inside the bricks."

With distribution handled by the secular Virgin label beginning in 1996, dc Talk experienced massive success with their albums *Jesus Freak* and *Supernatural*. Their music drew increasingly on rock's grunge sub-

genre as the band tried to reach fans of the late Seattle artist Kurt Cobain. After more than ten years of touring, recording, and making videos, however, the members of dc Talk found themselves creatively exhausted by the late 1990s. Not wishing to foreclose the possibility of a future reunion, they released an album, *Solo*, made up of solo contributions by each of its three members, and all three members went on to solo projects.

Tait's new direction took the form of a band bearing his own last name, which had its beginnings as early as 1996. He was inspired by Lajon Witherspoon of the metal band Sevendust, one of the few African-American frontmen in the rock genre, to form a band of his own, but his solo music generally fell into the straight-ahead Christian rock groove that had made dc Talk so popular. Tait's interest in social themes intensified. "With Tait, I'm going to write what's in my heart," he told Don Mayhew of the *Fresno Bee*. "It's social gospel. I sing about the poor, the left-out. There are people who live on the streets. They have mothers, fathers, sisters, brothers. But for whatever reason, they're out on the street. We walk by them. It's a real thing." He formed a group called the E.R.A.C.E. (Eliminating Racism and Creating Equality) Foundation that toured Christian campuses, combining workshops with Tait concerts.

Tait the band included drummer Chad Chapin (who doubled as Tait's housemate in Tennessee), bassist Lonnie Chapin, and guitarist Justin York (who replaced Pete Stewart). The band got off to a good start with appearances as part of the Billy Graham Crusade in 2001. Tait released two albums, *Empty* (2001) and *Lose This Life* (2003) to generally positive reviews; the *Christianity Today* Web site opined after the release of *Lose This Life* that Tait "has quickly evolved into one of the most potent and relevant bands on the contemporary scene. Michael Tait's songwriting matured as he drew on personal experiences such as the deaths of three family members over the course of one year."

Michael Tait also kept busy with other projects and continued to develop as an artist. He wrote songs for other performers, and in 2003 he took the starring role of Jesus in *Hero*, a Christian rock opera (written by Eddie DeGarmo of the duo DeGarmo & Key) that transplanted the setting for the story of the gospel narrative of the suffering of Christ to the present-day United States (Tait's Jesus was born in Bethlehem, Pennsylvania, and ministered to down-and-out congregants in New York City's streets). For Tait, the identity of Jesus lay beyond skin color. He didn't look like the blond, blue-eyed man Tait had seen in pictures of Jesus as a child, and "he didn't look like a black person, either, for that matter," he pointed out to the *Grand Rapids Press*. "The truth is, it didn't matter what color he was.... [H]e was the savior of the world." *Hero* appeared on DVD in 2005, and Tait and Toby McKeehan participated in the Winter Jam '05 tour that year. Discussions of a dc Talk reunion persisted, but even without one, Michael Tait continued to enjoy continued success.

Selected works

Albums with dc Talk

dc Talk, ForeFront, 1989.
Nu Thang, ForeFront, 1990.
Free at Last, ForeFront, 1992.
Jesus Freak, ForeFront, 1995.
Supernatural, Virgin, 1998.
Solo, ForeFront, 2001.

Albums with Tait

Empty, ForeFront, 2001.
Lose This Life, ForeFront, 2003.

Sources

Books

"dc Talk," *Contemporary Musicians,* volume 18, Gale, 1997.

Periodicals

Fresno Bee, October 5, 2001, p. E1.
Grand Rapids Press, April 1, 2001, p. B10; April 5, 2001, p. B6; April 14, 2001, p. B5; November 10, 2003, p. B1; January 13, 2005, p. 8.
Plain Dealer (Cleveland, OH), January 26, 2002, p. E7; November 13, 2003, p. F3.
San Diego Union-Tribune, February 1, 2002, p. E4.
Star Tribune (Minneapolis, MN), January 27, 2002, p. F10.
Washington Post, April 20, 1996, p. C6.
Washington Times, April 16, 1999, p. 12.

On-line

"Expect the Supernatural," *Christianity Today,* www.christianitytoday.com/music/interviews/tait.html (March 30, 2006).
"Tait," *Christianity Today,* www.christianitytoday.com/music/artists/tait.html (March 30, 2006).
"Tait: Lose This Life," *Christianity Today,* www.christianitytoday.com/music/reviews/2003/losethislife.html (March 30, 2006).

—James M. Manheim

Ralph Tresvant

1968—

Singer

Tresvant, Ralph, photograph. © Steve Azzara/Corbis.

When Ralph Tresvant embarked on the music scene in the late 1970s as a member of the R&B group New Edition, many compared him to Michael Jackson during his time as a member of The Jackson 5. Tresvant was only 15 years old, and—like the young star who grew up to be the King of Pop—his voice was a high falsetto. He helped make New Edition one of the premier musical groups of the 1980s. The group sold out concert venues, and its records consistently placed high on the R&B charts. Though the group disbanded in the late 1980s, its members experienced continued success. During his solo career in the 1990s, some reviewers compared Tresvant to R&B legend Marvin Gaye. Despite comparisons to other great singers, Tresvant found his own sound and came to be considered among the great R&B singers of the latter part of the 20th century. With his charm, good looks, and caring lyrics, Tresvant became known as "Mr. Sensitivity," thanks to his 1990 hit single, "Sensitivity."

Ralph Edward Tresvant, Jr. was born on May 16, 1968, to Patricia Ann and Ralph, Sr., in the Roxbury section of Boston, Massachusetts. Though the family lived in the projects, young Ralph and his older sister, LaTonya, were brought up in a close-knit family. He was taught to be respectful and to stay humble. Tresvant loved music. With one of his best friends, Ricky Bell, Tresvant and other boys from the same housing projects began to win local talent shows by singing as a group. They called the group New Edition. In the early 1980s, New Edition—which included Bell, Tresvant, Michael Bivins, Ronnie De-Voe, and Bobby Brown—impressed Maurice Starr, founder of Streetwise Records in Boston. Upon hearing the group, Starr immediately signed New Edition to a contract.

First Release a Hit

New Edition modeled itself after the Jackson 5 and the Temptations. Tresvant's voice most mimicked Michael Jackson's, and he provided the lead vocals for the majority of the group's songs. The group recorded its first album, *Candy Girl,* in 1983. The single "Candy Girl" topped the R&B charts, and was followed by successful songs: "Jealous Girl," and "Is This the End?"

Their first album brought New Edition to the attention of fans, as well as the MCA record label. Despite the

At a Glance . . .

Born Ralph Edward Tresvant, Jr. on May 16, 1968, in Boston, MA; son of Ralph, Sr. and Patricia Ann Tresvant (deceased); married Shelly, 1993 (divorced); married Amber Serrano, 2004; children: four.

Career: Member of highly successful R&B group, New Edition, 1979-89, 1996–; solo artist, 1990–; Xzault Media Group, partner.

Addresses: *Home*—Atlanta, GA. *Publicist*—It Girl Publications, 5301 Beethoven St., Ste. 220, Los Angeles, CA 90066; *Web*—www.ralphtresvant.com.

popular success of the group's first album, New Edition parted with Maurice Starr for financial reasons and signed with MCA Records in 1984.

The 1984 release of *New Edition* catapulted the group to enormous popularity. Songs like "Cool It Now," and "Mr. Telephone Man," kept New Edition at the top of the charts. With their identical outfits and precise choreography, New Edition entertained their mostly young female fans through concerts and videos. The group toured across the country, selling out at most venues.

Tresvant continued to lead many of the songs on this and later albums, but he also began to share lead vocals with Brown and Bell. On *New Edition* Tresvant led the vocals on "Cool It Now," but he shared the vocals on "Mr. Telephone Man" with Brown. In addition, Tresvant began penning lyrics. He wrote "I'm Leaving You Again" for *New Edition* with best friend Bell.

Changes in Group Brought More Success

The group's next album, *All for Love*, also showcased Tresvant's writing skills as he, Bell, Bivins, and DeVoe penned the raps on the single, "School." Though New Edition brought in profits for the record company, the group's members made little or no profit. After two years of heavy touring and being in the constant spotlight, every member of the group still lived in the projects.

Financial as well as musical goals splintered the group. Bobby Brown, who aspired to record solo, left the group in 1986 and released several hit songs. The quintet became a quartet. Tresvant continued to sing lead on most of the songs, and New Edition released a Christmas album, and *Under the Blue Moon*, a tribute to groups from the 1950s and the 1960s. Tresvant also

recorded tracks for a solo album, but it was never released.

The members of New Edition wanted to get the respect of the industry by releasing a more mature sound. They decided to replace Brown with Johnny Gill, an up-and-coming singer with a baritone voice. Their next album, *Heart Break,* with songs produced by Jimmy Jam and Terry Lewis—the hitmakers behind Janet Jackson's wildly popular *Control* album—was their most successful album in the 1980s. The addition of Gill, and a mature sound tinged with a street edge, garnered hits such as "If It Isn't Love," "N.E. Heartbreak," "Crucial," and "Can You Stand The Rain?," all placing in the top ten on the R&B charts. "If It Isn't Love" also crossed over to the pop charts, reaching as high as number seven.

Solo Career Took Off

Though the group was at the peak of their success, Tresvant and the others chose to disband in 1989. Out of the spotlight, Tresvant worked on his emergence as a solo artist. He stated to Allison Samuels of *Essence,* "Being in a group for that long a time makes you realize your individual talent a lot more, and you want others to see it...." Other members of New Edition also released albums, as Bell, Bivins and DeVoe became Bell Biv DeVoe, and released a more street-edged sound, complete with raps penned by Bivins and DeVoe. Johnny Gill released a self-titled solo album of his own in 1990. Both albums reached platinum status, and anticipation for Tresvant's solo release was high.

Not one to disappoint, Tresvant released his first single, "Sensitivity" in 1990. With a production team that included Jimmy Jam and Terry Lewis, and his own lyrics, his self-titled album sold more than a million copies thanks to his hit single, which also reached platinum status and climbed to number four on the pop charts. His album also reached number one on the R&B charts, where it remained in that position for two weeks. Tresvant also released "Stone Cold Gentleman" and "Rated R" to much fanfare.

In a trend that would continue well into the twenty-first century, Tresvant would appear on the song "Best Things in Life Are Free" with singers Luther Vandross, Janet Jackson, and fellow New Edition members turned hip-hop trio, Bell Biv DeVoe. Another hit single, "Money Can't Buy You Love," was also released on the *Mo' Money* soundtrack.

Group Reunited and Released Another Album

In the interim between the release of *Ralph Tresvant* and his second release, the lukewarm *It's Goin' Down* in 1994, Tresvant stayed busy. In addition to penning lyrics for other performers including Whitney Houston, he also made several guest appearances on television shows, including *Family Matters* and *New York Undercover,* and in films such as *House Party 2,* and *Brown Sugar.* He also found time to move to San Francisco and marry his childhood sweetheart, Shelly.

Tresvant's second album was a commercial disappointment, but he and the other members of New Edition began talks of releasing another album. With the return of Bobby Brown, the six members recorded *Home Again* in 1996. Ronnie DeVoe told the *Denver Post,* "We've had to check our egos at the door." While each artist had success on his own or in various groups, most of New Edition's fans longed for a new release from the group. Tresvant told *Jet,* "Our accomplishments with solo projects outsold the group. We came back and were able to do a successful project because of that. Those accomplishments mean something." Their first single, the hip-hop edged "Hit Me Off" was a hit and with Tresvant leading vocals, the ballad "I'm Still In Love With You," also placed on the charts.

While the reunion tour, which came on the heels of the group's 20th anniversary, was anxiously anticipated by many fans, it turned out to be a major disappointment. Brown, who was going through several personal issues, was constantly late to rehearsals and shows, and eventually quit the tour. His exit was followed by Michael Bivins, but Tresvant and the other three members continued to perform during both legs of the tour.

Began Acting as Group Returned

After the album and tour, Tresvant stepped out of the spotlight to regroup. In the late 1990s and early 2000s, he appeared in several traveling stage productions, and continued to write songs that were showcased on several soundtracks from such movies as *Love & Basketball* and *Barbershop.* The group reunited for several events, before signing a contract with Sean "Diddy" Combs' Bad Boy Records. As a quintet again, they released *One Love* in 2004. The first single off the new album, "Hot2Nite" combined the flavor of Bad Boy and Bell Biv Devoe while still representing the style of New Edition. However, album tracks such as "That's Why I Lied," and "Rekindling the Memories," were more reminiscent of the New Edition sound. Though the album did well, it still fell below the level of success to which the group was accustomed.

Tresvant and his fellow members felt that Combs was trying to mold the group into Bad Boy's image and that did not sit well with them. The group stepped away from the industry again. Tresvant released another solo album in 2006, *RizzWaFaire.* It, too, was met with mixed reviews. Amy Linden of *Vibe* declared, "This tendency toward anemic production and clumsy lyrics persists throughout the disc," while Rob Theakston on the *All Music* Web site noted that "[f]ans of his work will find this an enjoyable affair." Tresvant continued

appearing in stage productions, including *The Man of Her Dreams,* in 2006. Tresvant partnered with the Xzault Media Group in 2006 in order to continue his solo success and to branch out into film and animation. He and the other members of New Edition continued to reunite occasionally at functions such as the *Essence* Music Festival in July of 2006. Though many had dismissed the group as a passing fad, Ralph Tresvant and New Edition have endured with a sound that continues to thrill fans, both old and new.

Selected works

Albums, with New Edition

Candy Girl, Streetwise Records, 1983.
New Edition, MCA Records, 1984.
All for Love, MCA Records, 1985.
Under the Blue Moon, MCA Records, 1986.
Heart Break, MCA Records, 1988.
Home Again, MCA Records, 1996.
One Love, Bad Boy Records, 2004.

Solo Albums

Ralph Tresvant, MCA Records, 1990.
It's Goin' Down, MCA Records, 1994.
RizzWaFaire, Xzault, 2006.

Plays

The Man of Her Dreams, 2006.

Sources

Books

Who's Who Among African Americans, 18th Edition, Thomson Gale, 2005.

Periodicals

Billboard, January 29, 1994, pp. 22-23.
Denver Post, February 11, 1997, p. E-08.
Ebony, February 2005.
Essence, May 1991, p. 44.
Jet, November 15, 2004, pp. 52-59.
St. Louis Post-Dispatch, February 27, 1997.
USA Today, March 21, 2006.
Vibe, February 2006.
Virginian Pilot (Richmond, VA), January 19, 1997, p. E1.

On-line

"New Edition Reuniting Again—And This Time, Bobby's On Board," *VH1,* www.vh1.com/artists/news/1520836/01172006/new_edition.jhtml (March 21, 2006).

"One Love But Two Sounds: Classic New Edition And '04 BBD Flow," *VH1,* www.vh1.com/artists/news/1493545/11082004/new_edition.jhtml (March 21, 2006).

Ralph Tresvant, www.ralphtresvant.com (April 27, 2006).

"Ralph Tresvant," *Internet Movie Database,* www.imdb.com/name/nm0872285/bio (March 15, 2006).

"Ralph Tresvant," *It Girl Public Relations,* http://itgirlpublicrelations.com/?s=tresvant&submit=GO (March 1, 2006).

"*Ralph Tresvant,* Review" *All Music,* www.allmusic.com/cg/amg.dll?p=amg&sql=10:7vz1z88ajyv2 (March 28, 2006).

"*RizzWaFaire,* Review" *All Music,* www.allmusic.com/cg/amg.dll?p=amg&sql=10:hr63mpea9fco (March 28, 2006).

Other

Additional information was obtained through an internet radio interview at FWNTV available on-line at www.fwntv.net/fwntvaudio/ralpht_tresvant.htm (March 27, 2006).

—Ashyia N. Henderson

Nontombi Naomi Tutu

1960—

Educator, human rights activist

Being the child of a famous individual can be tough when one has talents and aspirations of one's own. The daughter of 1984 Nobel Peace Prize winner Archbishop Desmond Tutu, Naomi Tutu has in recent years emerged from her father's considerable shadow to gain recognition in her own right as a tireless fighter for human rights. She was given the name Nontombi—meaning "mother of girls"—by her grandmother. "I thought that that meant that I would only give birth to girls," Tutu was quoted as saying in a November 2004 *Detroit Free Press* article. "But when my son was born, I realized that it meant that I'd work with the young women of the world." Her grandmother's prescience has proven accurate. Naomi Tutu has spent her entire adult life advocating for the rights of women and people of color. An expert on race and gender relations, she has spread her human rights message to audiences across the United States and the world.

Nontombi Naomi Tutu, who generally goes by Naomi, was born in 1960 in Krugersdorp, South Africa, the fourth child and third daughter of Desmond and Leah Nomalizo Tutu. Like all of her siblings, Naomi received an international education. At age 6, she was sent from her home in Soweto to the Waterford KaMhlaba School, a boarding school located 1,000 miles away in Mbabane, Swaziland. The Waterford KaMhlaba School was one of eleven international United World Colleges, an educational movement that brings together students from all over the world based on merit, regardless of their ability to pay. Naomi also received portions of her early education in England, where her father spent much of his early career.

Inherited Mother's Determination

While it was her father who made headlines worldwide for his work on social justice, Naomi points to her mother as her greatest early influence. Leah Tutu had given up her teaching career to raise the family, but managed to remain engaged as a community activist and labor organizer while caring for four children and a famous husband. Leah played a prominent role in the formation of South Africa's first trade union for domestic workers in the 1980s. In the November 2004 *Detroit Free Press* article, Naomi recounted an example of her mother's strength and conviction. "I was in college when I found out my mom had been arrested for allegedly assaulting someone," she was quoted as saying. "She had confronted a white woman who had fired her domestic worker without notice. The woman slapped my mother and my mother fought back. The woman filed charges but was stunned when my mother filed countercharges."

After finishing her secondary education, Naomi continued her studies in the United States. She graduated from Berea College in Berea, Kentucky, where she received a bachelor's degree in Economics and French in 1983. She stayed in Kentucky for graduate school, earning a master's degree in International Economic Development from the Patterson School of Diplomacy and International Economic Development at the University of Kentucky.

After she received her master's degree, Tutu went to work for Equator Advisory Services, Ltd., a private homeland. Tutu went on to complete courses toward a PhD from the prestigious London School of Economics, but she was still working on her dissertation as of early 2006.

Naomi selected the writings for and wrote the introduction to the book *The Words of Desmond Tutu*, published by Newmarket Press in 1989. In her introduction, she touches on the difficulty in making a distinction between the Desmond Tutu who was her *tata* (father) and the Desmond Tutu who became an international symbol of the nonviolent struggle for a free South Africa. Having lived in both South Africa and the United States, and witnessing firsthand the contrast those two countries present for a person of color, Tutu has developed a unique perspective on race. "The major difference is that in the United States, when I run against prejudice, I can walk away from it," she was quoted as saying in a 1986 *Maclean's* magazine interview. "I can say that it's your loss if you're judging me by the color of my skin.... In South Africa, when you run up against prejudice, you can't walk away because it doesn't end with this person who is acting in that way. They can call in all the powers of the state to intervene on their side and you don't stand a chance as a black person." In the *Maclean's* interview, Tutu described the personal transformation that takes place as the plane approaches the airport in Johannesburg: The "free and easy" Naomi becomes "a black person—knowing the kind of humiliation and degradation that you face in South Africa if you are black."

Began Academic Career in the 1990s

Since 1990, Tutu's career has been three-fold: She has taught, she has administered programs focusing on race and gender relations, and she has guest lectured worldwide on those topics. From 1991 to 1993, she was a visiting professor of African-American Studies at the University of Hartford in Connecticut. She was a lecturer at the University of Connecticut from 1993 to 1996. She also taught African studies at Brevard College in North Carolina. In 1997, Tutu went to work for the African Gender Institute at the University of Cape Town in South Africa. There her work concentrated on issues of race, gender, and gender-based violence.

From 1999 to 2002, Tutu worked at Fisk University, a traditionally black school in Nashville, Tennessee. There she served as program coordinator for the school's Race Relations Institute, whose mission is to address issues of racism in the global community. Tutu's next stop was the newly formed Office of International Programs at Tennessee State University, also located in Nashville, where she held the position of associate director. The Office of International Programs is responsible for leading all of the university's international efforts, including recruiting faculty with international expertise, developing collaborative

consulting firm based in Hartford, Connecticut, specializing in economic development in sub-Saharan Africa. She also did consulting work on her own in South Africa, where she was particularly interested in educational and work opportunities for black women. Meanwhile, in the midst of her globetrotting lifestyle, Tutu found time to marry an American man, Corbin Seavers, in 1982. Her work in Africa was recognized by, among others, the Universal Orthodox College of Ogun State, Nigeria, which awarded her an honorary doctorate in 1985. That year, at age 24, Naomi founded the Tutu Foundation for Development and Relief, and served as its chairperson from 1985 to 1990. The Foundation provided scholarships to South African refugees in other African countries, helping them obtain skills to both sustain themselves in exile and find meaningful work upon their return to their projects with scholars in other countries, facilitating opportunities for students to study abroad, and promoting foreign language study.

Shifted Focus to Public Speaking

By the early 2000s, Tutu was recognized as a leading authority on race relations, gender issues, and the intersection between them. This, in combination with her famous name, placed her in greater demand than ever for public speaking engagements. She traveled the globe making presentations at schools, churches, conferences, community centers, and other venues on an array of social justice and human rights issues. By 2006, her public appearance schedule had become so active that she gave up her position at Tennessee State in order to devote herself to public speaking full time. Her speeches typically have inspiring titles, such as "Building a Global Community" and "Striving for Justice: Searching for Common Ground."

Tutu has described her life mission as being "to lift girls and women above the limitations of race, economics and gender," according to the 2004 *Detroit Free Press* article. To that end, she has worked in recent years to help women translate their skills at community building into a powerful voice in the political arena. Tutu has noted that because South African laws were hostile to both women and people of color until quite recently, she never voted until she was 34 years old; her grandmother voted for the first time at the age of 91. Consequently, serving as an election observer during South Africa's first democratic elections in 1994 was an extremely meaningful experience for Tutu. But it did nothing to make up for all the years of disenfranchisement. "For most of us, there will be a feeling of anger for the rest of our lives," she was quoted as saying in a 1996 *Cleveland Plain Dealer* article. "It may be important to stay angry, so it will never happen again." In her public addresses, Tutu often calls for the need to "open the wounds" of racism as a first step in moving forward on race relations in the United States. She was present at the meetings of the South African Truth and Reconciliation Commission, the body–chaired by her father–charged with the daunting task of healing the gaping wounds left by apartheid. Tutu believes a similar process to the Commission is necessary in communities across America, where a history of racism has been, if less overt, equally damaging. In a February 2006 talk at the University of North Carolina at Asheville, Tutu spoke about the problems inherent in confronting America's racist past. "For all of us, there are times when it is difficult to face the truth, some truth, about ourselves," Tutu said. She has devoted her career to forcing people to face those uncomfortable truths.

Sources

Books

Tutu, Naomi, ed., *The Words of Desmond Tutu,* Newmarket Press, 1989, pp. 11-17.

Periodicals

Cleveland Plain Dealer, November 16, 1996, p. 1B.
Detroit Free Press, November 2, 2004.
Maclean's, March 10, 1986, p. 8.
Milwaukee Journal Sentinel, July 28, 2001.
University Gazette, University of North Carolina, May 23, 2001.

On-line

"Nontombi Naomi Tutu,"*Kent State University, 6th Annual Symposium on Violence,*http://dept.kent.edu/violence_symposium/naomi_tutu.htm (August 28, 2006).
"Tutu to Give Keynote Address at NC State's King Commemoration," *North Carolina State University,* www.ncsu.edu/news/press_releases/06_01/002.htm (April 28, 2006).
"UNC Asheville to Host Talk by Nontombi Naomi Tutu; Daughter of South African Archbishop to Discuss 'Healing the Wounds of Racism,'" *University of North Carolina—Asheville,* www.unca.edu/news/releases/2006/tutu.html (April 28, 2006).

—Bob Jacobson

Dianne Walker

1951—

Dancer, dance educator

A mentor to tap dance luminary Savion Glover and an impressive dancer herself, Dianne "Lady Di" Walker has been a link between the classic age of tap dancing and its modern revival and development. One of a small but growing number of women to attain international recognition in the tap field, Walker studied with tap masters Leon Collins and Jimmy Slyde. Her dancing was featured in two of the key productions that rekindled interest in tap in the 1980s and 1990s: the film *Tap,* starring dancer Gregory Hines, and the stage revue *Black and Blue.* A tireless promoter of tap dancing, Walker has been richly honored for her contributions to the form.

Walker was born in Boston in 1951, and when she was two years old she became one of many individuals stricken by the childhood scourge of polio, a virus plaguing children that caused temporary, and sometimes permanent, paralysis until a vaccine was introduced in 1955. To rebuild her daughter's strength, Walker's mother enrolled her in dance classes after the debilitating disease. The plan worked—and it uncovered a passion for dance in the very young Walker. Taking instruction from Boston teacher Mildred Kennedy Bradic, Walker was enthusiastic about dance of all kinds, from ballet to jazz. But it was tap that she liked the most, especially after seeing the legendary dancer Bill "Bojangles" Robinson on television.

Taught Dance on Air Force Base

Many years passed before Walker could fulfill her dreams of becoming a dancer. Her father was in the United States Air Force, and the family soon left Boston for Edwards Air Force Base in the Southern California desert. Living there for five years, Walker taught dance classes on Saturday mornings to younger children. Her father's military career later took her to the Pacific island of Okinawa. Back in the United States, she earned an education degree from Boston University and an education master's from Antioch University in Yellow Springs, Ohio. She married her husband Rodney, and the couple had two children. In 1978 she was getting ready to enroll in law school, but her life changed when she attended a community event at a Prince Hall Masonic temple and met Willy "Prince" Spencer, an old vaudeville dancer there.

"He was interesting on all levels—interesting to look at, interesting to talk to, interesting to watch dance," Walker recalled in an interview broadcast on *The Connection,* on Boston radio station WBUR. Spencer suggested that she take lessons from Leon Collins, a famed tap dancer who still gave lessons at a Brookline studio. Few young dancers, and even fewer young women, were taking up tap in those years, but Walker was instantly hooked. "I knew from the moment I walked into his studio that I had found something that just made me happy," she told Jeni Tu of *DanceTeacher* magazine. "I had never felt such a connection to something, and that thing was connected to this wonderful family of people."

The "wonderful family of people" she mentioned was the community of tap dancers, several of whom were active in the Boston area. Walker studied not only with Collins but also with Jimmy Slyde, and through them she met earlier female tap dancers like Jeni LeGon, Marion Coles, Mabel Lee, and Harriet Brown. "These people I met were like a family, a really close family," she told Tu. "There's a lot of sharing, and wherever there's sharing there's a lot of compassion, a lot of love."

Took Over Dance Studio

Walker began to take over some of Collins's classes, and in 1985 she made her solo debut at a tap festival in Rome, Italy. "I gave you everything I had. I held nothing back," the dying Collins told Walker (as she recounted it to Carol Stocker of the *Boston Globe*). "Then he asked, 'Do you know what you're going to do in Rome next week? You dance for me.' And he was crying." Collins died three days later, and Walker made a triumphant debut before an audience of 2,000. Walker and another Collins student took over his Brookline studio, and Walker became its director.

She was coming on the tap scene at a propitious time. The decline of movie musicals in the 1960s and 1970s had dented the form's popularity, but by the mid-1980s a new generation, abroad as well as in the United States, had rediscovered it. She appeared in both the Paris and Broadway productions of *Black and Blue*, a revue celebrating the artistic achievements of African-American expatriates in Paris in the 1920s, and she was a featured shim-sham dancer in *Tap*, the 1989 film that did much to reintroduce tap dancing to mainstream audiences and to kick off a wave of troupes and films devoted to tap and other virtuoso popular dance forms. For the Broadway version of *Black and Blue* she served as assistant choreographer and dance captain. Considering herself a jazz percussionist of a sort, Walker frequently toured jazz clubs and festivals starting in the 1990s.

Mentored Savion Glover

One of Walker's co-stars in both *Black and Blue* and *Tap* was Savion Glover, who was 11 years old at the time. As Glover was appearing on the *Sesame Street* children's program and introducing yet another new generation to tap, Walker was becoming his mentor. Glover has referred to Walker affectionately as "Aunt Dianne," but a more frequent nickname that takes note of her elegant, seemingly almost effortless routines—her upper body seems almost not to move at all as her feet execute difficult patterns—is "Lady Di."

Keeping up a busy schedule of appearances as a dancer, Walker left the Collins studio in 1997 and became a full-time teacher on her own. She has held guest teaching positions at numerous prestigious colleges and universities, including Harvard University, Williams College, and the University of Michigan. Increasingly, she has turned her attention to the further popularization and expansion of tap dancing. Beginning in 1996 she served on the board of the Massachusetts Cultural Council, and she participated in the Dance USA Task Force on Dance Education.

"We did a damn good job!" Walker exclaimed to *DanceTeacher*, reflecting on the new generation of tap dancers she and other teachers had trained. "I'm happy when I see what's going on and what the level of dancing is in schools across the country." But, she said, young dancers needed more outlets for their talents. "I would like to see a tap dance company on the level of American Ballet Theatre, or Alvin Ailey American Dance Theater or Dance Theatre of Harlem. Or, I'd like to see the DTH and Alvin Ailey include tap dance. We've been so busy teaching that we don't have the business side together," she told *DanceTeacher*.

Walker's venerated status in the tap world was recognized with a slew of honors. In 1998 she became the first woman given the Living Treasure in American Dance Award from Oklahoma City University, and in 2003 she received the Flo-Bert Award (named for legendary stage performers Florence Mills and Bert Williams) from the New York Committee to Celebrate National Tap Dance Day. In 2004, Walker received the Hoofers Award from New York's Tap City group. Early in the following year, Walker toured nationally with Glover and Jimmy Slyde. Her dance career was far from over. "If I never tapped again and walked out the door right now, I would feel such as sense of accomplishment," she told *DanceTeacher*. But, she conceded, "I can't even find the door."

Selected works

Black and Blue (Broadway revue), 1989.
Tap (film), 1989.
Tap Dance in America (television documentary), 1989.
Honi Coles: The Class Act of Tap (documentary), 1994.
JUBA: Masters of Tap & Percussive Dance (television documentary), 1998.

Sources

Periodicals

Boston Globe, April 8, 1989, p. 9.

Boston Herald, May 24, 1997, p. 19; August 21, 1999, p. 27.
Dance Magazine, October 2003, p. 103; February 2005, p. 76.
DanceTeacher, January 2003.
Houston Chronicle, January 18, 2001, p. 10; January 22, 2001, p. 10.
New York Times, December 29, 1997, p. E1.

On-line

"Dianne Walker," *Tap Dance,* www.tapdance.org/tap/people/tapbios2.htm#DWALKER (April 6, 2006).
"Pioneering Dancer Tapped to Perform on Campus," *Massachusetts Institute of Technology* http://web.mit.edu/newsoffice.2005/arts-walker-0330.html (April 6, 2006).

Other

Additional material for this profile was taken from an interview with DianneWalker broadcast on *The Connection,* on radio station WBUR in Boston, March 29, 2005.

—James M. Manheim

Mary T. Washington

1906-2005

Accountant

Mary T. Washington was the first African-American woman to become a certified public accountant (CPA) in the United States, and she was the 13th African American to enter the profession. Her influence extended beyond her pioneer status as she helped train a whole generation of younger black CPAs, even though in so doing she was creating competition for her own growing firm. Washington's partner Hiram Pittman, whom she hired as a newly minted CPA, described their firm as an Underground Railroad for black accountants, who came from across the United States to gain work experience. With her exacting but warm personality, Washington was a central figure in Chicago's large African-American business community in the middle years of the twentieth century.

Washington was born Mary Thelma Morrison in Vicksburg, Mississippi, on April 21, 1906. Her father, a carpenter, was proud of her ability to read an entire newspaper. After her mother died when she was six, Washington was raised by her mother's parents in Chicago and was a star math student at Wendell Phillips High School. She worked late afternoons and weekends as a bookkeeper at Chicago's Douglas National Bank. After she graduated, she moved on to Binga State Bank, one of the city's prominent black-owned businesses in the 1920s. "She was just determined to achieve the highest thing she could achieve, and just set her goals high." her daughter Barbara Shepherd told Barbara Sherlock of the *Chicago Tribune*. In 1927 she married Seymour Washington; the couple had one daughter, Barbara, before divorcing in 1935.

At Binga State Bank, Washington became assistant to cashier and vice president Arthur J. Wilson, the country's second black CPA and the first in Illinois. In Wilson she found a mentor who inspired her even after the bank folded. She enrolled in an accounting program at Northwestern University's School of Business. She was the only woman in her class, but the issue of her blackness didn't come up—her skin was so light that she could pass for white if she chose to. While attending Northwestern, Washington opened an accounting and tax preparation business in the basement of her home in 1939. Her new husband, taxicab mechanic Donald Wylie, supported her ambitions and sometimes cooked dinners for Washington and the crowd of staffers she hired to work around the clock during tax season. Washington continued to use her first husband's surname professionally, but was also known as Mary T. Washington Wylie after her second marriage. That marriage produced a son, Donald Wylie Jr., and the couple adopted three more children.

Washington graduated from Northwestern in 1941 and did a required period of apprenticeship with Wilson. She passed the state's CPA exam in 1943 (once again as the only woman in the testing room) and became the first black female CPA in the country. There would not be another until 1968. Washington's firm, Mary T. Washington and Co., was flourishing as blacks joined the military during World War II and spent their earnings at new South Side businesses. Those businesses, including the cosmetics firm Fuller Products, sought out Washington's services. As her own business grew, she found a second mentor in the

At a Glance . . .

Born on April 21, 1906, in Vicksburg, MS; died on July 2, 2005, in suburban Chicago, IL; married Seymour Washington, 1927 (divorced 1935); married Donald Melvin Wylie, a taxicab mechanic; children: Barbara (from first marriage); Donald Jr., Donald II, Melanie, Ardelia (from second marriage). *Education:* Northwestern University, School of Business, BS, 1941.

Career: Mary T. Washington and Co.. accounting firm, founder, 1939; CPA, 1943; Washington & Pittman, founding partner, 1968; firm named changed to Washington, Pittman & McKeever, LLC, 1976; retired, 1985.

company's president, Samuel Fuller. She leased space in the offices of the Fuller Products Company, and for 35 years a $100 weekly check from Fuller served as the bedrock of her own company's income.

Fuller was not Washington's only client; the black-owned Seaway National Bank was another mainstay. Most white companies refused to hire blacks to provide financial services, but Washington, atypically, had white clients, many of them Jewish. Some of her larger black customers were pressured by banks to move their business to white-owned accounting firms, but her firm nevertheless continued to grow. Employment with Washington became a point of entry to the profession for young black accountants, and by the 1960s Chicago was said to have a higher concentration of black CPAs than any other city in the United States as a result.

Washington was generous but meticulous in training the next generation of accountants. "She was a stickler for details and for getting it right, and, for me anyhow, it was a wonderful place to get a start," accounting executive Frederick Ford, who joined Washington's firm in the late 1940s, recalled to Barbara Sherlock. "I learned how important it was to do as nearly to perfect work as you could." Chicago judge Willie M. Whiting worked for Washington while in college. "She was always very sweet, but it had to be correct," he recalled to Allison Enright of *Insight* on-line magazine. "I was hired to be a statistical typist, and a typist I was not. But never did she interfere except in a positive way. Eventually, I learned to type those reports." Ford told Enright that "None of the big CPA firms would hire blacks, so Ms. Washington offered to come and let me

work. She really opened the way for a number of black CPAs."

Washington joined with one of her protégés to form the firm of Washington & Pittman in 1968. With the addition of a third partner, Lester McKeever, the firm became known as Washington, Pittman & McKeever, LLC, in 1976. McKeever, who had joined Washington's staff as a part-time tax preparer, later became chairman of the Federal Reserve Bank of Chicago. "She was the pipeline," he told CNN. Washington, Pittman & McKeever remains a major force in the financial industry, with a roster of clients that includes the city of Chicago, Cook County, Chicago State and Western Illinois universities, the Chicago Public Library, Commonwealth Edison, and the telephone book printer R.R. Donnelly. Another client, early in his career, was boxer Muhammad Ali.

Washington was an important figure in Chicago's African-American business community, and her annual holiday parties were an essential stop for competitors and clients as well as her own employees. She retired in 1985, at the age of 79, and on July 2, 2005, at 99, she died in a suburban Chicago nursing home. Accounting historian Theresa Hammond told *Insight* that Washington "was not simply wealthy, successful, and highly regarded in the community. She set an example by creating opportunities for others and by generously supporting their careers, even after they had left her firm…. Her devotion to others' development…is a major reason that she is so well remembered today."

Sources

Books

Hammond, Theresa, *African American Certified Public Accountants since 1921,* University of North Carolina Press, 2002.

Periodicals

Chicago Sun-Times, July 13, 2005, p. 84.
Chicago Tribune, July 14, 2005, p. 12.
New York Times, July 25, 2005, p. B7.

On-line

Enright, Allison, "Remembering Ms. Washington," *Insight Magazine,* www.insight-mag.com./insight/05/11-12/col-1-pt-1-InMemoriam.asp (April 7, 2006).
"First Lady of Black CPAs," *CNN Money,* http://money.cnn.com/magazines/fsb/fsb_archive/2005/09/01/8277768/index.htm (April 7, 2006).

—James M. Manheim

Malinda Williams

1975—

Actress

Williams, Malinda, photograph. © Lisa O'Connor/Zuma/Corbis.

In the role of Tracy "Bird" Van Adams on the Showtime cable television program *Soul Food* from 2000 through 2004, actress Malinda Williams became famous as a cast member in the longest-running African-American television drama in history. The show marked a breakthrough for Williams, whose steadily rising career trajectory had impressed television executives who took note of her versatility. As Williams looked to new projects after the end of *Soul Food*'s run, she seemed to have unlimited possibilities. "Malinda has a career as an actress ahead of her—not an African-American actress," executive Felicia Henderson told Denene Millner of *Honey* magazine. "She is one of the few actresses who can play [age] 15 to 30, can play dramatic as well as comedy. Every door should be open to her and I think that will happen."

Williams was born in Elizabeth, New Jersey, outside of New York City, on December 3, 1975. Like her character in *Soul Food,* she was the youngest of three sisters. Williams broke into the entertainment industry as a child, making her television debut in a 1987 episode of *The Cosby Show* and appearing in 1990 in another *Cosby* episode and on *Miami Vice*. She took classes at New York's Actors Conservatory, and in 1993 she landed a major role in the HBO miniseries *Laurel Avenue*. An acting career didn't seem to be a promising prospect at the time, however, and Williams went to cosmetology school and got a job in a nail salon.

Benefited from Youthful Appearance

It was encouragement from Williams's *Laurel Avenue* costar Charles Dutton that changed her mind. Williams packed her bags and headed for Hollywood. Her acting career didn't exactly skyrocket, but she began to find small film and television roles almost immediately. Parts in the Martin Lawrence comedy *A Thin Line Between Love and Hate* (1995) and in the television series *Moesha* in 1996 helped pay the bills. One thing Williams had going for her was a naturally youthful appearance that allowed her to keep playing teenagers even as she was well into her third decade. "Part of it is genes," she explained to Tonya Pendleton of *Heart & Soul*. "I got it from my mom and my dad. And spiritedness is the key. I don't worry about anything. Negativity will wear you down and make you sick and old."

At a Glance . . .

Born December 3, 1975, in Elizabeth, NJ; married Mekhi Phifer, an actor, 1999 (divorced 2003); children: one son. *Education:* Studied at Actors Conservatory, New York.

Career: Actor, 1987–; Modern Goddess, lingerie line, 2006.

Awards: Two NAACP Image Award nominations for Outstanding Actress in a Drama Series, 2003 and 2004 (for *Soul Food*); Black Reel Award nomination for Best Actress, 2000 (for *The Wood*).

Addresses: *Agent*—West Entertainment, 6255 West Sunset Blvd., Suite 923, Los Angeles, CA 90028.

Another key to Williams's positive attitude at the time was her growing romance with actor Mekhi Phifer, who had won the lead in Spike Lee's film *Clockers* without benefit of formal acting studies. The two were introduced by a friend, and love bloomed when both appeared in the 1996 comedy *High School High*. After they dated for several years, Phifer proposed to Williams on New Year's Eve of 1998. Williams soon learned that she was pregnant, and the two were married in a wedding chapel on Valentine's Day of 1999.

In the meantime, Williams was actively involved in searching for a role that would make her a familiar face. It was a slow process, and at one point she was told (according to *Essence*) that she couldn't act her way out of a shoebox. Persistence brought Williams a recurring role in the series *Nick Freno: Licensed Teacher* in 1997 and 1998, and two films with good-sized roles for Williams appeared in 1999: in *The Wood* she played opposite actor Omar Epps as the ex-girlfriend of his character, and art imitated life as she played Phifer's girlfriend in *An Invited Guest*. Williams was frustrated by the low visibility of African Americans in the entertainment industry. "There simply aren't enough roles for black actresses here," she told *Essence*. "Sisters need to write their own screenplays," she said—and she worked on two of them, one of which told the story of the post-Civil War Freedmen's Savings Bank.

Crossed Border Daily to See Son

The year 2000 was a hectic one for Williams, but it was also the year things came together as she was signed to play the role of Bird in *Soul Food*. She had given birth to Omikaye, her son by Phifer. Filming on *Soul Food* took place in Toronto, Canada, and Williams formed a strong bond with co-stars Nicole Ari Parker and Vanessa Williams as the three lived and worked together in Toronto. Malinda Williams's nanny was unable to obtain a permit to work in Canada, so Williams made daily trips to Niagara Falls, New York—the nearest American city—to be with her new baby after a full day of work. "She had to spend most of her time on the road, and then she had to act during a first season where everything—hair, makeup, scripts—was heavily scrutinized," Vanessa Williams recalled to Pendleton. "And she was processing a very public breakup."

For it was true—Williams's marriage to Phifer began to fall apart after she found a phone number in their car, dialed it, and heard a woman answer, "Hey, baby!" The couple went to counseling, but further strains sank the marriage after Phifer didn't show up to see the birth of their child. (Phifer for his part told Millner that Williams had been unsupportive of his career, and that "I got love for her; I respect her. But we just weren't made for each other.") They hung on several years but were divorced in 2003.

Things were much more positive for Williams on the career front as *Soul Food* became a hit. With its mix of family dramas, love stories, career-related storylines, and insight into the African-American experience, the show locked up a strong black weekly viewership and broke out to a wider audience. Williams's character Bird was a hair salon owner married to Lem, an ex-convict who found work managing a grocery store. Bird's experiences formed a contrast with those of her older sister Teri, a career-driven lawyer, and the role came naturally to Williams. "Every family has a baby," she pointed out to *Jet*. "She [Bird] is still finding her way. In the end of the [final] season, she really fights for her place as that person who thinks she's found her way and makes her own decisions and sticks with them…. It's a great transition."

Performed Own Stunts

At the beginning of *Soul Food*'s run, Williams was resented by some fans of the film on which the series was based; some felt that she was unqualified to replace film star Nia Long in the role of Bird. By the time *Soul Food* wrapped up five successful years in 2004, she was a familiar face herself. She threw herself into the role of Bird, even once doing her own stunts during a volatile episode in which she was pursued by a stalker, a former high school teacher with whom she had an affair.

Williams's prospects looked strong as she looked to new opportunities after *Soul Food* ended. On the personal front, she began dating again and took up snowboarding. "If I'm having a funky day, I'm like, 'oooh, I need to go ride,'" she told Pendleton. It's sort of a metaphor for life." New acting projects for Williams included the film *Idlewild*, an ambitious Prohibition-era musical that was finished and ready for release in 2006. That year Williams branched out beyond acting to launch a line of lingerie and intimate accessories called Modern Goddess. With a solid footing in Hollywood and her new venture, Williams would likely continue to prosper.

Selected works

Films

A Thin Line Between Love and Hate, 1996.
High School High, 1996.
An Invited Guest, 1999.
The Wood, 1999.
Dancing in September, 2000.
Idlewild, 2006.

Television

Laurel Avenue (miniseries), 1993.

Nick Freno: Licensed Teacher, 1997-98.
Soul Food, 2000-04.

Sources

Periodicals

Boston Herald, February 24, 2004, p. 37.
Essence, June 1999.
Heart & Soul, February/March 2006.
Honey, June/July 2003.
Jet, February 16, 2004, p. 54.
New York Times, June 24, 2001, p. AR25.
Variety, August 16, 2004, p. 6.
Vibe, February 2006.

On-line

"Malinda Williams," *Internet Movie Database*, www.imbd.com (April 5, 2006).

—James M. Manheim

Montel Williams

1956—

Television talk show host, motivational speaker

Williams, Montel, photograph. © Lisa O'Connor/Zuma/Corbis.

Montel Williams joined the ranks of America's daytime talk show hosts in 1991 with his own program, the *Montel Williams Show*. Although he had made a name for himself as a motivational speaker, reaching out to inspire schoolchildren across the nation, few people believed that this former U.S. Navy intelligence officer would be ranked in the company of talk show celebrities Phil Donahue, Oprah Winfrey, and Sally Jessy Raphael. Yet, after only one year, his show was being broadcast to 80 percent of the television sets in America and in certain markets was getting a higher rating than *Donahue*. Fifteen years later, Montel Williams had made himself into a household name, with an Emmy Award for Outstanding Talk Show host, several Emmy nominations under his belt, and his inspirational approach to living with multiple sclerosis (MS).

Stood Out Among Other Hosts

"Williams doesn't fit the typical mold," Patrick Cole wrote in *Emerge* not long after Montel's emergence onto the talk show scene. "Instead of coming up through the broadcasting world's school of hard knocks, he honed his skills in the military." Though Williams admits that he didn't learn his craft by taking the traditional broadcasting route, he argued that he faced his own school of hard knocks. "I've traveled all over this country speaking," he told Michael Hill of the *Baltimore Sun*. "I know what it's like to wake up in the Quality Inn, the five-star hotel in some towns. I've talked to people in those little towns in Texas and Tennessee. I know what they want to know, what questions they want answered. Phil [Donahue], Oprah [Winfrey], Geraldo [Rivera] and Sally [Jessy Raphael] haven't done that."

Williams's physical charisma also separated him from his peers. At 6'2" and 210 pounds, he towered above most of his guests and audience members. His shaved head became a trademark to his many viewers. Yet aside from his physical characteristics, most people agreed that there was still something very different about Montel Williams himself. Carolyn Ramsay commented in the *Los Angeles Times* that "...maybe it's just his palpable confidence."

At a Glance . . .

Born Montel B. Williams on July 3, 1956, in Baltimore, MD; son of Herman (Baltimore commissioner of transportation) and Marjorie Williams; married Rochele See (divorced); married Grace Morley, 1992 (divorced 2000); engaged to Tara Fowler, 2006; children: (first marriage) Maressa, Ashley; (second marriage) Montel Jr., Wyntergrace. *Education*: U.S. Naval Academy, BS, 1980.

Career: Talk show host, producer, and motivational speaker. Reach for the American Dream Foundation, founder, 1988; motivational speaker, 1988–; *Montel Williams Show*, host and producer, 1991–, Out of My Way Productions, co-owner; Montel Williams MS Foundation, founder, 2000.

Awards: Best of Gannett Award; local Emmy Award for *The Fourth R–Kids Rap About Racism*; Emmy Award, for Outstanding Talk Show Host, 1996; New York State Psychological Association, Beacon Award, 2000.

Addresses: *Web*—www.montelshow.com.

Grew Up in the Ghetto

Montel gained confidence growing up in the Cherry Hill section of Baltimore, "one of the largest black ghettos of the era," he told Simi Horwitz of the *Washington Post*. "We lived three blocks from the dump. My parents were poor, but they worked very hard to give us the appearance of a lower-middle class lifestyle." While his parents did their part to give Montel a better life—his father worked three jobs and his mother two for most of his childhood—he didn't disappoint them.

As a high school student, Montel spent his summers working at the local McDonald's during the day and playing in a band at night. During his senior year at the predominantly white Andover High School in Linthicum, Maryland, Montel was voted class president. Yet politics was not the career he wanted to pursue when he graduated from high school in 1974. "I was going to be a rock star," he told Hill. The quick money that his band, Front Row, earned playing clubs around town, seemed more important to him than furthering his education. "I applied to some colleges but I didn't follow it up. Then two members of our band got busted and that ended that."

Broke Racial Barriers in the Military

Montel found himself with two options when his band suddenly dissolved: he could go to a vocation technical school and learn a trade or he could do what many other black males at the time were doing—join the military. Montel's decision to enlist in the Navy proved to be the right one. Within the first six months, he received two meritorious promotions and was accepted into the U.S. Naval Academy Preparatory School right after boot camp.

As the first black man to be accepted into the academy's prep school, Montel was determined to succeed. As one of forty Marines to enter the school in 1976, he was one of only four to actually graduate. Williams continued on at the U.S. Naval Academy and earned a bachelor's degree in engineering with minors in international security affairs and Mandarin Chinese in 1980.

As a special intelligence officer, Williams traveled the world doing top-secret communications work for the military. His ability to speak fluent Chinese and Russian, which he mastered at the Defense Language Institute in Monterey, California, helped him climb the ladder of success. During his 15-year stint in the military, Williams was decorated nine times, including two Meritorious Service Medals. "I was shooting to be an admiral," he told Horwitz.

Inspired to Motivate Others

Williams's career aspirations quickly changed direction when he started recruiting minorities for officer training in the Navy. While stationed in Norfolk, Virginia, he was asked by a friend to speak at a black leadership conference in Kansas. "That presentation garnered 12 requests for me to speak at high schools," Williams recalled to Horwitz. Williams was so taken by the response he received from students that he mounted a one-man campaign to lecture kids on the importance of education and the evils of drug abuse.

The number of requests for Williams to speak amassed quickly, especially after he was featured on the *Today Show* and *NBC Nightly News* in 1988. Soon after, he formed the Denver-based, non-profit Reach the American Dream Foundation, which provided everything from personal counseling to college scholarships for underprivileged teens.

Though he had reached the rank of lieutenant commander in the Navy, Williams knew that he could not continue to travel the country talking with kids about everything from drugs to suicide to acquired immune deficiency syndrome (AIDS) at his current pace and be an effective naval commander. So with only nine years left until his retirement and without a steady income, Williams resigned from active duty. He told Wallace

Terry of *Parade* that it was the hardest and easiest decision of his life. "Since kids are listening to me," he explained, "I know this is what I'm supposed to be doing. Maybe I won't win the war, but I'll liberate a lot of prisoners."

Montel began a grueling motivational speaking tour, working 26 days out of every month. With a hectic travel schedule, it didn't take long before Williams "carried his message to more than 700 schools and two million students," according to Marian Dozer of the *Detroit Free Press*. Yet kids were not the only ones coming out to hear him speak. The message that Montel was carrying to students—a person can move mountains by practicing the "three R's": responsibility, restraint, and respect—was also aimed at parents. "He told his audience," Margaret Friedrich wrote in the *Baltimore Sun* after seeing Williams at Howard Community College, "that each parent should follow his 'three R's'—taking the responsibility to show children how to use restraint and delay gratification, to assume responsibility for the future of the community and to show self-respect and respect for others."

Captured Television Audiences

Montel's first significant television appearance came during one of his many speaking engagements. A Jacksonville, Florida, school district wanted to televise his talk on a local station, WTLV, owned by the Gannett Company. After Williams added a talk show to the end of his speech, the message he had been delivering to students around the country proved to have a greater impact. In fact, at the end of the year the program was so successful that it was honored with a Best of Gannett Award.

Other television appearances to explain his motivational speeches and special broadcasts of his speeches, including ones in Washington, D.C., and Detroit, followed. In 1990 he hosted a program in Denver called *The 4th R–Kids Rap About Racism* that won a local Emmy Award. And when Pepsico, which had helped fund some of Williams's speeches, was looking for someone to narrate an introduction to a special version of the 1991 film *Glory*—a chronicle of a troop of black soldiers in the Civil War—to be used as an educational tool in schools, Williams was given the job.

It didn't take long for Williams to attract the attention of entertainment executives in Hollywood. According to Ramsay, "When Freddie Fields, who produced *Glory*, saw the one minute intro, he thought Williams was a star." At first, Fields and his associates wanted to develop a dramatic series that centered around Williams. "But after watching a talk show special for which he won a local Emmy in Denver," Ramsay continued, "they decided talk was the proper vehicle."

In the summer of 1991 the *Montel Williams Show* was launched on nine stations throughout the country.

Though the program—produced and taped in Los Angeles by Out of My Way Productions, of which Williams owns 50 percent—was only seen in a few cities in the United States, they were some of the biggest, including New York, Los Angeles, and Dallas. The *Montel Williams Show*, Steve McClellan wrote in *Broadcasting*, "got off to a shaky start, both critically and in the ratings." It didn't take long, however, before the ratings began to improve and the number of stations carrying the show increased.

Created Unique Show

Part of the reason the show began to do so well was its informal town hall-meeting approach. The one hour program was designed to follow the traditional talk show format by sticking to one topic, usually of a serious nature. Though the range of topics covered on the program—rape, child molestation, drug abuse, transsexualism, suicide, etc.—are considered by many to be sensationalistic, Williams maintained that his approach was different. "If we are talking about rape, for example, and have a panel of rape survivors, we don't belabor what actually happened during the rape," he pointed out to Horwitz. "Other shows will spend three or four segments going over every gory detail. Our aim is to find out how the survivors are handling the experience."

During the summer of 1992 the *Montel Williams Show* moved to New York City to remain competitive with the other talk shows, something that the three-hour time difference between coasts had prohibited. Though the decision brought him closer to his competition, it also instilled in Williams the need to make his program even more unique by focusing on topics not normally covered on daytime talk shows.

For one particular program Williams and his crew spent nearly 24 hours traveling through Manhattan interviewing homeless people and their advocates at soup kitchens, shelters, and subway stations. Scott Williams of the *Baltimore Sun* questioned Williams's decision to devote an entire program to the plight of the homeless. "That's part of the reason we are so different," the talk show host responded. "You'd think this is something you'd see in another type of show, but in the way we format our field pieces, there's time for conversation, time for discussion, time for questions. I think our viewing audience wants to see a little difference."

As the talk show genre faced increased competition in the late 1990s and early 2000s, many critics feared that shows would go to extremes to increase ratings. "It's a TV show, and we know that we have to entertain, and we will do that," Williams admitted to Hill. "But you don't have to get down in the sleaze like the other talk shows. I think it's time we have one that doesn't just titillate the libido, but that titillates the intellect." Williams pursued that aim with vigor. Williams shunned the sensationalism of other talk shows and instead focused on offering something different. Williams sought out guests who could discuss psychological aspects of life and frequently featured licensed psychologist Debbie Magids. In 1992 he began an After-Care Program to help his troubled guests obtain needed psychological counseling, weight-loss and eating disorder help, and drug rehabilitation after their appearance on his show. Williams also followed up with those guests to highlight their progress. Discussing his show with *AskMen.com* in 2004, Williams differentiated it from other shows by highlighting his interest in helping his viewers as much as entertaining them, saying: "You know when you tune into our show every single day of the week, like a buffet, you are going to get a well-balanced diet, with the other shows, you're just going to get candy. That's the reason I think we're still on the air, because after a while, you get sick of candy."

Although the *Montel Williams Show* was Williams's first priority, he also pursued acting. He starred in the television drama *Matt Waters* in 1996, and made guest appearances on *All My Children, JAG, Second Time Around,* and *Touched by an Angel.* He also played roles in the 1997 movie *The Peacemaker* and the 2002 thriller *Noon Blue Apples.*

Continued to Inspire Others

Williams never abandoned the crusade that brought him to the television screen. In 1992 he hosted *Mountain! Get Out of My Way*, a prime time television special that addressed the issues of AIDS, addiction, crime, and suicide as experienced by children. "Most of *Mountain!* takes place outside the talk-show format," Susan Stewart noted in the *Detroit Free Press.* "There's a fine line between exploring this painful stage in life and exploiting it; Williams walks the line well. Three stars." Williams skill at handling difficult issues came to the fore in 1999 when he was diagnosed with multiple sclerosis (MS), an autoimmune disease affecting the brain and spinal cord.

Despite the disease, Williams continued his characteristic ways: setting goals and working toward them. "This disease is not going to stop me," said Williams, according to the *Seattle Times.* He set up the Montel Williams MS Foundation and the Mountain Movers Press in 2000 to increase awareness of MS, raise funds for research, and to provide inspiration for those suffering from the disease. Williams set up the foundation so that all donated money could be used to support MS, using corporate sponsors to cover the administrative costs of the foundation. To fund the foundation, Williams organized such events as an annual bike-a-thon, art shows, bowling events, and even went on a charitable singing tour with country star Hal Ketchum.

Not only did MS not stop Williams, it may have actually added fuel to his already brightly burning fire. In addition to his charitable work, Williams continued his

television show, which was entering his 15th season in 2006. He regularly toured the United States giving motivational talks on such diverse topics as drug abuse and racial harmony. In addition, Williams produced various films and television shows and co-authored bestselling books, including *Climbing Higher,* an absorbing memoir of his life with MS. Williams remained true the philosophy that brought him out of the ghetto and into the limelight. He wrote in *Mountain, Get Out of My Way*: "I don't believe that things happen by mistake. If you ask me, things happen because you make them happen. Things happen for a reason. God gave me the ability to stand on my feet and speak my piece, and it was up to me to put these tools to use."

Selected writings

Books

(With Daniel Paisner) *Mountain, Get Out Of My Way,* Warner Books, 1996.
(With Jill Kramer) *Life Lessons and Reflections,* Mountain Movers Press, 2000.
(With Jeffrey Gardère) *Practical Parenting,* Mountain Movers Press, 2000.
(With Wini Linguvic) *Body Change: The 21-Day Fitness Program for Changing Your Body—and Changing Your Life.* Mountain Movers Press, 2001.
(With Lawrence Grobel) *Climbing Higher,* Penguin, 2004.

Sources

Periodicals

Art Business News, June 2005, p. 22.
Baltimore Sun, February 27, 1991; July 3, 1991; July 25, 1991; August 28, 1991; June 8, 1992.
Broadcasting, October 14, 1991; January 21, 1992.
Crisis, February-March 1996, p.34.
Detroit Free Press, October 26, 1988; February 20, 1991; December 4, 1991; August 31, 1992.
Detroit News, April 8, 1992; August 25, 1992.
Emerge, May 1992.
Los Angeles Times, July 8, 1991.
Parade, January 12, 1992.
Seattle Times, August 24, 1999, p. A5.
Times (Tampa, FL), May 16, 1992.
USA Today, June 17, 1992; August 27, 1992.
USA Weekend, July 3-5, 1992.
Variety, April 22, 1991; October 28, 1991.
Washington Post, August 30, 1992.

On-line

Montel Williams, www.montelshow.com (July 21, 2006).
Montel Williams MS Foundation, www.montelms.org (July 21, 2006).
"Montel Williams…Still the Talk of the Town," *Ask-*

Men.com, www.askmen.com/toys/interview_100/ 140_montel_williams_interview.html (July 21, 2006).

—Joe Kuskowski and Sara Pendergast

Ronald A. Williams

1949—

Business executive

Ronald A. Williams rose to a become one of the most powerful African-American business leaders in the United States. As Chief Executive Officer of Aetna, Inc., one of the nation's leading health insurance providers, Williams oversaw some 27,000 employees and services delivered to nearly 15 million insurance plan members. He earned respect throughout the insurance industry as a talented problem-solver who has always been willing to toil outside of the limelight to strengthen the companies he has managed.

Rose from Working-Class Neighborhood

Ronald A. Williams was born in 1949 in Chicago, Illinois. During his childhood, Williams had no reason to expect that he would become a big-time success in the corporate world. He grew up in a working-class Chicago neighborhood. His father worked as a parking lot attendant, later advancing to a somewhat better job driving a bus. His mother worked part time in a beauty salon. Williams' goals were quite modest; he did not try to imagine much beyond going to college. He managed to achieve that goal with the help of student loans, taking classes at night, and working during the day. He graduated from Roosevelt University in Chicago in 1970 with a degree in psychology.

Shortly after graduating, Williams landed a job as a junior aide in the office of the Governor of Illinois. While working there, he began to realize that he was capable of accomplishing much more than he had ever

imagined. For the first time, he began to see African-American men in high-ranking positions, and it occurred to him that there was nothing stopping him from similar achievements. Being a person of color did not, as experience had led him to believe, mean that he could only work at low-paying occupations. "It started with an awareness that there were significantly greater opportunities, and many of the limitations that my parents faced were not limitations that I would face," Williams was quoted as saying in a January 2006 article in the *Hartford Courant*.

Williams took a major step toward business success by enrolling at the Sloan School of Management at the Massachusetts Institute of Technology (MIT), where he earned a master's degree in the mid-1980s. Interested primarily in service industries, Williams gravitated toward health care early in his business career. He was co-founder and senior vice president at Vista Health Corp. Other positions included group marketing executive at Control Data Corp.; and president and co-founder of Integrative Systems, a mid-career assessment and testing firm.

Excelled in Insurance Industry

In 1987, Williams joined Blue Cross of California as Vice-President for Corporate Services. Over the next several years, he worked his way up the Blue Cross organizational chart. In October of 1995, Williams was named president of Blue Cross of California, a role he filled from October of 1995 to March of 1999. At the same time, he was Executive Vice President of Blue

At a Glance . . .

Born Ronald A. Williams in 1949, in Chicago, IL; married Cynthia Williams; child: Christopher. *Education:* Roosevelt University, BA, Psychology, 1970; Sloan School of Management, Massachusetts Institute of Technology, MS, Business Management, 1984.

Career: Vista Health Corp., co-founder and senior vice president; Control Data Corp, group marketing executive; Integrative Systems, president and co-founder; Blue Cross of California, various executive positions, 1987-1994, president, 1995-99; WellPoint Health Networks, Inc., executive vice president, 1995-2001, group president, Large Group Division, 1999-2001; Aetna Corp., executive vice president and chief of health operations, 2001-02, president, 2002–, CEO, 2006–.

Memberships: Lucent Technologies, Board of Directors, 2003–; The Conference Board, trustee, 2003–; Dean's Advisory Council and Corporate Visiting Committee, Massachusetts Institute of Technology.

Awards: *Fortune Magazine's* "Top 50 Most Powerful Black Executives in America," 2002; *Black Enterprise,* "75 Most Powerful African Americans in Corporate America," 2005.

Addresses: *Office*—Aetna, Inc., 151 Farmington Ave., Hartford, CT 06156.

data into information for meaningful decision making." Williams led the team that created Aetna's Executive Management Information System, a powerful data analysis and reporting system capable of collecting data from all corner's of the company and translating it into a wide variety of reports on many different performance measures.

In a short time frame, the management team of Rowe and Williams righted Aetna's finances and turned the company into an industry innovator. They cut costs dramatically by laying off a lot of employees, dumping unprofitable units, and streamlining remaining operations. The pair also gave Aetna an influential voice in the public policy arena on health care issues. Their styles, however, could scarcely have been more different. In contrast to Rowe, an outspoken and charismatic manager often called a "visionary," Williams is a soft-spoken, behind-the-scenes leader whose reputation was built on a record of putting practical operations ideas into action and seeing them actually work. In May of 2002, Williams was named Aetna's President, with Rowe retaining the title of CEO. Williams was appointed to the company's board of directors a few months later. That year, *Fortune* magazine included Williams on its list of the "Top 50 Most Powerful Black Executives in America."

At Aetna, Williams was more involved in day-to-day operations than other executives. He set up his office on the first floor of the company's Hartford, Connecticut headquarters rather than on the eighth floor like the other high-ranking officials. He initiated quarterly meetings with about 5,000 managers and supervisors, and maintains an active presence on the company's internal computer network, where employers from anywhere in the company can ask him questions—and actually expect to receive a response.

Recognized for His Skill

In October of 2003, Williams was elected to the Board of Directors of Lucent Technologies, Inc. and to the Board of Trustees of The Conference Board, an independent, nonprofit membership organization that collects and disseminates information about management and markets. In 2005, *Black Enterprise* concurred with *Fortune's* assessment of Williams a few years earlier, naming him to the magazine's "75 Most Powerful African Americans in Corporate America" list.

Under the leadership of Williams and Rowe, Aetna's stock rose some 700 percent between May of 2001 and January of 2006, and the company's net income grew from $127 million in 2000 to $1.6 billion in 2005. When Rowe announced his impending retirement in 2005, Williams was the obvious choice to succeed him as CEO of Aetna. Williams took over on February 14, 2006. The transition was so seamless—nobody expected any significant changes in the way things were run—that it was barely noticed outside of the company. Even inside Aetna, the changing of the

Cross' parent company, WellPoint Health Networks. In April of 1999, Williams was promoted to Group President of WellPoint's Large Group Division, serving in addition as Executive Vice President of WellPoint's Large Group Businesses.

In March of 2001, Williams was hired by insurance giant Aetna, Inc., a direct competitor of WellPoint, initially coming on board as Executive Vice President and Chief of Health Operations. Williams quickly became the right hand of Aetna president Jack Rowe, who had joined the company a year earlier. When Williams was hired, Aetna was experiencing serious financial problems. Williams immediately became one of the company's point people in addressing the crisis. The chief problem he identified, according to his comments on MIT's Sloan School Alumni Web site, was that the company "had simply not organized our guard lacked the drama that often accompanies such events. Williams' calm demeanor and methodical intelligence had long ago earned the confidence of colleagues and industry insiders.

"He exudes confidence and is careful and deliberate in his thinking and action," Alan White, senior associate dean of MIT's Sloan School of Management was quoted as saying in *Newsday.* "You don't want someone to come in and make a bunch of splashy decisions. He won't take an unwise action. I've never known him to." Industry analysts and investors seemed to agree; the week Williams took the helm at Aetna, the company's stock reached its highest value ever.

Sources

Periodicals

Black Enterprise, February 2005; January 27, 2006.

Business Week, December 8, 2003; January 16, 2006, p. 47.

Business Wire, January 4, 2006.

Hartford Courant, January 5, 2006.

Newsday, February 13, 2006.

On-line

"A New Doctor for Aetna," *Business Week Online,* www.businessweek.com/bwdaily/dnflash/jan2006/nf2006014_9348_db035.htm?campaign_id=search (April 28, 2006).

"Featured Alumni," *MIT Sloan School of Management,* http://mitsloan.mit.edu/mba/alumni/williams.php (April 28, 2006).

"Ronald A. Williams," *Aetna Inc,* www.aetna.com/presscenter/williams.htm (April 28, 2006).

—Bob Jacobson

Stanley "Tookie" Williams

1953-2005

Activist, writer, death row inmate

Williams, Stanley, photograph. UPI/Landov.

Stanley "Tookie" Williams was a man with a type of charisma that few people possess; he could get his message across. Half his life he spent spreading a destructive message. From age 17 in 1971 to 1981, Williams' message was violence. He founded one of the most notorious, violent gangs in America: the Crips. From the drug-infested, crime-ridden streets of South Central Los Angeles, Williams built the Crips into a powerful rival to the Bloods, and the gangs' antagonism toward each other, and other gangs, caused unrest and bloodshed that eventually spread a gang culture and violence throughout the nation. Imprisoned on death row for a murder conviction in 1981, Williams began a transformation into an anti-gang activist. In an effort of atonement, he created a series of books for children warning against the dangers of gang involvement and spoke out against violence. Before his death in 2005, Williams made a name for himself as a promoter of peace, winning multiple nominations for the Nobel Peace Prize.

Built Powerful Gang

Williams was raised by his mother—his father left when

Williams was a toddler. Without a father figure, he learned about black men through stereotypes that labeled them as violent, promiscuous, and criminal. Williams internalized those negative stereotypes and grew up, as he told the *San Francisco Chronicle*, "mimicking pimps and drug dealers." As a teenager, he rarely attended high school. By the age of 16, he had already earned a reputation outside of the classroom as a street warrior on the South Central's west side. Williams told *Contemporary Black Biography* (*CBB*) that he was considered a "bully slayer" because he fought kids who picked on his relatives and friends.

In 1971, when small gangs were invading South Central communities and stealing from residents, 17-year-old Williams and his friend, Raymond Lee Washington, organized the Crip—a derivative of "Crib"—gang. The original Crips, with a membership of approximately twenty to thirty young men, formed a front to protect themselves from other gangs. The early Crips divided into the Westside Crips and the Eastside Crips. By 1979 the Crips, who were known to wear blue bandanas, had manifested into a statewide organization. Although the Crips had organized at first in an

At a Glance . . .

Born Stanley Tookie Williams III, on December 29, 1953, in New Orleans, LA; executed on December 13, 2005, San Quentin State Prison, California; children: Travon and Stan "Lil' Tookie."

Career: Gang leader, 1971-1981; anti-gang activist, 1980-2005.

Awards: Five-time nominee for Nobel Peace Prize; four-time nominee for Nobel Peace Prize in Literature; President's Call to Service Award, for good deeds on death row, 2005.

attempt to defend themselves and their neighborhoods, according to the tookie.com Web site, the Crips became "just like the gang members they had once sought to protect themselves from—Crips had become gangbangers who terrorized their own neighborhoods."

But there was another, more alluring, side to gang life besides violence. The Crips gave Williams a false, but deeply felt sense of security, recognition, and belonging; all of which he had not found outside of gang life. "Let's face it, there weren't any black rotary clubs out there; there weren't any cricket clubs.... So there was a void." Williams told *Contemporary Black Biography* (*CBB*). "The gang life actually filled that void, though negative as it was, and negative as it is today, it filled a void that nothing else could fill."

In 1979 the co-founders of the Crips no longer ran the streets of South Central Los Angeles. Their terrorist reign abruptly ended when Washington was gunned down and murdered by a rival gang member, and Williams was charged with killing four people in a motel robbery. Two years later, Williams was found guilty of committing the four murders, and he was sent to San Quentin's death row. Although Williams admitted to his violent past, he denied committing those particular murders to the day he died.

Changed His Life in Prison

As a leader of one of California's most notorious gangs, Williams was often approached and praised by other prisoners who either sought or held membership in gangs. During his incarceration, Williams realized that his motivating reality for gang membership was self-hatred. Williams told *CBB* that when a child is subjected to lies and disparaging myths about his people, "That child, as I did, eventually develops a psychological complex about himself and his people.

That's why it was exceptionally easy for me to lash out at my own people...without remorse." Such children, Williams explained to *CBB*, end up "trying to destroy one another to prove they're better than other blacks who happen to personify that...negative image."

From 1988 to 1994, Williams spent his days and nights between four small walls in solitary confinement. He turned to the Bible, a dictionary, and thesaurus, for education and guidance. While in solitary, Williams underwent a gradual transformation that he has attributed to God. "Gradually I rediscovered that I had a conscience...it took me years, many long years of re-edification, soul searching, and a battle against my so-called hypocritical mentality," he told *CBB*.

Promoted Positive Behavior

After realizing his mistakes, Williams felt obligated to reach out to young people, with a message debunking the glorified image of gang membership. He decided to channel his message through a series of children's books entitled *Tookie Speaks Out*. In 1996 Barbara Cottman Becnel, Williams's co-author, sold the idea for the children's books to the Rosen Publishing Group and the wheels were in motion to distribute Williams's books.

Written for children from kindergarten through fourth grade, the books were used in schools and juvenile correction facilities in the United States, Africa, and Switzerland, and drew attention from people across the country. All the proceeds from Williams's books goes non-profit organizations including Mothers Against Gang Violence, a group based in South Central. The series prompted Dr. Allen Cohen, executive director of Pacific Institute for Research and Evaluation, to contact Williams and Becnel about launching other anti-gang measures in schools. "The themes in the book were entirely congruent with what I think is the best knowledge of the potential of young people to get associated with negative behavior," Cohen said in the *Los Angeles Times*.

After learning that the Crips had spread with a vengeance, setting up shop in 42 states and on at least one other continent by the late 1990s, Williams wanted to launch an Internet project to promote his anti-gang message on another level. He conferred with Becnel who oversaw the inception of Internet Project for Street Peace and who maintained the Web site, tookie. com. The Internet project aimed at building literacy and peer leadership, and it promoted an anti-gang online chat with youth in America and abroad. On the Web site, Williams posted an apology for pioneering an organization that has sunk its venomous teeth into the lives of so many young people. On the Web site, Williams said that he "didn't expect the Crips to end up ruining the lives of so many young people, especially young black men who have hurt other young black men." Williams also apologized to the children of

America and South Africa who face the wrath and temptation of street gangs on a daily basis.

Won Accolades for Message of Peace

In November of 2000 Mario Fehr, a member of the Swiss Parliament, made an unprecedented move and nominated Williams for the 2001 Nobel Peace Prize. It was the first time a death row inmate has ever been nominated for the prize. Fehr presented his nomination to the Nobel Peace Prize Committee in Oslo, Norway, on the basis that Williams's books and Internet project have had a positive influence on children and encouraged them to resist gangs. "As far as the nomination, all I can say is it does show the impossible is possible even for an individual on death row. It proves that the most phenomenal of things can be accomplished from the abyss of a prison cell. It shows what perseverance and initiative can accomplish," Williams told CBB.

Williams's nomination was greeted with considerable controversy. Many people lauded Williams's efforts at atonement. Corey Weinstein, a physician and board member of California Prison Focus, a prisoner advocacy group, told the San Francisco Chronicle that society is not forgiving of criminals. "It's interesting to say that a person will get out of a bad marriage, turn their life around, go to school, change their religion or do a variety of things to alter their direction. It's so ordinary." Weinstein added, "It's only with criminals we try to freeze people in their worst moments in life." But, as Mario Fehr said in the San Francisco Chronicle, "This is something that you can show to young people…that no matter what mistakes you have made in your life, you can change for the better." Community Activist Malik Spellman told the Los Angeles Times that he was "elated" to hear the news of Williams's nomination, explaining, "I was so honored because people who are peacemakers in the streets should be nominated."

Still, a number of people felt that a man convicted of multiple murders should not be considered for such a prestigious award. Richard MacMahon, director of the gang unit for the Los Angeles County Probation Department, told the Los Angeles Times, "I do not see [Williams'] contributions as being comparable to those of Desmond Tutu and Mother Teresa." Deputy Attorney General Lisa J. Brault told the San Francisco Chronicle that Williams's nomination "was an insult to the victims and an affront to the award itself." In addition, San Quentin prison officials alleged, based on information from inmates in other prisons, that Williams was still involved with the Crips.

When asked about such criticisms, Williams told CBB, "One thing for sure is I'm no Desmond Tutu, nor a Martin Luther King, or a Nelson Mandela. What it boils down to is I'm not in control over other people's prejudgmental (sic) types of opinions." Williams contin-

ued, "All I say is this: no one in this world is absolutely loved, nor absolutely hated. It's an impossibility for me to even try to convince everybody to like me or to agree with what I'm doing. The fact of the matter is they can stone me, but they can't stone the message. The message is greater than I am." Williams would be nominated several more times for the Nobel Peace Prize and other prestigious awards. Just before his death in 2005, Williams became the first person on death row to be awarded the President's Call to Service Award.

Found Personal Redemption

With his death sentence looming, Williams spent much of his time praying, studying, writing, exercising, and drawing. In 2004, he published his memoir Blue Rage, Black Redemption. The FXChannel released a made-for-television movie based on the book later in the year. In what Back Stage called an "inspiring story," Jamie Foxx portrayed Williams' "evolution from violent street thug to a beacon of hope."

Despite his focus on peace and personal outreach, Williams' status as a death row inmate remained. In December of 2005, Williams' lawyers sought clemency for Williams from California Governor Arnold Schwarzenegger. But Schwarzenegger ultimately denied clemency because Williams did not express regret or remorse for the murders of a clerk at a 7-Eleven store and three motel owners in 1979, the crime for which he was sentenced to death. "Am I guilty?" Williams told Jet: "No, not culpable of those crimes. I've done many things, but that isn't one of them, and I believe that's why I'm in here because of karma, the things I got away with many moons ago." Williams' execution was scheduled for December of 2005.

Williams was not downtrodden in his final days. "I know of my redemption. Believe me. Mine is real," Williams expressed to Jet. "If you knew me in the beginning and would see me now, you wouldn't believe it. It's like night and day. I have literally made a 720-degree turnaround. A 360-degree wouldn't have been enough." He noted in Jet that he would not change his life if he had it to do over again. "I know for a fact that had I stayed out there in society I would have eventually—the fool that I was thinking that I was invincible—would have gotten a bullet to the back of my cranium—I know that…" He went on to say that his prison sentence enabled him "to help a multitude of young people. Had I been out there, I never would have been able to do that." Williams was executed by lethal injection on December 13, 2005, while more than 2,000 people held vigil outside the San Quentin State Prison walls.

Selected writings

(With Barbara Cottman Becnel), Gangs and Your Neighborhood, Power Kids Press, 1996.

(With Becnel), *Gangs and the Abuse of Power*, Kids Press, 1996.

(With Becnel), *Gangs and Violence*, Kids Press, 1996.

(With Becnel), *Gangs and Wanting to Belong*, Kids Press, 1996.

(With Becnel), *Gangs and Drugs*, Kids Press, 1996.

(With Becnel), *Gangs and Self-Esteem*, Kids Press, 1996.

(With Becnel), *Gangs and Weapons*, Kids Press, 1996.

(With Becnel), *Gangs and Your Friends*, Kids Press, 1996.

(With Becnel), *Life in Prison*, Chronicle Books, 1998.

Blue Rage, Black Redemption: A Memoir, Damamli Publishing Company, 2004.

Sources

Periodicals

America's Intelligence Wire, December 8, 2005.

Back Stage, January 20, 2005, p. 18.

Jet, September 5, 2005; January 9, 2006, p. 46.

Los Angeles Times, December 27, 1996 p.5; December 7, 2000, p. B-1; January 3, 2001.

New York Times, December 6, 2000, p. A18.

San Francisco Chronicle, November 26, 2000 p. A 31; December 11, 2000 p. A 17.

Sentinel (Los Angles, CA), December 8-14, 2005, p. A6.

Washington Post, November 26, 2005, p. A3.

On-line

The Coroner's Report, www.gangwar.com (July 19, 2006).

StreetGangs, www.streetgangs.com (July 19, 2006).

Tookie's Corner, www.tookie.com (July 19, 2006).

Other

Additional information was obtained through a personal interview between Stanley Tookie Williams and *Contemporary Black Biography* on March 20, 2001.

—Ashyia Henderson, Shellie M. Saunders, Jennifer M. York, and Sara Pendergast

Chandra Wilson

1969—

Actor

Wilson, Chandra, photograph. Stephen Shugerman/Getty Images.

Chandra Wilson's star has risen with the acclaim of the ABC series *Grey's Anatomy* in which she plays Dr. Miranda Bailey, the supervisor of a team of doctors-in-training whose formidable manner prompts the nervous underlings to refer to her as "the Nazi." A veteran of the New York stage who spent the better part of the 1990s looking for meaningful, steady work in the entertainment industry, Wilson agreed with *Houston Chronicle* writer Mike McDaniel that her character was a bit fierce, but confessed, "I had never thought of...the stereotype of the angry black woman. But I never thought of her as angry. I always saw her as firm."

Born in Houston, Texas, in 1969, Wilson's talent for performing became evident at an early age. At the age of five, she began appearing in musicals at Theatre Under the Stars, a Houston venue, and followed that with a busy after-school schedule. "My mom said I was not going to be an idle child," she said in the interview with McDaniel, "so I had things to do every day after school. Between dance and theater classes...three days a week, every single minute was accounted for."

After graduating from Houston's High School for the Performing and Visual Arts in 1987, Wilson went on to New York University and its prestigious Tisch School of the Arts. Her course of study included workshops in Method acting at the esteemed Lee Strasberg Theatre Institute, and before she graduated in 1991 with a Bachelor of Fine Arts degree in drama she won her first solid role in a well-received play by cartoonist Lynda Barry, *The Good Times Are Killing Me.* Her portrayal of Bonna Willis, a young woman in a Chicago neighborhood in the changing racial climate of the 1960s, brought her the Theatre World Award for Outstanding Debut Performance.

Though she was determined to forge a career in theater, Wilson took the occasional television role. Her small-screen debut came in a 1989 episode of *The Cosby Show* in which the Huxtable house is overrun with party-goers thanks to son Theo's unwise decision to host a get-together there when his parents leave town. After college, Wilson appeared in a 1992 episode of *Law & Order,* and had a small role in the 1993 Tom Hanks film *Philadelphia.* After becoming a

At a Glance . . .

Born on August 27, 1969, in Houston, TX; married; children: Joy, Serena, Michael. *Education:* New York University, BFA., 1991; studied at the Lee Strasberg Theatre Institute, New York, NY.

Career: Stage actor, 1975–; television actor, 1989–; film actor, 1993–.

Awards: Theatre World Award for Outstanding Debut Performance, 1991, for *The Good Times Are Killing Me.*

Addresses: *Office*—c/o ABC Television, 500 S. Buena Vista St., Burbank, CA 91521.

mother in 1992, with a second daughter born in 1994, she took a few years off, and then struggled to find steady work in New York City. She worked as a temp at Deutsche Bank in Manhattan in the mid-1990s, and stayed on almost until her breakout role in *Grey's Anatomy.* Additional income came thanks to parts in television commercials she appeared in for Burger King, Scope mouthwash, Blockbuster Video, and the United Negro College Fund.

Wilson's other credits during this period include that of Jason Alexander's klutzy personal assistant in an ill-fated ABC sitcom, *Bob Patterson,* in 2001. The show took such a vicious drubbing from critics that of the ten episodes filmed, only five ever aired. She continued to find occasional work on the New York stage, appearing in *On the Town,* a 1998 Broadway musical revue from acclaimed director George C. Wolfe. She was also an understudy in the Tony Award-winning musical *Avenue Q* in 2004.

Wilson won an impressive Broadway role in 2004's *Caroline, or Change,* a musical from Tony Kushner (*Angels in America*) and Jeanine Tesori. The story is set in the early 1960s, and featured Tonya Pinkins in the title role. Wilson was cast as Caroline's longtime friend, Dotty Moffet. The musical opened in May of 2004 at the Eugene O'Neill Theatre, but closed just three months later. One of its highlights was a confrontation between the two women in Wilson's show-stopping number. "When I get offstage, the first thing I do is say to myself, 'Thank you, God, for letting me hit those notes,'" she told Jason Zinoman in the *New York Times.*

Wilson's truly lucky break came when she was cast in *Grey's Anatomy,* which began airing on Sunday nights in March of 2005. The show stars Ellen Pompeo as Meredith Grey, a first-year intern at a Seattle hospital,

and many of the plotlines revolve around various mini-crises in the hospital and the tangle of romantic relationships among Meredith and her fellow medical-school graduates. Wilson portrays their supervising doctor, Miranda Bailey—a tough, no-nonsense boss whom they all fear. *Entertainment Weekly* critic Lisa Schwarzbaum confessed that despite the constant melodrama in each hour-long episode, she was addicted to *Grey's Anatomy.* "Legions of viewers can't wait to discuss the next shift in the romantic geometry" among the interns, Schwarzbaum wrote, but went on to confess, "I am not such a viewer.... Myself, I'd build a whole show around the competence and womanly maturity of Chandra Wilson's Dr. Miranda Bailey, but that's why I'm not in showbiz."

Thanks to ABC's support for the show—which included an ad campaign and a highly coveted time slot following the ratings heavy-hitter *Desperate Housewives*—Wilson's new job quickly pulled in a similarly addicted viewership and comparably favorable reviews. Yet *Houston Chronicle* journalist McDaniel asserted that "the show distinguishes itself in other ways," and listed among these "its mix of humor and drama, its use of sex as a plot device and the colorblind way it employs its diverse cast." McDaniel mentioned Wilson, along with two other African-American actors on the show, Isaiah Washington and James Pickens Jr., "all in positions of responsibility. And no big deal is made of it." It was a quiet triumph of multiculturalism on television also noticed by the *New York Times*'s Matthew Fogel. "Although medical shows have become the cough syrup of television—sturdy, dependable and widely available—'Grey's Anatomy' has differentiated itself by creating a diverse world of doctors—almost half the cast are men and women of color—and then never acknowledging it," Fogel wrote.

There were plans to expand some of *Grey's Anatomy* storylines to focus more on Dr. Bailey's personal life in coming seasons. Wilson, for her part, was happy to have found steady work, and rejected the idea that the show had suddenly catapulted her to a celebrity. In the *Houston Chronicle* interview with McDaniel, which she conducted via mobile phone, she laughingly told the writer from her hometown paper that she was currently just "walking down the street like a regular New Yorker, going about life. There's no big star thing happening. I can still go to the store and run my little errands, and it's OK."

Selected works

Films

Philadelphia, 1993.
Mad Dog and Glory, 1993.
Lone Star, 1996.

Plays

The Good Times Are Killing Me, 1991.

On the Town, 1998.
Caroline, or Change, 2004.

Television

Bob Patterson, 2001.
Grey's Anatomy, 2005—.

Sources

Periodicals

American Theatre, March 2004.
Entertainment Weekly, December 16, 2005, p. 70.
Houston Chronicle, May 4, 2005, p. 1.
New York Times, February 22, 2004, p. AR13; May 8, 2005, p. AR16.

—Carol Brennan

Kimberlydawn Wisdom

1956—

Michigan surgeon general

Wisdom, Kimberlydawn, Dr., photograph. Photo courtesy of Dr. Kimberlydawn Wisdom. Reproduced by permission.

In February of 2003, Dr. Kimberlydawn Wisdom rose to the top of her profession when she was appointed surgeon general of the State of Michigan—the nation's first state surgeon general. For more than 30 years, Dr. Wisdom, an emergency-room physician, researcher, and public-health advocate, devoted herself to promoting preventative medicine within the black community. As surgeon general she launched a public-health promotional campaign and led the state's disease-prevention efforts. Wisdom and Governor Jennifer Granholm made racial and ethnic health disparities a strategic priority for the state.

Fought Racial Discrimination

Kimberlydawn Edmunds was born on October 8, 1956, in New London, Connecticut. She grew up in the predominantly white town of Mystic, Connecticut, where her father, McKinley Hoff Edmunds, Jr., an architectural engineer, worked on the design of the first atomic submarine. Her mother, Florence Jackson Edmunds, was a homemaker whose goal of becoming a nurse had been interrupted by marriage and a family that included young Wisdom, her twin sisters, and a brother. No one in Mystic would sell a black family a house or land, until a white farmer sold the Edmunds some land as revenge on a neighbor. McKinley Edmunds turned the barn into a home for his family.

Wisdom knew from early experience the benefits of helping others. Her mother often suffered with migraine headaches and ear problems, and as a youth Wisdom learned to care for her. By the age of seven, Wisdom knew that she wanted to be a doctor. But her road to that goal would be difficult. In school Wisdom experienced racism. Her sixth-grade teacher told her not to take French because she would never have the opportunity to visit France. In her 1998 presentation "Into the Heart of Darkness," Wisdom recalled her guidance counselor warning her that there was "no such thing as a black doctor," that she would never succeed as a physician, and that she should pursue a career that reflected her race and gender. However her parents supported her ambitions and the high-school classmates who had once harassed her elected Wisdom class president.

At a Glance . . .

Born Kimberlydawn Edmunds on October 8, 1956, in New London, CT; married Garth A. Wisdom, 1978; children: Garth A., Jr., Kristina, Brandon. *Education:* University of Pennsylvania, BS, Biology, 1978; University of Michigan Medical School, MD, 1982; Henry Ford Hospital, intern, internal medicine, 1982-83, resident, emergency medicine, 1983-85; University of Michigan School of Public Health, MS, 1991.

Career: Henry Ford Health System, Detroit, MI, senior staff physician, 1985–, Center for Medical Treatment Effectiveness Programs in Diverse Populations, researcher, 1995-02, Institute on Multicultural Health, founder and director, 2003; University of Michigan Medical School, Ann Arbor, Department of Medical Education, instructor, 1988-95, assistant director, academic programs, 1990-97, assistant professor, 1995–; Case Western Reserve University, Cleveland, OH, Department of Epidemiology and Biostatistics, assistant professor, 1997-02; University of Michigan, School of Public Health, adjunct assistant professor, 2003–; State of Michigan, Lansing, Surgeon General, 2003–.

Selected memberships: American College of Emergency Physicians, fellow; ADA, Task Force to Revise the National Standards for Diabetes Self-Management Education Programs, Diabetes Education Program for Pharmacists, Michigan Affiliate Board of Directors and Minority Affairs Committee; American Medical Association; American Public Health Association; Michigan State Medical Society, Concerns of Women Physicians, Public Awareness Committee.

Selected awards: University of Pennsylvania, Onyx Senior Honor Society, 1978; *Crain's Detroit Business*, Healthcare Heroes Award, 2002; National Association of Negro Business and Professional Women's Clubs, Inc., National Sojourner Truth Meritorious Award, 2003, 2005; Detroit Community Health Connection, Inc., Community Health Warrior Award, 2005; Morehouse School of Medicine, honorary doctorate, 2005.

Addresses: *Office*—Office of the Surgeon General, Michigan Department of Community Health, 201 Townsend St., Capital View Building, 7th Floor, Lansing, MI 48913.

Wisdom learned how much she could accomplish by speaking out. After enduring racial discrimination at the hands of YWCA (Young Women's Christian Association) camp counselors, Wisdom—who had been elected YWCA representative for the Eastern Region—traveled with a group of girls to New York City where they picketed the national YWCA board meeting. In response, the board invited them into the meeting with Wisdom as their spokesperson. At the age of 14, she became a member of the YWCA National Board of Directors. Wisdom told *Contemporary Black Biography* (*CBB*) that this experience "had a very great influence on my future career."

Specialized in Emergency Medicine

After graduating from the University of Pennsylvania in 1978, Kimberlydawn Edmunds married Garth A. Wisdom, a mechanical engineer who later became a financial planner. She also entered the University of Michigan Medical School as one of a few black female students.

After earning her medical degree in 1982, Wisdom joined the Henry Ford Health System in Detroit, Michigan, where she remained for more than two decades. She trained as an emergency room physician and became board-certified. Eventually Wisdom held dual appointments as a senior staff physician and researcher. In 1988 she joined the faculty of the University of Michigan Medical School and the following year began studying at the university's School of Public Health, where she earned her master's degree in clinical research design and statistical analysis in 1991.

Whereas Wisdom's early research focused on emergency and internal medicine and medical education, in the 1990s she began concentrating her efforts on health issues within the black community. Between 1996 and 2000, Wisdom directed the National Institutes of Health Community Liaison Core of the Resource Center for Minority Aging Research. During this period she also investigated medical-treatment effectiveness with the Agency for Healthcare Policy Research.

Addressed Racial Disparities in Healthcare

Wisdom often treated black patients with medical complications from diabetes. Her initial study documented the disparities in blood-sugar levels among black and non-black patients with diabetes. In 1998 Wisdom told the African American Women on Tour conference in Detroit, as quoted in the *Michigan Chronicle*: "There is no such thing as 'borderline' diabetes caused by a touch of sugar - you have it. One person dies every 1.2 hours from diabetes. African American bodies have insulin resistance; sugar needs to get into the cell.

Newly diagnosed diabetes is devastating, especially in the midst of amputating a foot or leg when it could have been prevented. Ninety-five percent of diabetes care is self care." Wisdom led the establishment of the Detroit chapter of the American Diabetes Association (ADA) and she worked with the Centers for Disease Control and Prevention on diabetes care.

Wisdom created and directed the African-American Initiative for Male Health Improvement (AIM-HI). With an outfitted van, AIM-HI staff visited churches, fraternities, and even barbershops, screening black men for diabetes and high-blood pressure and educating them about the effects of these diseases. Although geared toward men, about half of those screened were women. The results were worse than Wisdom had imagined. About one-third of the 7,000 adults required follow-up testing and care. Federal funding enabled AIM-HI to open two centers in Detroit that offered screening for diabetes, hypertension, stroke risk, and eye disease, as well as follow-up care and access to primary healthcare. Classes and support groups were established for diabetes and hypertension self-management, nutrition, and fitness training.

In 2003 Wisdom obtained grant money to establish the Institute on Multicultural Health. She told *CBB* that she was most proud of her accomplishments with AIM-HI and this new institute, as well as her early research publications on emergency medicine and her later research documenting racial disparities in healthcare. Her article "The Healing Process: Reflections on African American History and Diabetes Care" was based on the presentation "Into the Heart of Darkness" in which Wisdom and a white colleague presented pictures and personal stories of healthcare inequalities to a predominately white audience. This risky undertaking was so well-received, Wisdom told *CBB*, that it "set the stage for future presentations on understanding cultural racism."

Appointed State Surgeon General

Upon being named surgeon general, Wisdom was given the opportunity to promote preventative medicine throughout Michigan. As the state's chief public health officer, Wisdom told *CBB* that she saw herself as "the people's doctor" with responsibility for utilizing the best scientific data and resources to improve public health, work with legislators and policy-makers, and build partnerships to promote the health of the state's citizens. She told *CBB*, "two-thirds of healthcare costs and deaths are due to chronic diseases and the etiology of these diseases is unhealthy lifestyles."

As of 2005, almost 40 percent of black men in Michigan died before age 65 and black infants were almost three times as likely to die as white infants. In 2004 Wisdom directed the development of "Michigan Steps Up," a statewide healthy lifestyles campaign that called for preventative measures including exercise and healthier food in schools and workplaces. As a result of her 2004 report on the health status of Michigan residents, Wisdom was able to create "A Prescription for a Healthier Michigan," which dealt with protecting families and communities, eliminating healthcare disparities, and promoting healthy lifestyles. She also established the "Childhood Lead Poisoning Prevention" initiative and focused attention on HIV/AIDS, tobacco use, infant mortality, unwanted pregnancies, school health programs, and access to healthcare. The *Michigan Chronicle* quoted Wisdom in May of 2004: "Too many Michigan residents are uninsured, including children and working adults. Too many lack health care coverage or are unable to get medical care; and too many Michigan residents have no personal healthcare provider."

Following Wisdom's appointment, other states began to consider creating surgeon-general or equivalent positions. Wisdom told *CBB* that state surgeon generals could help promote healthy lifestyles by reaching out to community advocates who can "empower themselves to create environments that support healthy behaviors."

Wisdom authored many reports and research publications and was the recipient of numerous honors and awards. She told *CBB* that in the future she hoped to use her research, publications, speaking engagements, and teaching to have an even greater impact on the health of underserved communities.

Selected writings

Book chapters

(With M. D. Rush and S. Winslett) "Diabetes Mellitus," in *Emergency Medicine: A Comprehensive Study Guide*, 5th Ed., McGraw Hill, 2000.

Periodicals

"Crossing Boundaries," *Diabetes Spectrum*, Vol. 8, No. 5, 1995, p. 310.

(With others) "Comparison of Laboratory Test Frequency and Test Results Between African-Americans and Caucasians with Diabetes: Opportunity for Improvement," *Diabetes Care*, Vol. 20, No. 6, June 1997, pp. 971-977.

"The Healing Process: Reflections on African American History and Diabetes Care," *The Diabetes Educator*, Vol. 24, No. 6, 1998, pp. 690-700.

"Strategies for Community Participation in Diabetes Prevention: A Detroit Experience," *Ethnicity and Disease*, Vol. 13, No. 3, Supplement 3, 2003.

Sources

Periodicals

Crain's Detroit Business, August 26, 2002, p. 12.
Health & Medicine Week, May 24, 2004, p. 502.

Lansing State Journal, November 26, 2005.

Michigan Chronicle, June 28, 1998, p. 1-C; May 28, 2003, p. C2; October 20-26, 2004, p. B1; September 7-13, 2005, p. A6.

On-line

"Into the Heart of Darkness: Reflections on Racism and Diabetes Care," *Michigan Diabetes Research and Training Center,* www.med.umich.edu/mdrtc/education/profedu.htm (February 10, 2006).

"Michigan's First Surgeon General," *Michigan Department of Community Health,* www.michigan.gov/textonly/1,2964,7-132–65525–,00.html (February 10, 2006).

Other

Additional information for this profile was obtained through an interview with Dr. Kimberlydawn Wisdom on February 26, 2006.

—Margaret Alic

Georgie Woods

1927-2005

Disc jockey, radio talk show host

George "Georgie" Woods, known as "the guy with the goods," became a radio legend in Philadelphia during his four-decade-long career that started in the 1950s. Starting at a time when there were few African Americans on mainstream media outlets, Woods created a popular show that broke new ground for a long list of performers, from Sam Cooke to the Beatles. The broadcast pioneer was also an ardent supporter of the civil rights movement, and used his high profile in the city to draw his listeners into the causes he championed. "In the 1950's and the 1960's, he was it—the person everyone listened to," former Philadelphia mayor W. Wilson Goode was quoted as saying in the New York Times. "He was an outstanding community and civil rights leader."

Woods was born in Barnett, Georgia, in 1927, as one of Clinton and Ludelia Lewis Woods's 13 children. Clinton Woods was an itinerant Baptist preacher who died when his son Georgie was nine. After her husband's death, Ludelia Woods took her family to Harlem, New York's thriving African American neighborhood. She died, too, when Woods was just 14. Forced to quit school in order to support his siblings, Woods worked as a dishwasher, truck driver, dockworker, and mail sorter at the post office before joining the U.S. Navy during World War II, when he was 16. His experience with Armed Services Radio, the information and entertainment network for U.S. military forces serving overseas, helped him find his calling, and when he returned to civilian life he enrolled in a three-month radio announcers' course. His first job was on the New York City station WWRL in late 1952, but he moved on to Philadelphia when he was hired at an AM station there, WHAT, in January of 1953.

Woods was one of just four African-American radio announcers, or disc jockeys (DJs) on the air in Philadelphia, at a time when radio was at the height of popularity as an entertainment medium. In 1956, he moved over to another AM station in Philly, WDAS, and would spend the remainder of his career at one of these two stations, both of which geared their programming to the city's black community. Early on, his distinctive baritone voice was popular with listeners, but he also proved to have a good ear for a potential hit record. In 1957, Woods began playing a new song from a moderately well known gospel singer who had stopped recording religious music to concentrate on making pop records. The singer was Sam Cooke, and the track was "You Send Me," which went on to spend six weeks at number one on the charts.

Woods even played a catchy tune from an unknown British group called the Beatles in 1962, "Please, Please Me." Two years later, he claimed that a record from an all-white act, the Righteous Brothers, was "blue-eyed soul." The term came into widespread use a few years later when the Osmond Brothers were mocked as the white copycat version of an African-American singing family, the Jackson 5.

Woods spent four years in the mid-1960s back at WHAT after a dispute with the management of WDAS. On both outlets he called himself "Georgie Woods, the man with the goods." By then he had already emerged as well-known local champion of the civil rights move-

At a Glance . . .

Born on May 11, 1927, in Barnett, GA; died of a heart attack on June 18, 2005, in Boynton Beach, FL; married Gilda (second wife); children: Janet, Lynne (from first marriage); George Jr. (second marriage); Devin (with companion Doris Harris).

Career: WWRL-AM, New York City, disk jockey, 1952; WHAT-AM, Philadelphia, disk jockey, 1953-56, 1964-68, and 1990-94; WDAS, disk jockey, 1956-64, and 1968-78, talk-show host, 1978-90; WGPR, disk jockey, 1994-96; host, *17 Canteen* (television dance show), WPHL TV17, Philadelphia, 1960s and '70s; produced his own line of potato chips, 1988-?.

Memberships: NAACP.

Awards: March of Dimes Achievement in Radio Award, 2002; inductee, Broadcast Pioneers of Philadelphia Hall of Fame, 2005.

ment. He organized a Philadelphia caravan of 21 buses to the 1963 March on Washington, interviewed Malcolm X, and began hosting Motown-star-studded "Freedom Shows" that were fundraisers for various civil rights organizations. He also served as vice president of the local chapter of the National Association for the Advancement of Colored People (NAACP), and sometimes stopped playing records to discuss issues important to the city's black community. In 1967, he ran for a seat on the Philadelphia city council, and seemed to win by a narrow margin. An overnight recount, done under questionable circumstances, showed otherwise, and Woods never ventured near electoral politics again.

After the assassination of Dr. Martin Luther King in April of 1968, Woods urged his listeners to stay calm and keep the slain civil rights leader's message of peace in mind. That same year he returned to WDAS, and as music programming on AM stations declined thanks to the better sound quality of the FM signal, WDAS decided to give Woods his own talk show in 1978. It drew excellent ratings, and lasted for nearly twenty years. Eventually he became the program director for WDAS as well.

The talk-show forum gave Woods an opportunity to discuss race, city politics, and other topics full-time, but his opinions occasionally landed him in trouble. One of the most heated controversies came in 1988, when

Woods responded to hints of resentment in the black community against stores owned by Korean immigrants. Woods suggested on the air that African Americans boycott the businesses owned by Korean Americans, asserting that "they take our money; they suck our blood," according to a *Philadelphia Inquirer* profile by Joe Logan. The radio station issued an apology, but Woods refused to do so, saying, "I will not apologize for speaking out on behalf of blacks," Logan quoted him as saying.

Logan interviewed Woods in 1993, when the DJ was being honored on the occasion of his 66th birthday for his 40 years in radio and legacy of community involvement. The celebrations included the unveiling of a mural located at 5531 Germantown Avenue in a tribute to his life. At the time, Woods admitted to Logan that his skirmish with the city's Korean-American business owners was misguided. "One thing I will have to say about them is they come into the community and work hard," he told the *Inquirer.* "There's a void there and they've filled it. That's our fault, not their fault. It took me a long time to understand that." Looking back, Woods also told the *Philadelphia Inquirer* that his support for integration, the goal of the civil rights struggle, in the 1960s was also a mistake. "I think integration has hurt the blacks, because we used to be a unit.... We had black hotels, we had our own restaurants, our own shopping centers, our own clothing stores—and we lost it all through integration."

Woods retired from the airwaves in 1996. In 1997 Woods moved to Florida, and the city sent him off with a heartfelt celebration of his career. "We would like him to leave with the feeling that his work in radio, television, public affairs, politics, and the many other arenas have not been without the love and appreciation of those who have shared his life...," Diane Brown said in her farewell speech to Woods, according to the *Philadelphia Tribune.* He died in Boynton, Beach, Florida, in June of 2005.

Sources

Periodicals

Billboard, July 2, 2005, p. 68.
New York Times, June 26, 2005, p. A33.
Philadelphia Inquirer, May 11, 1993, p. E1.
Philadelphia Tribune, May 14, 1993, p. A1; May 30, 1997, p. A1; July 7, 2000, p. E8.

On-line

Broadcast Pioneers of Philadelphia, www.broadcastpioneers.com/georgiewoods.html (March 28, 2006).

—Carol Brennan

Donald Young Jr.

1989—

Athlete

Young, Donald, photograph. © David Gray/Reuters/Corbis.

Tennis player Donald Young Jr. has made a career out of setting records. At age 14, the left-handed player was the first African American to win the Orange Bowl's 16-and-under division, and became the youngest male to win a junior Grand Slam title. As Douglas Robson of the *Washington Post* put it in 2005, Young "may be the best 15-year-old male in the history of U.S. tennis."

Donald Jr., the only child of Donald and Illonah Young, was born on July 23, 1989, in Chicago, Illinois. Both of Young's parents played tennis in college, and Donald Jr. started playing the game at age two. Home schooled by his mother, he was coached from the beginning by his parents. By the time Young was ten, his exceptional talent was obvious. He worked that year as a ball boy at a seniors' tournament, where he had the chance to fill in briefly when John McEnroe's hitting partner was late. According to William C. Rhoden in the *New York Times*, McEnroe was so impressed that he told his agent that Young was "the first person I ever saw that has hands like me."

Young excelled in junior tennis tournaments. In 1999 Young won the boys' (age) 10 singles title at the American Tennis Association National Championships. He then advanced to the quarterfinals in the boys' 12 doubles. The following year he won five titles: boys' 11 singles at the Little Mo Sectionals, Little Mo Regionals, and Little Mo Nationals; boys' 12 singles at the USTA Midwest Boys Designated; and boys' 12 singles at the Copper Bowl. Also that year he advanced to the boys' 14 singles quarterfinals at the Midwest Closed, and to the boys' 14 doubles quarterfinals (with Rozell Hodges) at the USTA National Open Championships.

Young accumulated even more wins in 2001. Ranked number one in under 12s that year by the USTA, he took the boys' 12 singles trophies at the Franklin Winter Junior Championships and the USTA National Opens. With Rozell Hodges he won the boys' 14 doubles at the MidWest Closed, and was runner-up in singles in that tournament. At the Super National Hard Court Championships he won the boys' 12 singles title and, with Denis Nevolo, took third place in doubles. Young won the boys' 16 singles at the Mary Lou Piatek Munster Open, and at the USTA Super National Clay Court Championships took the boys' 12 singles title and advanced to the doubles final (with Andrew

At a Glance . . .

Born on July 23, 1989, in Chicago, IL. *Education:* Private education at home.

Career: Professional tennis player, 2004–.

Awards: *Newsweek,* "Individuals to Watch," 2005.

Addresses: *Agent*—Gary Swain, IMG, One Lincoln Center, Oakbrook Terrace, IL 60181.

McCarthy). Young captured three boys' 14 singles titles: the Designated Midwest Tennis Series, the Harvest Day Open, and the NTC Junior Open. He also advanced to the boys' 14 doubles round of 16, with Michael Cameron, at the USTA Super National Winter Championships. He finished third in the boys' 12 Junior Orange Bowl, and won the boys' 12 doubles (with Dennis Nevolo) at the Eddie Herr International.

Ranked number one in under 14s by the USTA in 2002, Young continued to take title after title. He won the boys' 16 singles at the Lockport Junior Open, the Clarence Walker Jr. Memorial Open, and Sandburg Open, where he also won the boys' 18 doubles (with Adam Wright). He took boys' 16 singles and doubles trophies (with Austin Travis) at the Mary Lou Piatek-Daniels Munster Classic, where he also won the boys' 18 doubles (with Porter Myrick). He won the boys' 14 singles and doubles titles (again with Austin Travis) at the Midwest Closed. Young won the boys' 14 singles title at the Midwest Open and the doubles title (with Leo Rosenberg) at the USTA Super National Hard Court Championships. He won the boys' 14 doubles (with Calvin Kemp) at the Eddie Herr International Junior Tennis Championships, and took boys' 14 singles and doubles titles (with Spencer Vegosen) at the USTA Super National Winter Championships. He also finished fourth at the boys' 14 Junior Orange Bowl.

In 2003, at age 14, Young turned professional. It was an early age to take this step, and sports analysts wondered how he would respond to the pressure of increased competition. Robson, for example, pointed out that Young puts tremendous pressure on himself to win, noting that the player "engages in self-critical muttering, slouches his head on missed shots, constantly eyes his parents in the crowd and occasionally slams balls into the backstop." But Young's mother noted that, for a boy of such talent, there is no prior example to follow. She sees to it that her son has time to play his favorite video games and enjoy other adolescent activities. According to managing director of the USTA's USA Tennis High Performance Program Paul Roetert, quoted by Robson, Young's parents were doing an exceptional job with him, and he added that he considered Young to be "a pretty levelheaded kid."

In 2003 Young became the first African American in the 57-year history of the Orange Bowl International Championships to win a singles title, in the boys' 16s final. "That was when I knew I had ability," he told *BBC Sport* writer Sarah Holt. That year Young also won both singles and doubles titles (with Leo Rosenberg) at the most prestigious international event for players age 14 and under at Les Petits As in Tarbes, France. He took the boys' 14 singles title at the USTA Super National Spring Championships and won the boys' 18 doubles title (with Calvin Kemp) at the Interscholastics-East at the University of Kentucky. Young won both singles and doubles titles (with Jean Ives Aubone) at the El Paso Youth Tennis Center ITF Tournament, and won the boys' 18 singles title at the Chanda Rubin American ITF Junior Classic-Texas. At the World Junior Tennis Championships he led Team USA to its second consecutive title.

Young captured the Easter Bowl 18 singles title in 2004, a feat that not even Pete Sampras or John McEnroe was able to achieve. He made history again when he became the youngest male ever to win a junior Grand Slam, at age 15 in Australia in 2005. "Being number one is awesome," he said in remarks quoted on *BBC Sport Academy.* "I've wanted to be number one since I started playing tournaments." That year he also became the youngest player to reach number one in the ITF World Junior Rankings. Young went on to win the boys' 18 singles title at the USTA National Championships and win his second Grand Slam title of the year in doubles at the US Open, with Alex Clayton.

But 2005 held disappointments as well. Young was eliminated early in the French Open Junior Tournament, which he entered as one of the favorites. Also favored to win the Junior World Championship, he lost in the quarterfinals. Still, he finished the year as the top-ranked junior boy in the world, and he won the ITF's World Junior Champion title.

Young showed great maturity and a willingness to improve his game. "I'd say my biggest weapon is my mental strength," he told *BBC Sport.* "I'm a fighter on court." Still at an early point in his career, Young has the potential, many tennis analysts believe, to become one of the top players in the world.

Sources

Periodicals

Black Enterprise, September 1, 2005.
New York Times, June 1, 2005.
Washington Post, April 18, 2005.

On-line

"Donald Blows Them Away," *BBC Sport Academy,* http://news.bbc.co.uk/sportacademy/hi/sa/tennis/features/newsid_3914000/3914281.stm (March 10, 2006).

"Donald Young: Junior Spotlight of the Week," *U.S. Tennis Association,* www.usta.com/juniors/ (March 10. 2006).

"Juniors: 2005 Year in Review," *United States Tennis Association,* www.usta.com/juniors/fullstory.sps?iNewsid=287295 (March 10, 2006).

"Young American," *BBC Sport,* http://news.bbc.co.uk (February 19, 2006).

"Young Not Number One Junior Yet," *Pro Tennis* Fan, www.protennisfan.com/2005 (March 10, 2006).

—E. M. Shostak

Cumulative Nationality Index

Volume numbers appear in **bold**

American

Aaliyah **30**
Aaron, Hank **5**
Abbott, Robert Sengstacke **27**
Abdul-Jabbar, Kareem **8**
Abdur-Rahim, Shareef **28**
Abele, Julian **55**
Abernathy, Ralph David **1**
Abu-Jamal, Mumia **15**
Ace, Johnny **36**
Adams Earley, Charity **13, 34**
Adams, Eula L. **39**
Adams, Floyd, Jr. **12**
Adams, Johnny **39**
Adams, Leslie **39**
Adams, Oleta **18**
Adams, Osceola Macarthy **31**
Adams, Sheila J. **25**
Adams, Yolanda **17**
Adams-Ender, Clara **40**
Adderley, Julian "Cannonball" **30**
Adderley, Nat **29**
Adkins, Rod **41**
Adkins, Rutherford H. **21**
Agyeman, Jaramogi Abebe **10**
Ailey, Alvin **8**
Al-Amin, Jamil Abdullah **6**
Albright, Gerald **23**
Alert, Kool DJ Red **33**
Alexander, Archie Alphonso **14**
Alexander, Clifford **26**
Alexander, Joyce London **18**
Alexander, Khandi **43**
Alexander, Margaret Walker **22**
Alexander, Sadie Tanner Mossell **22**
Ali, Hana Yasmeen **52**
Ali, Laila **27**
Ali, Muhammad **2, 16, 52**
Allain, Stephanie **49**
Allen, Byron **3, 24**
Allen, Debbie **13, 42**
Allen, Ethel D. **13**
Allen, Marcus **20**
Allen, Robert L. **38**
Allen, Samuel W. **38**
Allen, Tina **22**
Allen-Buillard, Melba **55**
Alston, Charles **33**
Amerie **52**
Ames, Wilmer **27**
Amos, John **8**
Amos, Wally **9**
Anderson, Anthony **51**

Anderson, Carl **48**
Anderson, Charles Edward **37**
Anderson, Eddie "Rochester" **30**
Anderson, Elmer **25**
Anderson, Jamal **22**
Anderson, Marian **2, 33**
Anderson, Michael P. **40**
Anderson, Norman B. **45**
Anderson, William G(ilchrist), D.O. **57**
Andrews, Benny **22**
Andrews, Bert **13**
Andrews, Raymond **4**
Angelou, Maya **1, 15**
Ansa, Tina McElroy **14**
Anthony, Carmelo **46**
Anthony, Wendell **25**
Archer, Dennis **7, 36**
Archie-Hudson, Marguerite **44**
Arkadie, Kevin **17**
Armstrong, Louis **2**
Armstrong, Robb **15**
Armstrong, Vanessa Bell **24**
Arnez J. **53**
Arnwine, Barbara **28**
Arrington, Richard **24**
Arroyo, Martina **30**
Artest, Ron **52**
Asante, Molefi Kete **3**
Ashanti **37**
Ashe, Arthur **1, 18**
Ashford, Emmett **22**
Ashford, Nickolas **21**
Ashley-Ward, Amelia **23**
Atkins, Cholly **40**
Atkins, Erica **34**
Atkins, Juan **50**
Atkins, Russell **45**
Atkins, Tina **34**
Aubert, Alvin **41**
Auguste, Donna **29**
Austin, Junius C. **44**
Austin, Lovie **40**
Austin, Patti **24**
Avant, Clarence **19**
Ayers, Roy **16**
Babatunde, Obba **35**
Bacon-Bercey, June **38**
Badu, Erykah **22**
Bailey, Buster **38**
Bailey, Clyde **45**
Bailey, DeFord **33**
Bailey, Radcliffe **19**
Bailey, Xenobia **11**

Baines, Harold **32**
Baiocchi, Regina Harris **41**
Baisden, Michael **25**
Baker, Anita **21, 48**
Baker, Augusta **38**
Baker, Dusty **8, 43**
Baker, Ella **5**
Baker, Gwendolyn Calvert **9**
Baker, Houston A., Jr. **6**
Baker, Josephine **3**
Baker, LaVern **26**
Baker, Maxine B. **28**
Baker, Thurbert **22**
Baldwin, James **1**
Ballance, Frank W. **41**
Ballard, Allen Butler, Jr. **40**
Ballard, Hank **41**
Bambaataa, Afrika **34**
Bambara, Toni Cade **10**
Bandele, Asha **36**
Banks, Ernie **33**
Banks, Jeffrey **17**
Banks, Tyra **11, 50**
Banks, William **11**
Banner, David **55**
Baraka, Amiri **1, 38**
Barber, Ronde **41**
Barber, Tiki **57**
Barboza, Anthony **10**
Barclay, Paris **37**
Barden, Don H. **9, 20**
Barker, Danny **32**
Barkley, Charles **5**
Barlow, Roosevelt **49**
Barnes, Roosevelt "Booba" **33**
Barnes, Steven **54**
Barnett, Amy Du Bois **46**
Barnett, Etta Moten **56**
Barnett, Marguerite **46**
Barney, Lem **26**
Barnhill, David **30**
Barrax, Gerald William **45**
Barrett, Andrew C. **12**
Barrett, Jacquelyn **28**
Barrino, Fantasia **53**
Barry, Marion S(hepilov, Jr.) **7, 44**
Barthe, Richmond **15**
Basie, Count **23**
Basquiat, Jean-Michel **5**
Bass, Charlotta Spears **40**
Bassett, Angela **6, 23**
Bates, Daisy **13**
Bates, Karen Grigsby **40**
Bates, Peg Leg **14**

Bath, Patricia E. **37**
Baugh, David **23**
Baylor, Don **6**
Baylor, Helen **36**
Beach, Michael **26**
Beal, Bernard B. **46**
Beals, Jennifer **12**
Beals, Melba Patillo **15**
Bearden, Romare **2, 50**
Beasley, Jamar **29**
Beasley, Phoebe **34**
Beatty, Talley **35**
Bechet, Sidney **18**
Beckford, Tyson **11**
Beckham, Barry **41**
Belafonte, Harry **4**
Bell, Derrick **6**
Bell, James "Cool Papa" **36**
Bell, James A. **50**
Bell, James Madison **40**
Bell, Michael **40**
Bell, Robert Mack **22**
Bellamy, Bill **12**
Belle, Albert **10**
Belle, Regina **1, 51**
Belton, Sharon Sayles **9, 16**
Benét, Eric **28**
Ben-Israel, Ben Ami **11**
Benjamin, Andre **45**
Benjamin, Regina **20**
Benjamin, Tritobia Hayes **53**
Bennett, George Harold "Hal" **45**
Bennett, Lerone, Jr. **5**
Benson, Angela **34**
Bentley, Lamont **53**
Berry, Bertice **8, 55**
Berry, Chuck **29**
Berry, Fred "Rerun" **48**
Berry , Halle **4, 19, 57**
Berry, Mary Frances **7**
Berry, Theodore **31**
Berrysmith, Don Reginald **49**
Bethune, Mary McLeod **4**
Betsch, MaVynee **28**
Beverly, Frankie **25**
Bibb, Eric **49**
Bibb, Henry and Mary **54**
Bickerstaff, Bernie **21**
Biggers, John **20, 33**
Bing, Dave **3**
Bishop, Sanford D. Jr. **24**
Black, Albert **51**
Black, Barry C. **47**
Black, Keith Lanier **18**

Cumulative Occupation Index

Volume numbers appear in **bold**

Art and design

Abele, Julian **55**
Adjaye, David **38**
Allen, Tina **22**
Alston, Charles **33**
Anderson, Ho Che **54**
Andrews, Benny **22**
Andrews, Bert **13**
Armstrong, Robb **15**
Bailey, Radcliffe **19**
Bailey, Xenobia **11**
Barboza, Anthony **10**
Barnes, Ernie **16**
Barthe, Richmond **15**
Basquiat, Jean-Michel **5**
Bearden, Romare **2, 50**
Beasley, Phoebe **34**
Benjamin, Tritobia Hayes **53**
Biggers, John **20, 33**
Blacknurn, Robert **28**
Brandon, Barbara **3**
Brown, Donald **19**
Burke, Selma **16**
Burroughs, Margaret Taylor **9**
Camp, Kimberly **19**
Campbell, E. Simms **13**
Campbell, Mary Schmidt **43**
Catlett, Elizabeth **2**
Chase-Riboud, Barbara **20, 46**
Cortor, Eldzier **42**
Cowans, Adger W. **20**
Crite, Alan Rohan **29**
De Veaux, Alexis **44**
DeCarava, Roy **42**
Delaney, Beauford **19**
Delaney, Joseph **30**
Delsarte, Louis **34**
Donaldson, Jeff **46**
Douglas, Aaron **7**
Driskell, David C. **7**
Edwards, Melvin **22**
El Wilson, Barbara **35**
Ewing, Patrick A.**17**
Fax, Elton **48**
Feelings, Tom **11, 47**
Freeman, Leonard **27**
Fuller, Meta Vaux Warrick **27**
Gantt, Harvey **1**
Gilliam, Sam **16**
Golden, Thelma **10, 55**
Goodnight, Paul **32**
Green, Jonathan **54**
Guyton, Tyree **9**

Harkless, Necia Desiree **19**
Harrington, Oliver W. **9**
Hathaway, Isaac Scott **33**
Hayden, Palmer **13**
Hayes, Cecil N. **46**
Honeywood, Varnette P. **54**
Hope, John **8**
Hudson, Cheryl **15**
Hudson, Wade **15**
Hunt, Richard **6**
Hunter, Clementine **45**
Hutson, Jean Blackwell **16**
Jackson, Earl **31**
Jackson, Vera **40**
John, Daymond **23**
Johnson, Jeh Vincent **44**
Johnson, William Henry **3**
Jones, Lois Mailou **13**
Kitt, Sandra **23**
Knox, Simmie **49**
Lawrence, Jacob **4, 28**
Lee, Annie Francis **22**
Lee-Smith, Hughie **5, 22**
Lewis, Edmonia **10**
Lewis, Norman **39**
Lewis, Samella **25**
Loving, Alvin, Jr., **35, 53**
Manley, Edna **26**
Mayhew, Richard **39**
McGee, Charles **10**
McGruder, Aaron **28, 56**
Mitchell, Corinne **8**
Moody, Ronald **30**
Morrison, Keith **13**
Motley, Archibald Jr. **30**
Moutoussamy-Ashe, Jeanne **7**
Mutu, Wangechi **44**
N'Namdi, George R. **17**
Nugent, Richard Bruce **39**
Olden, Georg(e) **44**
Ouattara **43**
Perkins, Marion **38**
Pierre, Andre **17**
Pindell, Howardena **55**
Pinderhughes, John **47**
Pinkney, Jerry **15**
Pippin, Horace **9**
Porter, James A. **11**
Prophet, Nancy Elizabeth **42**
Puryear, Martin **42**
Reid, Senghor **55**
Ringgold, Faith **4**
Ruley, Ellis **38**
Saar, Alison **16**

Saint James, Synthia **12**
Sallee, Charles **38**
Sanders, Joseph R., Jr. **11**
Savage, Augusta **12**
Sebree, Charles **40**
Serrano, Andres **3**
Shabazz, Attallah **6**
Simpson, Lorna **4, 36**
Sims, Lowery Stokes **27**
Sklarek, Norma Merrick **25**
Sleet, Moneta, Jr. **5**
Smith, Bruce W. **53**
Smith, Marvin **46**
Smith, Morgan **46**
Smith, Vincent D. **48**
Steave-Dickerson, Kia **57**
Tanksley, Ann **37**
Tanner, Henry Ossawa **1**
Thomas, Alma **14**
Thrash, Dox **35**
Tolliver, William **9**
VanDerZee, James **6**
Wainwright, Joscelyn **46**
Walker, A'lelia **14**
Walker, Kara **16**
Washington, Alonzo **29**
Washington, James, Jr. **38**
Wells, James Lesesne **10**
White, Charles **39**
White, Dondi **34**
White, John H. **27**
Williams, Billy Dee **8**
Williams, O. S. **13**
Williams, Paul R. **9**
Williams, William T. **11**
Wilson, Ellis **39**
Woodruff, Hale **9**

Business

Abbot, Robert Sengstacke **27**
Abdul-Jabbar, Kareem **8**
Adams, Eula L. **39**
Adkins, Rod **41**
Ailey, Alvin **8**
Al-Amin, Jamil Abdullah **6**
Alexander, Archie Alphonso **14**
Allen, Byron **24**
Allen-Buillard, Melba **55**
Ames, Wilmer **27**
Amos, Wally **9**
Auguste, Donna **29**
Avant, Clarence **19**
Baker, Dusty **8, 43**
Baker, Ella **5**

Baker, Gwendolyn Calvert **9**
Baker, Maxine **28**
Banks, Jeffrey **17**
Banks, William **11**
Barden, Don H. **9, 20**
Barrett, Andrew C. **12**
Beal, Bernard B. **46**
Beamon, Bob **30**
Beasley, Phoebe **34**
Bell, James A. **50**
Bennett, Lerone, Jr. **5**
Bing, Dave **3**
Blackshear, Leonard **52**
Blackwell Sr., Robert D. **52**
Blayton, Jesse B., Sr. **55**
Bolden, Frank E. **44**
Borders, James **9**
Boston, Kelvin E. **25**
Boston, Lloyd **24**
Boyd, Gwendolyn **49**
Boyd, John W., Jr. **20**
Boyd, T. B., III **6**
Bradley, Jennette B. **40**
Bridges, Shelia **36**
Bridgforth, Glinda **36**
Brimmer, Andrew F. **2, 48**
Bronner, Nathaniel H., Sr. **32**
Brown, Eddie C. **35**
Brown, Les **33**
Brown, Marie Dutton **12**
Brunson, Dorothy **1**
Bryant, John **26**
Burgess, Marjorie L. **55**
Burrell, Tom **21, 51**
Burroughs, Margaret Taylor **9**
Burrus, William Henry "Bill" **45**
Busby, Jheryl **3**
Cain, Herman **15**
CasSelle, Malcolm **11**
Chamberlain, Wilt **18, 47**
Chapman, Nathan A. Jr. **21**
Chappell, Emma **18**
Chase, Debra Martin **49**
Chase, Leah **57**
Chenault, Kenneth I. **4, 36**
Cherry, Deron **40**
Chisholm, Samuel J. **32**
Clark, Celeste **15**
Clark, Patrick **14**
Clay, William Lacy **8**
Clayton, Xernona **3, 45**
Cobbs, Price M. **9**
Colbert, Virgis William **17**
Coleman, Donald A. **24**

Tyson, Asha 39
Ussery, Terdema, II 29
Utendahl, John 23
Van Peebles, Melvin 7
VanDerZee, James 6
Vaughn, Gladys Gary 47
Vaughns, Cleopatra 46
Walker, A'lelia 14
Walker, Cedric "Ricky" 19
Walker, Madame C. J. 7
Walker, Maggie Lena 17
Walker, T. J. 7
Ward, Lloyd 21, 46
Ware, Carl H. 30
Washington, Alonzo 29
Washington, Mary T. 57
Washington, Regynald G. 44
Washington, Val 12
Wasow, Omar 15
Watkins, Donald 35
Watkins, Walter C. Jr. 24
Wattleton, Faye 9
Wek, Alek 18
Welburn, Edward T. 50
Wells-Barnett, Ida B. 8
Westbrook, Kelvin 50
Wharton, Clifton R., Jr. 7
White, Linda M. 45
White, Walter F. 4
Wiley, Ralph 8
Wilkins, Ray 47
Williams, Armstrong 29
Williams, O. S. 13
Williams, Paul R. 9
Williams, Ronald A. 57
Williams, Terrie 35
Williams, Walter E. 4
Wilson, Phill 9
Wilson, Sunnie 7, 55
Winfrey, Oprah 2, 15
Woods, Jacqueline 52
Woods, Sylvia 34
Woodson, Robert L. 10
Wright, Charles H. 35
Wright, Deborah C. 25
Yoba, Malik 11
Zollar, Alfred 40

Dance
Acogny, Germaine 55
Ailey, Alvin 8
Alexander, Khandi 43
Allen, Debbie 13, 42
Atkins, Cholly 40
Babatunde, Obba 35
Baker, Josephine 3
Bates, Peg Leg 14
Beals, Jennifer 12
Beatty, Talley 35
Byrd, Donald 10
Clarke, Hope 14
Collins, Janet 33
Davis, Chuck 33
Davis, Sammy Jr. 18
Dove, Ulysses 5
Dunham, Katherine 4
Ellington, Mercedes 34
Fagan, Garth 18
Falana, Lola 42
Glover, Savion 14
Guy, Jasmine 2
Hall, Arthur 39
Hammer, M. C. 20

Henson, Darrin 33
Hines, Gregory 1, 42
Horne, Lena 5
Jackson, Michael 19, 53
Jamison, Judith 7
Johnson, Virginia 9
Jones, Bill T. 1, 46
King, Alonzo 38
McQueen, Butterfly 6, 54
Miller, Bebe 3
Mills, Florence 22
Mitchell, Arthur 2, 47
Moten, Etta 18
Muse, Clarence Edouard 21
Nash, Joe 55
Nicholas, Fayard 20, 57
Nicholas, Harold 20
Nichols, Nichelle 11
Powell, Maxine 8
Premice, Josephine 41
Primus, Pearl 6
Ray, Gene Anthony 47
Rhoden, Dwight 40
Ribeiro, Alfonso, 17
Richardson, Desmond 39
Robinson, Bill "Bojangles" 11
Robinson, Cleo Parker 38
Robinson, Fatima 34
Rodgers, Rod 36
Rolle, Esther 13, 21
Sims, Howard "Sandman" 48
Spears, Warren 52
Tyson, Andre 40
Vereen, Ben 4
Walker, Cedric "Ricky" 19
Walker, Dianne 57
Washington, Fredi 10
Williams, Vanessa L. 4, 17
Zollar, Jawole Willa Jo 28

Education
Achebe, Chinua 6
Adams, Leslie 39
Adams-Ender, Clara 40
Adkins, Rutherford H. 21
Aidoo, Ama Ata 38
Ake, Claude 30
Alexander, Margaret Walker 22
Allen, Robert L. 38
Allen, Samuel W. 38
Allen-Buillard, Melba 55
Alston, Charles 33
Amadi, Elechi 40
Anderson, Charles Edward 37
Archer, Dennis 7
Archie-Hudson, Marguerite 44
Aristide, Jean-Bertrand 6, 45
Asante, Molefi Kete 3
Aubert, Alvin 41
Awoonor, Kofi 37
Bacon-Bercey, June 38
Baiocchi, Regina Harris 41
Baker, Augusta 38
Baker, Gwendolyn Calvert 9
Baker, Houston A., Jr. 6
Ballard, Allen Butler, Jr. 40
Bambara, Toni Cade 10
Baraka, Amiri 1, 38
Barboza, Anthony 10
Barnett, Marguerite 46
Bath, Patricia E. 37
Beckham, Barry 41
Bell, Derrick 6

Benjamin, Tritobia Hayes 53
Berry, Bertice 8, 55
Berry, Mary Frances 7
Bethune, Mary McLeod 4
Biggers, John 20, 33
Black, Albert 51
Black, Keith Lanier 18
Blassingame, John Wesley 40
Blockson, Charles L. 42
Bluitt, Juliann S. 14
Bogle, Donald 34
Bolden, Tonya 32
Bosley, Freeman, Jr. 7
Boyd, T. B., III 6
Bradley, David Henry, Jr. 39
Branch, William Blackwell 39
Brathwaite, Kamau 36
Braun, Carol Moseley 4, 42
Briscoe, Marlin 37
Brooks, Avery 9
Brown, Claude 38
Brown, Joyce F. 25
Brown, Sterling 10
Brown, Uzee 42
Brown, Wesley 23
Brown, Willa 40
Bruce, Blanche Kelso 33
Brutus, Dennis 38
Bryan, Ashley F. 41
Burke, Selma 16
Burke, Yvonne Braithwaite 42
Burks, Mary Fair 40
Burnim, Mickey L. 48
Burroughs, Margaret Taylor 9
Burton, LeVar 8
Butler, Paul D. 17
Callender, Clive O. 3
Campbell, Bebe Moore 6, 24
Campbell, Mary Schmidt 43
Cannon, Katie 10
Carby, Hazel 27
Cardozo, Francis L. 33
Carnegie, Herbert 25
Carruthers, George R. 40
Carter, Joye Maureen 41
Carter, Kenneth 53
Carter, Warrick L. 27
Cartey, Wilfred 47
Carver, George Washington 4
Cary, Lorene 3
Cary, Mary Ann Shadd 30
Catlett, Elizabeth 2
Cayton, Horace 26
Cheney-Coker, Syl 43
Clark, Joe 1
Clark, Kenneth B. 5, 52
Clark, Septima 7
Clarke, Cheryl 32
Clarke, George 32
Clarke, John Henrik 20
Clayton, Constance 1
Cleaver, Kathleen Neal 29
Clements, George 2
Clemmons, Reginal G. 41
Clifton, Lucille 14
Cobb, Jewel Plummer 42
Cobb, W. Montague 39
Cobbs, Price M. 9
Cohen, Anthony 15
Cole, Johnnetta B. 5, 43
Collins, Janet 33
Collins, Marva 3
Comer, James P. 6

Cone, James H. 3
Coney, PonJola 48
Cook, Mercer 40
Cook, Samuel DuBois 14
Cook, Toni 23
Cooper Cafritz, Peggy 43
Cooper, Afua 53
Cooper, Anna Julia 20
Cooper, Edward S. 6
Copeland, Michael 47
Cortez, Jayne 43
Cosby, Bill 7, 26
Cotter, Joseph Seamon, Sr. 40
Cottrell, Comer 11
Cox, Joseph Mason Andrew 51
Creagh, Milton 27
Crew, Rudolph F. 16
Crew, Spencer R. 55
Cross, Dolores E. 23
Crouch, Stanley 11
Cruse, Harold 54
Cullen, Countee 8
Daly, Marie Maynard 37
Dathorne, O.R. 52
Davis, Allison 12
Davis, Angela 5
Davis, Arthur P. 41
Davis, Charles T. 48
Davis, Erroll B., Jr. 57
Davis, George 36
Dawson, William Levi 39
Deconge-Watson, Lovenia 55
Delany, Sadie 12
Delany, Samuel R., Jr. 9
Delco, Wilhemina R. 33
Delsarte, Louis 34
Dennard, Brazeal 37
DePriest, James 37
Dickens, Helen Octavia 14
Diop, Cheikh Anta 4
Dixon, Margaret 14
Dodson, Howard, Jr. 7, 52
Dodson, Owen Vincent 38
Donaldson, Jeff 46
Douglas, Aaron 7
Dove, Rita 6
Dove, Ulysses 5
Draper, Sharon Mills 16, 43
Driskell, David C. 7
Drummond, William J. 40
Du Bois, David Graham 45
Dumas, Henry 41
Dunbar-Nelson, Alice Ruth Moore 44
Dunnigan, Alice Allison 41
Dunston, Georgia Mae 48
Dymally, Mervyn 42
Dyson, Michael Eric 11, 40
Early, Gerald 15
Edelin, Ramona Hoage 19
Edelman, Marian Wright 5, 42
Edley, Christopher 2, 48
Edley, Christopher F., Jr. 48
Edwards, Harry 2
Elders, Joycelyn 6
Elliot, Lorris 37
Ellis, Clarence A. 38
Ellison, Ralph 7
Epps, Archie C., III 45
Evans, Mari 26
Fauset, Jessie 7
Favors, Steve 23

Feelings, Muriel **44**
Figueroa, John J. **40**
Fleming, Raymond **48**
Fletcher, Bill, Jr. **41**
Floyd, Elson S. **41**
Ford, Jack **39**
Foster, Ezola **28**
Foster, Henry W., Jr. **26**
Franklin, John Hope **5**
Franklin, Robert M. **13**
Frazier, E. Franklin **10**
Freeman, Al, Jr. **11**
Fryer, Roland G. **56**
Fuller, A. Oveta **43**
Fuller, Arthur **27**
Fuller, Howard L. **37**
Fuller, Solomon Carter, Jr. **15**
Futrell, Mary Hatwood **33**
Gaines, Ernest J. **7**
Gates, Henry Louis, Jr. **3, 38**
Gates, Sylvester James, Jr. **15**
Gayle, Addison, Jr. **41**
George, Zelma Watson **42**
Gerima, Haile **38**
Gibson, Donald Bernard **40**
Giddings, Paula **11**
Giovanni, Nikki **9, 39**
Golden, Marita **19**
Gomes, Peter J. **15**
Gomez, Jewelle **30**
Granville, Evelyn Boyd **36**
Greenfield, Eloise **9**
Guinier, Lani **7, 30**
Guy-Sheftall, Beverly **13**
Hageman, Hans and Ivan **36**
Hale, Lorraine **8**
Halliburton, Warren J. **49**
Handy, W. C. **8**
Hansberry, William Leo **11**
Harkless, Necia Desiree **19**
Harper, Michael S. **34**
Harris, Alice **7**
Harris, Jay T. **19**
Harris, Patricia Roberts **2**
Harsh, Vivian Gordon **14**
Harvey, William R. **42**
Haskins, James **36, 54**
Hathaway, Isaac Scott **33**
Hayden, Carla D. **47**
Hayden, Robert **12**
Haynes, George Edmund **8**
Henderson, Stephen E. **45**
Henries, A. Doris Banks **44**
Herenton, Willie W. **24**
Hill, Anita **5**
Hill, Bonnie Guiton **20**
Hill, Errol **40**
Hill, Leslie Pinckney **44**
Hine, Darlene Clark **24**
Hinton, William Augustus **8**
Hoagland, Everett H. **45**
Hogan, Beverly Wade **50**
Holland, Endesha Ida Mae **3, 57**
Holt, Nora **38**
Hooks, Bell **5**
Hope, John **8**
Houston, Charles Hamilton **4**
Hoyte, Lenon **50**
Hrabowski, Freeman A. III **22**
Huggins, Nathan Irvin **52**
Hughes, Ebony **57**
Hull, Akasha Gloria **45**
Humphries, Frederick **20**

Hunt, Richard **6**
Hutcherson, Hilda Yvonne **54**
Hutson, Jean Blackwell **16**
Imes, Elmer Samuel **39**
Jackson, Fred James **25**
Jackson, Vera **40**
Jarret, Vernon D. **42**
Jarvis, Charlene Drew **21**
Jeffries, Leonard **8**
Jenifer, Franklyn G. **2**
Jenkins, Ella **15**
Johns, Vernon **38**
Johnson, Hazel **22**
Johnson, James Weldon **5**
Jones, Bobby **20**
Jones, Clara Stanton **51**
Jones, Edward P. **43**
Jones, Gayl **37**
Jones, Ingrid Saunders **18**
Jones, Lois Mailou **13**
Joplin, Scott **6**
Jordan, Barbara **4**
Jordan, June **7, 35**
Josey, E. J. **10**
Just, Ernest Everett **3**
Karenga, Maulana **10**
Kay, Ulysses **37**
Keith, Damon J. **16**
Kennedy, Florynce **12, 33**
Kennedy, Randall **40**
Kilpatrick, Carolyn Cheeks **16**
Kimbro, Dennis **10**
King, Preston **28**
Kittles, Rick **51**
Komunyakaa, Yusef **9**
Kunjufu, Jawanza **3, 50**
Ladner, Joyce A. **42**
Lawrence, Jacob **4, 28**
Lawrence-Lightfoot, Sara **10**
Lee, Annie Francis **22**
Lee, Joe A. **45**
Leevy, Carrol M. **42**
Leffall, LaSalle, Jr. **3**
Lester, Julius **9**
Lewis, David Levering **9**
Lewis, Norman **39**
Lewis, Samella **25**
Lewis, Shirley A. R. **14**
Lewis, Thomas **19**
Liberia-Peters, Maria Philomena **12**
Lincoln, C. Eric **38**
Lindsey, Tommie **51**
Locke, Alain **10**
Logan, Rayford W. **40**
Lorde, Audre **6**
Loury, Glenn **36**
Loving, Jr., Alvin **35, 53**
Lucy Foster, Autherine **35**
Lyttle, Hulda Margaret **14**
Madhubuti, Haki R. **7**
Major, Clarence **9**
Malveaux, Floyd **54**
Manley, Audrey Forbes **16**
Marable, Manning **10**
Markham, E.A. **37**
Marsalis, Wynton **16**
Marshall, Paule **7**
Masekela, Barbara **18**
Mason, Ronald **27**
Massey, Walter E. **5, 45**
Massie, Samuel P., Jr. **29**
Mayhew, Richard **39**
Maynard, Robert C. **7**

Maynor, Dorothy **19**
Mayo, Whitman **32**
Mays, Benjamin E. **7**
McCarty, Osceola **16**
McKay, Nellie Yvonne **17, 57**
McMillan, Terry **4, 17, 53**
McMurray, Georgia L. **36**
McWhorter, John **35**
Meek, Carrie **6**
Mell, Patricia **49**
Memmi, Albert **37**
Meredith, James H. **11**
Millender-McDonald, Juanita **21**
Mitchell, Corinne **8**
Mitchell, Sharon **36**
Mofolo, Thomas Mokopu **37**
Mollel, Tololwa **38**
Mongella, Gertrude **11**
Mooney, Paul **37**
Moore, Barbara C. **49**
Moore, Harry T. **29**
Moore, Melba **21**
Morrison, Keith **13**
Morrison, Toni **15**
Moses, Robert Parris **11**
Mphalele, Es'kia (Ezekiel) **40**
Mullen, Harryette **34**
Murray, Pauli **38**
N'Namdi, George R. **17**
N'Namdi, George R. **17**
Nabrit, Samuel Milton **47**
Naylor, Gloria **10, 42**
Neal, Larry **38**
Newman, Lester C. **51**
Norman, Maidie **20**
Norton, Eleanor Holmes **7**
Nour, Nawal M. **56**
Ogletree, Charles, Jr. **12, 47**
Onwueme, Tess Osonye **23**
Onwurah, Ngozi **38**
Owens, Helen **48**
Owens, Major **6**
Page, Alan **7**
Paige, Rod **29**
Painter, Nell Irvin **24**
Palmer, Everard **37**
Parker, Kellis E. **30**
Parks, Suzan-Lori **34**
Patterson, Frederick Douglass **12**
Patterson, Mary Jane **54**
Patterson, Orlando **4**
Payton, Benjamin F. **23**
Perry, Warren **56**
Peters, Margaret and Matilda **43**
Pickett, Cecil **39**
Pinckney, Bill **42**
Pindell, Howardena **55**
Player, Willa B. **43**
Porter, James A. **11**
Poussaint, Alvin F. **5**
Price, Florence **37**
Price, Glenda **22**
Price, Richard **51**
Primus, Pearl **6**
Prophet, Nancy Elizabeth **42**
Puryear, Martin **42**
Quarles, Benjamin Arthur **18**
Quigless, Helen G. **49**
Rahman, Aishah **37**
Ramphele, Mamphela **29**
Reagon, Bernice Johnson **7**
Reddick, Lawrence Dunbar **20**
Redding, J. Saunders **26**

Redmond, Eugene **23**
Reid, Irvin D. **20**
Rice, Louise Allen **54**
Richards, Hilda **49**
Ringgold, Faith **4**
Robinson, Sharon **22**
Robinson, Spottswood **22**
Rogers, Joel Augustus **30**
Rollins, Charlemae Hill **27**
Russell-McCloud, Patricia **17**
Salih, Al-Tayyib **37**
Sallee, Charles Louis, Jr. **38**
Satcher, David **7, 57**
Schomburg, Arthur Alfonso **9**
Sears, Stephanie **53**
Senior, Olive **37**
Shabazz, Betty **7, 26**
Shange, Ntozake **8**
Shipp, E. R. **15**
Shirley, George **33**
Simmons, Ruth J. **13, 38**
Sinkford, Jeanne C. **13**
Sisulu, Sheila Violet Makate **24**
Sizemore, Barbara A. **26**
Smith, Anna Deavere **6**
Smith, Barbara **28**
Smith, Jessie Carney **35**
Smith, John L. **22**
Smith, Mary Carter **26**
Smith, Tubby **18**
Southern, Eileen **56**
Sowande, Fela **39**
Soyinka, Wole **4**
Spears, Warren **52**
Spikes, Dolores **18**
Stanford, John **20**
Steele, Claude Mason **13**
Steele, Shelby **13**
Stephens, Charlotte Andrews **14**
Stewart, Maria W. Miller **19**
Stone, Chuck **9**
Sudarkasa, Niara **4**
Sullivan, Louis **8**
Swygert, H. Patrick **22**
Tanksley, Ann **37**
Tatum, Beverly Daniel **42**
Taylor, Helen (Lavon Hollingshed)
 30
Taylor, Susie King **13**
Terrell, Mary Church **9**
Thomas, Alma **14**
Thurman, Howard **3**
Tillis, Frederick **40**
Tolson, Melvin **37**
Tribble, Israel, Jr. **8**
Trueheart, William E. **49**
Tucker, Rosina **14**
Turnbull, Walter **13**
Tutu, Desmond **6**
Tutu, Nontombi Naomi **57**
Tutuola, Amos **30**
Tyson, Andre **40**
Tyson, Asha **39**
Tyson, Neil de Grasse **15**
Usry, James L. **23**
van Sertima, Ivan **25**
Velez-Rodriguez, Argelia **56**
Wade-Gayles, Gloria Jean **41**
Walcott, Derek **5**
Walker, George **37**
Wallace, Michele Faith **13**
Wallace, Perry E. **47**
Wallace, Phyllis A. **9**

Bailey, DeFord **33**
Baiocchi, Regina Harris **41**
Baker, Anita **21**, **48**
Baker, Josephine **3**
Baker, LaVern **26**
Ballard, Hank **41**
Bambaataa, Afrika **34**
Banner, David **55**
Barker, Danny **32**
Barnes, Roosevelt "Booba" **33**
Barrino, Fantasia **53**
Basie, Count **23**
Bassey, Shirley **25**
Baylor, Helen **36**
Bebey, Francis **45**
Bechet, Sidney **18**
Beenie Man **32**
Belafonte, Harry **4**
Belle, Regina **1**, **51**
Benét, Eric **28**
Benjamin, Andre **45**
Bentley, Lamont **53**
Berry, Chuck **29**
Beverly, Frankie **25**
Bibb, Eric **49**
Blake, Eubie **29**
Blakey, Art **37**
Blanchard, Terence **43**
Bland, Bobby "Blue" **36**
Blige, Mary J. **20**, **34**
Blondy, Alpha **30**
Blow, Kurtis **31**
Bolden, Buddy **39**
Bond, Beverly **53**
Bonds, Margaret **39**
Bonga, Kuenda **13**
Brandy **14**, **34**
Braxton, Toni **15**
Bridgewater, Dee Dee **32**
Brooks, Avery **9**
Brooks, Hadda **40**
Brown, Angela M. **54**
Brown, Charles **23**
Brown, Foxy **25**
Brown, Oscar, Jr. **53**
Brown, Patrick "Sleepy" **50**
Brown, Uzee **42**
Bumbry, Grace **5**
Burke, Solomon **31**
Burleigh, Henry Thacker **56**
Burns, Eddie **44**
Burnside, R.L. **56**
Busby, Jheryl **3**
Butler, Jerry **26**
Butler, Jonathan **28**
Caesar, Shirley **19**
Cage, Byron **53**
Calloway, Cab **1**
Campbell Martin, Tisha **8**, **42**
Cannon, Nick **47**
Carey, Mariah **32**, **53**
Carr, Kurt **56**
Carr, Leroy **49**
Carroll, Diahann **9**
Cartíer, Xam Wilson **41**
Carter, Benny **46**
Carter, Betty **19**
Carter, Nell **39**
Carter, Regina **23**
Carter, Warrick L. **27**
Chanté, Keshia **50**
Chapman, Tracy **26**
Charlemagne, Manno **11**

Charles, Ray **16**, **48**
Cheatham, Doc **17**
Checker, Chubby **28**
Chenault, John **40**
Christie, Angella **36**
Chuck D **9**
Ciara **56**
Clarke, Kenny **27**
Clark-Sheard, Karen **22**
Clemons, Clarence **41**
Cleveland, James **19**
Cliff, Jimmy **28**
Clinton, George **9**
Cole, Nat King **17**
Cole, Natalie Maria **17**
Coleman, Ornette **39**
Collins, Albert **12**
Collins, Bootsy **31**
Collins, Lyn **53**
Coltrane, John **19**
Combs, Sean "Puffy" **17**, **43**
Common **31**
Cook, Charles "Doc" **44**
Cook, Will Marion **40**
Cooke, Sam **17**
Cortez, Jayne **43**
Count Basie **23**
Cowboy Troy **54**
Cox, Deborah **28**
Cox, Ida **42**
Craig, Carl **31**
Crawford, Randy **19**
Cray, Robert **30**
Creagh, Milton **27**
Crocker, Frankie **29**
Crothers, Scatman **19**
Crouch, Andraé **27**
Crouch, Stanley **11**
Crowder, Henry **16**
D'Angelo **27**
Dash, Damon **31**
Dash, Darien **29**
David, Craig **31**, **53**
Davis, Anthony **11**
Davis, Gary **41**
Davis, Guy **36**
Davis, Miles **4**
Davis, Sammy, Jr. **18**
Davis, Tyrone **54**
Dawson, William Levi **39**
de Passe, Suzanne **25**
Deezer D, **53**
Dennard, Brazeal **37**
Dickenson, Vic **38**
Diddley, Bo **39**
Dixon, Willie **4**
DJ Jazzy Jeff **32**
DMX **28**
Dobbs, Mattiwilda **34**
Donegan, Dorothy **19**
Dorsey, Thomas **15**
Downing, Will **19**
Dr. Dre **10**
Dre, Dr. **14**, **30**
Duke, George **21**
Dumas, Henry **41**
Dunner, Leslie B. **45**
Duplechan, Larry **55**
Dupri, Jermaine **13**, **46**
Dupri, Jermaine **13**
Dworkin, Aaron P. **52**
Earthquake, **55**
Eckstine, Billy **28**

Edmonds, Kenneth "Babyface" **10**, **31**
Edmonds, Tracey **16**
Edwards, Esther Gordy **43**
Eldridge, Roy **37**
Ellington, Duke **5**
Elliott, Missy "Misdemeanor" **31**
Escobar, Damien **56**
Escobar, Tourie **56**
Estes, Simon **28**
Estes, Sleepy John **33**
Eubanks, Kevin **15**
Europe, James Reese **10**
Evans, Faith **22**
Eve **29**
Evora, Cesaria **12**
Falana, Lola **42**
Farmer, Art **38**
Fats Domino **20**
Fela **1**, **42**
Ferrell, Rachelle **29**
Ferrer, Ibrahim **41**
50 Cent **46**
Fitzgerald, Ella **8**, **18**
Flack, Roberta **19**
Flash, Grandmaster **33**
Foster, George "Pops" **40**
Foxx, Jamie **15**, **48**
Franklin, Aretha **11**, **44**
Franklin, Kirk **15**, **49**
Freelon, Nnenna **32**
Freeman, Paul **39**
Freeman, Yvette **27**
Fuqua, Antoine **35**
Gaines, Grady **38**
Garrett, Sean **57**
Gaye, Marvin **2**
Gaye, Nona **56**
Gaynor, Gloria **36**
George, Zelma Watson **42**
Gibson, Althea **8**, **43**
Gil , Gilberto **53**
Gill, Johnny **51**
Gillespie, Dizzy **1**
Ginuwine **35**
Glover, Corey **34**
Goapele, **55**
Golson, Benny **37**
Gordon, Dexter **25**
Gordy, Berry, Jr. **1**
Gotti, Irv **39**
Grae, Jean **51**
Graves, Denyce Antoinette **19**, **57**
Gray, F. Gary **14**, **49**
Gray, Macy **29**
Greaves, William **38**
Greely, M. Gasby **27**
Green, Al **13**, **47**
Green, Grant **56**
Griffin, LaShell **51**
Griffiths, Marcia **29**
Guy, Buddy **31**
Haddon, Dietrick **55**
Hailey, JoJo **22**
Hailey, K-Ci **22**
Hall, Aaron **57**
Hammer, M. C. **20**
Hammond, Fred **23**
Hammond, Lenn **34**
Hampton, Lionel **17**, **41**
Hancock, Herbie **20**
Handy, W. C. **8**
Hardin Armstrong, Lil **39**

Harper, Ben **34**
Harrell, Andre **9**, **30**
Harris, Corey **39**
Hathaway, Donny **18**
Hathaway, Lalah **57**
Hawkins, Coleman **9**
Hawkins, Erskine **14**
Hawkins, Screamin' Jay **30**
Hawkins, Tramaine **16**
Hayes, Isaac **20**
Hayes, Roland **4**
Hayes, Teddy **40**
Hemphill, Jessie Mae **33**
Henderson, Fletcher **32**
Hendricks, Barbara **3**
Hendrix, Jimi **10**
Hendryx, Nona **56**
Henry, Clarence "Frogman" **46**
Higginbotham, J. C. **37**
Hill, Lauryn **20**, **53**
Hinderas, Natalie **5**
Hines, Earl "Fatha" **39**
Hinton, Milt **30**
Holiday, Billie **1**
Holland-Dozier-Holland **36**
Holmes, Clint **57**
Holt, Nora **38**
Hooker, John Lee **30**
Horn, Shirley **32**, **56**
Horne, Lena **5**
House, Son **8**
Houston, Cissy **20**
Houston, Whitney **7**, **28**
Howlin' Wolf **9**
Humphrey, Bobbi **20**
Hunter, Alberta **42**
Hyman, Phyllis **19**
Ice Cube **8**, **30**
Ice-T **6**, **31**
India.Arie **34**
Isley, Ronald **25**, **56**
Ja Rule **35**
Jackson, Fred James **25**
Jackson, George **19**
Jackson, Hal **41**
Jackson, Isaiah **3**
Jackson, Janet **6**, **30**
Jackson, John **36**
Jackson, Mahalia **5**
Jackson, Michael **19**, **53**
Jackson, Millie **25**
Jackson, Milt **26**
Jackson, Randy **40**
Jacquet, Illinois **49**
Jamelia **51**
James, Etta **13**, **52**
James, Rick **17**
James, Skip **38**
Jarreau, Al **21**
Jay-Z **27**
Jean, Wyclef **20**
Jean-Baptiste, Marianne **17**, **46**
Jenkins, Ella **15**
Jerkins, Rodney **31**
Jimmy Jam **13**
Johnson, Beverly **2**
Johnson, Buddy **36**
Johnson, J. J. **37**
Johnson, James Weldon **5**
Johnson, Johnnie **56**
Johnson, Robert **2**
Jones, Bobby **20**
Jones, Donell **29**

Watson, Johnny "Guitar" 18
Watts, Andre 42
Watts, Reggie 52
Webster, Katie 29
Welch, Elisabeth 52
Wells, Mary 28
West, Kanye 52
Whalum, Kirk 37
White, Barry 13, 41
White, Josh, Jr. 52
White, Maurice 29
White, Willard 53
Williams, Bert 18
Williams, Clarence 33
Williams, Deniece 36
Williams, Denise 40
Williams, Joe 5, 25
Williams, Mary Lou 15
Williams, Pharrell 47
Williams, Saul 31
Williams, Vanessa L. 4, 17
Wilson, Cassandra 16
Wilson, Charlie 31
Wilson, Gerald 49
Wilson, Mary 28
Wilson, Nancy 10
Wilson, Natalie 38
Wilson, Sunnie 7, 55
Winans, Angie 36
Winans, BeBe 14
Winans, CeCe 14, 43
Winans, Debbie 36
Winans, Marvin L. 17
Winans, Ronald 54
Winans, Vickie 24
Wonder, Stevie 11, 53
Woods , Scott 55
Woods, Georgie 57
Yarbrough, Camille 40
Yoba, Malik 11
York, Vincent 40
Young, Lester 37

Religion

Abernathy, Ralph David 1
Adams, Yolanda 17
Agyeman, Jaramogi Abebe 10
Al-Amin, Jamil Abdullah 6
Anthony, Wendell 25
Arinze, Francis Cardinal 19
Aristide, Jean-Bertrand 6, 45
Armstrong, Vanessa Bell 24
Austin, Junius C. 44
Banks, William 11
Baylor, Helen 36
Bell, Ralph S. 5
Ben-Israel, Ben Ami 11
Black, Barry C. 47
Boyd, T. B., III 6
Bryant, John R. 45
Burgess, John 46
Butts, Calvin O., III 9
Bynum, Juanita 31
Cage, Byron 53
Caldwell, Kirbyjon 55
Cardozo, Francis L. 33
Carr, Kurt 56
Caesar, Shirley 19
Cannon, Katie 10
Chavis, Benjamin 6
Cleaver, Emanuel 4, 45
Clements, George 2
Cleveland, James 19

Colemon, Johnnie 11
Collins, Janet 33
Cone, James H. 3
Cook, Suzan D. Johnson 22
Crouch, Andraé 27
DeLille, Henriette 30
Divine, Father 7
Dyson, Michael Eric 11, 40
Elmore, Ronn 21
Farrakhan, Louis 2, 15
Fauntroy, Walter E. 11
Flake, Floyd H. 18
Foreman, George 15
Franklin, Kirk 15, 49
Franklin, Robert M. 13
Gilmore, Marshall 46
Gomes, Peter J. 15
Gray, William H., III 3
Green, Al 13, 47
Gregory, Wilton 37
Grier, Roosevelt 13
Haddon, Dietrick 55
Haile Selassie 7
Harris, Barbara 12
Hawkins, Tramaine 16
Hayes, James C. 10
Healy, James Augustine 30
Hooks, Benjamin L. 2
Howard, M. William, Jr. 26
Jackson, Jesse 1, 27
Jakes, Thomas "T.D." 17, 43
Jemison, Major L. 48
Johns, Vernon 38
Jones, Absalom 52
Jones, Bobby 20
Jones, E. Edward, Sr. 45
Kelly, Leontine 33
King, Barbara 22
King, Bernice 4
King, Martin Luther, Jr. 1
Kobia, Rev. Dr. Samuel 43
Lester, Julius 9
Lewis-Thornton, Rae 32
Lincoln, C. Eric 38
Little Richard 15
Long, Eddie L. 29
Lowery, Joseph 2
Lyons, Henry 12
Majors, Jeff 41
Marino, Eugene Antonio 30
Mays, Benjamin E. 7
McClurkin, Donnie 25
McKenzie, Vashti M. 29
Muhammad, Ava 31
Muhammad, Elijah 4
Muhammad, Khallid Abdul 10, 31
Muhammed, W. Deen 27
Murray, Cecil 12, 47
Otunga, Maurice Michael 55
Patterson, Gilbert Earl 41
Pierre, Andre 17
Powell, Adam Clayton, Jr. 3
Price, Frederick K.C. 21
Reems, Ernestine Cleveland 27
Reese, Della 6, 20
Riley, Helen Caldwell Day 13
Rugambwa, Laurean 20
Scott, George 1929-2005 55
Shabazz, Betty 7, 26
Sharpton, Al 21
Shaw, William J. 30
Shuttlesworth, Fred 47
Slocumb, Jonathan 52

Somé, Malidoma Patrice 10
Stallings, George A., Jr. 6
Stampley, Micah 54
Steinberg, Martha Jean "The Queen" 28
Sullivan, Leon H. 3, 30
Tillard, Conrad 47
Thurman, Howard 3
Tonex, 54
Turner, Henry McNeal 5
Tutu, Desmond (Mpilo) 6, 44
Vanzant, Iyanla 17, 47
Waddles, Charleszetta "Mother" 10, 49
Walker, Hezekiah 34
Walker, John T. 50
Washington, James Melvin 50
Waters, Ethel 7
Weems, Renita J. 44
West, Cornel 5, 33
White, Reggie 6, 50
Williams, Hosea Lorenzo 15, 31
Wilson, Natalie 38
Winans, BeBe 14
Winans, CeCe 14, 43
Winans, Marvin L. 17
Winans, Ronald 54
Wright, Jeremiah A., Jr. 45
Wright, Nathan, Jr. 56
Wyatt, Addie L. 56
X, Malcolm 1
Youngblood, Johnny Ray 8

Science and technology

Adkins, Rod 41
Adkins, Rutherford H. 21
Alexander, Archie Alphonso 14
Allen, Ethel D. 13
Anderson, Charles Edward 37
Anderson, Michael P. 40
Anderson, Norman B. 45
Anderson, William G(ilchrist), D.O. 57
Auguste, Donna 29
Auguste, Rose-Anne 13
Bacon-Bercey, June 38
Banda, Hastings Kamuzu 6, 54
Bath, Patricia E. 37
Benjamin, Regina 20
Benson, Angela 34
Black, Keith Lanier 18
Bluford, Guy 2, 35
Bluitt, Juliann S. 14
Bolden, Charles F., Jr. 7
Brown, Vivian 27
Brown, Willa 40
Bullard, Eugene 12
Callender, Clive O. 3
Canady, Alexa 28
Cargill, Victoria A. 43
Carroll, L. Natalie 44
Carruthers, George R. 40
Carson, Benjamin 1, 35
Carter, Joye Maureen 41
Carver, George Washington 4
CasSelle, Malcolm 11
Chatard, Peter 44
Chinn, May Edward 26
Christian, Spencer 15
Cobb, W. Montague 39
Cobbs, Price M. 9
Cole, Rebecca 38
Coleman, Bessie 9

Coleman, Ken 57
Comer, James P. 6
Coney, PonJola 48
Cooper, Edward S. 6
Daly, Marie Maynard 37
Davis, Allison 12
Dean, Mark 35
Deconge-Watson, Lovenia 55
Delany, Bessie 12
Delany, Martin R. 27
Dickens, Helen Octavia 14
Diop, Cheikh Anta 4
Drew, Charles Richard 7
Dunham, Katherine 4
Dunston, Georgia Mae 48
Elders, Joycelyn 6
Ellington, E. David 11
Ellis, Clarence A. 38
Emeagwali, Dale 31
Emeagwali, Philip 30
Ericsson-Jackson, Aprille 28
Fields, Evelyn J. 27
Fisher, Rudolph 17
Flipper, Henry O. 3
Flowers, Sylester 50
Foster, Henry W., Jr. 26
Freeman, Harold P. 23
Fulani, Lenora 11
Fuller, A. Oveta 43
Fuller, Arthur 27
Fuller, Solomon Carter, Jr. 15
Gates, Sylvester James, Jr. 15
Gayle, Helene D. 3, 46
Gibson, Kenneth Allen 6
Gibson, William F. 6
Gourdine, Meredith 33
Granville, Evelyn Boyd 36
Gray, Ida 41
Gregory, Frederick 8, 51
Griffin, Bessie Blout 43
Hall, Lloyd A. 8
Hannah, Marc 10
Harris, Mary Styles 31
Henderson, Cornelius Langston 26
Henson, Matthew 2
Hinton, William Augustus 8
Hutcherson, Hilda Yvonne 54
Imes, Elmer Samuel 39
Irving, Larry, Jr. 12
Jackson, Shirley Ann 12
Jawara, Sir Dawda Kairaba 11
Jemison, Mae C. 1, 35
Jenifer, Franklyn G. 2
Johnson, Eddie Bernice 8
Johnson, Lonnie G. 32
Jones, Randy 35
Jones, Wayne 53
Joseph, Kathie-Ann 56
Julian, Percy Lavon 6
Juma, Dr. Calestous 57
Just, Ernest Everett 3
Kenney, John A., Jr. 48
Kittles, Rick 51
Knowling, Robert E., Jr. 38
Kong, B. Waine 50
Kountz, Samuel L. 10
Latimer, Lewis H. 4
Lavizzo-Mourey, Risa 48
Lawless, Theodore K. 8
Lawrence, Robert H., Jr. 16
Leevy, Carrol M. 42
Leffall, LaSalle, Jr. 3
Lewis, Delano 7

Cumulative Subject Index

Volume numbers appear in **bold**

Iman **4, 33**
Ingram, Rex **5**
Ja Rule **35**
Jackson, Janet **6, 30**
Jackson, Michael **19, 53**
Jackson, Millie **25**
Jackson, Samuel L. **8, 19**
Jean-Baptiste, Marianne **17, 46**
Johnson, Dwayne "The Rock" **29**
Johnson, Rafer **33**
Johnson, Rodney Van **28**
Jones, James Earl **3, 49**
Jones, Orlando **30**
Kennedy-Overton, Jayne Harris **46**
Khumalo, Leleti **51**
King, Regina **22, 45**
King, Woodie, Jr. **27**
Kirby, George **14**
Kitt, Eartha **16**
Knight, Gladys **16**
Knowles, Beyoncé **39**
Kodhoe, Boris **34**
Kotto, Yaphet **7**
L. L. Cool J., **16, 49**
LaBelle, Patti **13, 30**
La Salle, Eriq **12**
Lampley, Oni Faida **43**
Lane, Charles **3**
Lassiter, Roy **24**
Lathan, Sanaa **27**
Lawrence, Martin **6, 27**
Lee, Canada **8**
Lee, Joie **1**
Lee, Spike **5, 19**
Lemmons, Kasi **20**
LeNoire, Rosetta **37**
Lester, Adrian **46**
Lewis, Emmanuel **36**
(Lil') Bow Wow **35**
Lil' Kim **28**
Lincoln, Abbey **3**
Lindo, Delroy **18, 45**
LisaRaye **27**
Love, Darlene **23**
Lumbly, Carl **47**
Mabley, Jackie "Moms" **15**
Mac, Bernie **29**
Marrow, Queen Esther **24**
Martin, Helen **31**
Martin, Jesse L. **31**
Master P **21**
Mayo, Whitman **32**
McDaniel, Hattie **5**
McDonald, Audra **20**
Mckee, Lonette **12**
McKinney, Nina Mae **40**
McQueen, Butterfly **6, 54**
Meadows, Tim **30**
Merkerson, S. Epatha **47**
Michele, Michael **31**
Mitchell, Brian Stokes **21**
Mo'Nique **35**
Moore, Chante **26**
Moore, Melba **21**
Moore, Shemar **21**
Morris, Garrett **31**
Morris, Greg **28**
Morton, Joe **18**
Mos Def **30**
Moten, Etta **18**
Murphy, Eddie **4, 20**
Muse, Clarence Edouard **21**
Nash, Johnny **40**

Neal, Elise **29**
Newton, Thandie **26**
Nicholas, Fayard **20, 57**
Nicholas, Harold **20**
Nichols, Nichelle **11**
Norman, Maidie **20**
Notorious B.I.G. **20**
Ntshona, Winston **52**
O'Neal, Ron **46**
Orlandersmith, Dael **42**
Orman, Roscoe **55**
Parker, Nicole Ari **52**
Payne, Allen **13**
Peete, Holly Robinson **20**
Perrineau, Harold, Jr. **51**
Perry, Tyler **40, 54**
Phifer, Mekhi **25**
Pinkett Smith, Jada **10, 41**
Poitier, Sidney **11, 36**
Pratt, Kyla **57**
Premice, Josephine **41**
Prince **18**
Pryor, Richard **3, 24, 56**
Queen Latifah **1, 16**
Randle, Theresa **16**
Rashad, Phylicia **21**
Raven, **44**
Ray, Gene Anthony **47**
Reddick, Lance **52**
Reese, Della **6, 20**
Reid, Tim **56**
Reuben, Gloria **15**
Rhames, Ving **14, 50**
Rhymes, Busta **31**
Ribeiro, Alfonso **17**
Richards, Beah **30**
Richards, Lloyd **2**
Robeson, Paul **2**
Robinson, Shaun **36**
Rock, Chris **3, 22**
Rodgers, Rod **36**
Rolle, Esther **13, 21**
Ross, Diana **8, 27**
Ross, Tracee Ellis **35**
Roundtree, Richard **27**
Rowell, Victoria **13**
Rudolph, Maya **46**
Shakur, Tupac **14**
Simmons, Henry **55**
Sinbad **1, 16**
Sisqo **30**
Smith, Anjela Lauren **44**
Smith, Anna Deavere **6, 44**
Smith, Barbara **11**
Smith, Roger Guenveur **12**
Smith, Will **8, 18, 53**
Snipes, Wesley **3, 24**
Snoop Dogg **35**
St. Jacques, Raymond **8**
St. John, Kristoff **25**
St. Patrick, Mathew **48**
Tamia **24, 55**
Tate, Larenz **15**
Taylor, Meshach **4**
Taylor, Regina **9, 46**
Taylor, Ron **35**
Thomas, Sean Patrick **35**
Thomason, Marsha **47**
Thompson, Kenan **52**
Thompson, Tazewell **13**
Torres, Gina **52**
Torry, Guy **31**
Toussaint, Lorraine **32**

Townsend, Robert **4, 23**
Tucker, Chris **13, 23**
Turner, Tina **6, 27**
Tyler, Aisha N. **36**
Tyrese **27**
Tyson, Cicely **7, 51**
Uggams, Leslie **23**
Underwood, Blair **7, 27**
Union, Gabrielle **31**
Usher **23, 56**
Van Peebles, Mario **2, 51**
Van Peebles, Melvin **7**
Vance, Courtney B. **15**
Vereen, Ben **4**
Walker, Eamonn **37**
Ward, Douglas Turner **42**
Warfield, Marsha **2**
Warner, Malcolm-Jamal **22, 36**
Warren, Michael **27**
Washington, Denzel **1, 16**
Washington, Fredi **10**
Washington, Kerry **46**
Waters, Ethel **7**
Wayans, Damon **8, 41**
Wayans, Keenen Ivory **18**
Wayans, Marlon **29**
Wayans, Shawn **29**
Weathers, Carl **10**
Webb, Veronica **10**
Whitaker, Forest **2, 49**
Whitfield, Lynn **18**
Williams, Bert **18**
Williams, Billy Dee **8**
Williams, Clarence, III **26**
Wilson, Chandra **57**
Wilson, Dorien **55**
Williams, Joe **5, 25**
Williams, Malinda **57**
Williams, Samm-Art **21**
Williams, Saul **31**
Williams, Vanessa **32**
Williams, Vanessa L. **4, 17**
Williamson, Mykelti **22**
Wilson, Debra **38**
Wilson, Flip **21**
Winfield, Paul **2, 45**
Winfrey, Oprah **2, 15**
Witherspoon, John **38**
Woodard, Alfre **9**
Wright, Jeffrey **54**
Yarbrough, Cedric **51**
Yoba, Malik **11**

Active Ministers Engaged in Nurturance (AMEN)
King, Bernice **4**

Actors Equity Association
Lewis, Emmanuel **36**

Actuarial science
Hill, Jessie, Jr. **13**

ACT UP
See AIDS Coalition to Unleash Power

Acustar, Inc.
Farmer, Forest **1**

ADC
See Agricultural Development Council

Addiction Research and Treatment Corporation
Cooper, Andrew W. **36**

Adoption and foster care
Baker, Josephine **3**
Clements, George **2**
Gossett, Louis, Jr. **7**
Hale, Clara **16**
Hale, Lorraine **8**
Oglesby, Zena **12**

Adventures in Movement (AIM)
Morgan, Joe Leonard **9**

Advertising
Barboza, Anthony **10**
Burrell, Tom **21, 51**
Campbell, E. Simms **13**
Chisholm, Samuel J. **32**
Coleman, Donald A. **24**
Cullers, Vincent T. **49**
Johnson, Beverly **2**
Jones, Caroline R. **29**
Jordan, Montell **23**
Lewis, Byron E. **13**
McKinney Hammond, Michelle **51**
Mingo, Frank **32**
Olden, Georg(e) **44**
Pinderhughes, John **47**
Roche, Joyce M. **17**

Advocates Scene
Seale, Bobby **3**

Aetna
Williams, Ronald A. **57**

AFCEA
See Armed Forces Communications and Electronics Associations

Affirmative action
Arnwine, Barbara **28**
Berry, Mary Frances **7**
Carter, Stephen L. **4**
Edley, Christopher F., Jr. **48**
Higginbotham, A. Leon Jr. **13, 25**
Maynard, Robert C. **7**
Norton, Eleanor Holmes **7**
Rand, A. Barry **6**
Thompson, Bennie G. **26**
Waters, Maxine **3**

AFL-CIO
See American Federation of Labor and Congress of Industrial Organizations

African/African-American Summit
Sullivan, Leon H. **3, 30**

African American Catholic Congregation
Stallings, George A., Jr. **6**

African American Dance Ensemble
Davis, Chuck **33**

African American folklore
Bailey, Xenobia **11**
Brown, Sterling **10**
Driskell, David C. **7**
Ellison, Ralph **7**

Dungy, Tony **17**, **42**
Fowler, Reggie **51**
Gilliam, Frank **23**
Green, Dennis **5**, **45**
Moon, Warren **8**
Moss, Randy **23**
Page, Alan **7**
Rashad, Ahmad **18**
Stringer, Korey **35**
Walker, Herschel **1**

Minority Business Enterprise Legal Defense and Education Fund
Mitchell, Parren J. **42**

Minority Business Resource Center
Hill, Jessie, Jr. **13**

Minority Enterprise Small Business Investment Corporations (MESBICs)
Lewis, Reginald F. **6**

Minstrel shows
McDaniel, Hattie **5**

Miracle Network Telethon
Warner, Malcolm-Jamal **22**, **36**

Miss America
Dunlap, Ericka **55**
Harold, Erika **54**
Vincent, Marjorie Judith **2**
Williams, Vanessa L. **4**, **17**

Miss Collegiate African-American Pageant
Mercado-Valdes, Frank **43**

Miss USA
Gist, Carole **1**

Miss World
Darego, Agbani **52**

Mississippi Freedom Democratic Party (MFDP)
Baker, Ella **5**
Blackwell, Unita **17**
Hamer, Fannie Lou **6**
Henry, Aaron **19**
Norton, Eleanor Holmes **7**

Mississippi state government
Hamer, Fannie Lou **6**

MLA
See Modern Language Association of America

Model Inner City Community Organization (MICCO)
Fauntroy, Walter E. **11**

Modeling
Allen-Buillard, Melba **55**
Banks, Tyra **11**, **50**
Beckford, Tyson **11**
Berry, Halle **4**, **19**, **57**
Campbell, Naomi **1**, **31**
Darego, Agbani **52**
Dirie, Waris **56**
Hardison, Bethann **12**
Hounsou, Djimon **19**, **45**
Houston, Whitney **7**, **28**

Iman **4**, **33**
Johnson, Beverly **2**
Kodjoe, Boris **34**
Langhart, Janet **19**
Leslie, Lisa **16**
LisaRaye **27**
Michele, Michael **31**
Onwurah, Ngozi **38**
Powell, Maxine **8**
Rochon, Lela **16**
Simmons, Kimora Lee **51**
Sims, Naomi **29**
Smith, Barbara **11**
Tamia **24**, **55**
Taylor, Karin **34**
Tyrese **27**
Tyson, Cicely **7**, **51**
Watley, Jody **54**
Webb, Veronica **10**
Wek, Alek **18**

Modern dance
Ailey, Alvin **8**
Allen, Debbie **13**, **42**
Byrd, Donald **10**
Collins, Janet **33**
Davis, Chuck **33**
Dove, Ulysses **5**
Fagan, Garth **18**
Faison, George **16**
Henson, Darrin **33**
Jamison, Judith **7**
Jones, Bill T. **1**, **46**
King, Alonzo **38**
Kitt, Eartha **16**
Miller, Bebe **3**
Primus, Pearl **6**
Spears, Warren **52**
Vereen, Ben **4**

Modern Language Association of America (MLA)
Baker, Houston A., Jr. **6**

Modern Records
Brooks, Hadda **40**

Monoprinting
Honeywood, Varnette P. **54**

Montgomery bus boycott
Abernathy, Ralph David **1**
Baker, Ella **5**
Burks, Mary Fair **40**
Jackson, Mahalia **5**
Killens, John O. **54**
King, Martin Luther, Jr. **1**
Parks, Rosa **1**, **35**, **56**
Rustin, Bayard **4**

Montgomery County Police Department
Moose, Charles **40**

Montreal Canadians hockey team
Brashear, Donald **39**

Montreal Expos baseball team
Doby, Lawrence Eugene Sr. **16**, **41**

Moore Black Press
Moore, Jessica Care **30**

Morehouse College
Brown, Uzee **42**
Hope, John **8**

Mays, Benjamin E. **7**

Morgan Stanley
Lewis, William M., Jr. **40**

Morna
Evora, Cesaria **12**

Morris Brown College
Cross, Dolores E. **23**

Moscow World News
Khanga, Yelena **6**
Sullivan, Louis **8**

Mother Waddles Perpetual Mission, Inc.
Waddles, Charleszetta "Mother" **10**, **49**

Motivational speaking
Brown, Les **5**
Bunkley, Anita Richmond **39**
Creagh, Milton **27**
Grant, Gwendolyn Goldsby **28**
Jolley, Willie **28**
July, William **27**
Kimbro, Dennis **10**
Russell-McCloud, Patricia **17**
Tyson, Asha **39**

Motor City Giants baseball team
Kaiser, Cecil **42**

Motorcyle racing
Showers, Reggie **30**

Motwon Historical Museum
Edwards, Esther Gordy **43**

Motown Records
Atkins, Cholly **40**
Bizimungu, Pasteur **19**
Busby, Jheryl **3**
de Passe, Suzanne **25**
Edwards, Esther Gordy **43**
Gaye, Marvin **2**
Gordy, Berry, Jr. **1**
Harrell, Andre **9**, **30**
Holland-Dozier-Holland **36**
Jackson, George **19**
Jackson, Michael **19**, **53**
Kendricks, Eddie **22**
Massenburg, Kedar **23**
Powell, Maxine **8**
Richie, Lionel **27**
Robinson, Smokey **3**, **49**
Ross, Diana **8**, **27**
Terrell, Tammi **32**
Wells, Mary **28**
Wilson, Mary **28**
Wonder, Stevie **11**, **53**

Mt. Holyoke College
Tatum, Beverly Daniel **42**

Mouvement Revolutionnaire National pour la Developpement (Rwanda; MRND)
Habyarimana, Juvenal **8**

MOVE
Goode, W. Wilson **4**
Wideman, John Edgar **5**

Movement for Assemblies of the People
Bishop, Maurice **39**

Movement for Democratic Change (MDC)
Tsvangirai, Morgan **26**

Movement for the Survival of the Ogoni People
Saro-Wiwa, Kenule **39**

Moviement Popular de Libertação de Angola (MPLA)
dos Santos, José Eduardo **43**
Neto, António Agostinho **43**

MPLA
See Moviement Popular de Libertação de Angola

MPS
See Patriotic Movement of Salvation

MRND
See Mouvement Revolutionnaire National pour la Developpement

MTV Jams
Bellamy, Bill **12**

Muddy Waters
Little Walter **36**

Multimedia art
Bailey, Xenobia **11**
Robinson, Aminah **50**
Simpson, Lorna **4**, **36**

Multiple Sclerosis
Falana, Lola **42**

Muppets, The
Clash, Kevin **14**

Murals
Alston, Charles **33**
Biggers, John **20**, **33**
Douglas, Aaron **7**
Lee-Smith, Hughie **5**
Walker, Kara **16**

Murder Inc.
Ashanti **37**
Gotti, Irv **39**
Ja Rule **35**

Museum of Modern Art
Pindell, Howardena **55**

Music Critics Circle
Holt, Nora **38**

Music One, Inc.
Majors, Jeff **41**

Music publishing
Combs, Sean "Puffy" **17**, **43**
Cooke, Sam **17**
Edmonds, Tracey **16**
Gordy, Berry, Jr. **1**
Handy, W. C. **8**
Holland-Dozier-Holland **36**
Humphrey, Bobbi **20**
Ice Cube **8**, **30**
Jackson, George **19**
Jackson, Michael **19**, **53**

Ruff Ryders Records
Eve 29

Rugby
Mundine, Anthony 56

Rush Artists Management Co.
Simmons, Russell 1, 30

Russell-McCloud and Associates
Russell-McCloud, Patricia A. 17

Rutgers University
Davis, George 36
Gibson, Donald Bernard 40

Rwandan Government
Kagame, Paul 54

Rwandese Patriotic Front
Kagame, Paul 54

SAA
See Syndicat Agricole Africain

SACC
See South African Council of Churches

Sacramento Kings basketball team
Russell, Bill 8
Webber, Chris 15, 30

Sacramento Monarchs basketball team
Griffith, Yolanda 25

SADCC
See Southern African Development Coordination Conference

Sailing
Pinckney, Bill 42

St. Kitts and Nevis government
Douglas, Denzil Llewellyn 53

St. Louis Browns baseball team
Brown, Willard 36

St. Louis Blues hockey team
Brathwaite, Fred 35
Mayers, Jamal 39

St. Louis Browns baseball team
Paige, Satchel 7

St. Louis Cardinals baseball team
Baylor, Don 6
Bonds, Bobby 43
Brock, Lou 18
Flood, Curt 10
Gibson, Bob 33
Lankford, Ray 23

St. Louis city government
Bosley, Freeman, Jr. 7
Harmon, Clarence 26

St. Louis Giants baseball team
Charleston, Oscar 39

St. Louis Hawks basketball team
See Atlanta Hawks basketball team

St. Louis Rams football team
Bruce, Isaac 26
Faulk, Marshall 35
Pace, Orlando 21

St. Louis Stars baseball team
Bell, James "Cool Papa" 36

Sainte Beuve Prize
Beti, Mongo 36

SAMM
See Stopping AIDS Is My Mission

Sammy Davis Jr. National Liver Institute University Hospital
Leevy, Carrol M. 42

San Antonio Spurs basketball team
Duncan, Tim 20
Elliott, Sean 26
Lucas, John 7
Robinson, David 24

San Diego Chargers football team
Barnes, Ernie 16
Lofton, James 42

San Diego Conquistadors
Chamberlain, Wilt 18, 47

San Diego Gulls hockey team
O'Ree, Willie 5

San Diego Hawks hockey team
O'Ree, Willie 5

San Diego Padres baseball team
Carter, Joe 30
Gwynn, Tony 18
McGriff, Fred 24
Sheffield, Gary 16
Winfield, Dave 5

San Francisco 49ers football team
Edwards, Harry 2
Green, Dennis 5, 45
Lott, Ronnie 9
Rice, Jerry 5, 55
Simpson, O. J. 15

San Francisco Giants baseball team
Baker, Dusty 8
Bonds, Barry 6, 34
Bonds, Bobby 43
Carter, Joe 30
Mays, Willie 3
Morgan, Joe Leonard 9
Robinson, Frank 9
Strawberry, Darryl 22

San Francisco Opera
Mitchell, Leona 42

Sankofa Film and Video
Blackwood, Maureen 37
Julien, Isaac 3

Sankofa Video and Bookstore
Gerima, Haile 38

Saturday Night Live
Meadows, Tim 30
Morris, Garrett 31
Murphy, Eddie 4, 20
Rock, Chris 3, 22
Rudolph, Maya 46
Thompson, Kenan 52

Savoy Ballroom
Johnson, Buddy 36

Saxophone
Adderley, Julian "Cannonball" 30
Albright, Gerald 23
Bechet, Sidney 18
Clemons, Clarence 41
Coltrane, John 19
Golson, Benny 37
Gordon, Dexter 25
Hawkins, Coleman 9
Jacquet, Illinois 49
Kay, Ulysses 37
Kenyatta, Robin 54
Parker, Charlie 20
Redman, Joshua 30
Rollins, Sonny 37
Washington, Grover, Jr. 17, 44
Waters, Benny 26
Whalum, Kirk 37
York, Vincent 40
Young, Lester 37

Schomburg Center for Research in Black Culture
Andrews, Bert 13
Dodson, Howard, Jr. 7, 52
Hutson, Jean Blackwell 16
Morrison, Sam 50
Reddick, Lawrence Dunbar 20
Schomburg, Arthur Alfonso 9

School desegregation
Fortune, T. Thomas 6
Hamer, Fannie Lou 6
Hobson, Julius W. 44

Scotland Yard
Griffin, Bessie Blout 43

Science fiction
Barnes, Steven 54
Bell, Derrick 6
Butler, Octavia 8, 43
Delany, Samuel R., Jr. 9

SCLC
See Southern Christian Leadership Conference

Score One for Kids
Cherry, Deron 40

Screen Actors Guild
Fields, Kim 36
Howard, Sherri 36
Lewis, Emmanuel 36

Poitier, Sidney 11, 36

Screenplay writing
Brown, Cecil M. 46
Campbell-Martin, Tisha 8, 42
Elder, Lonne III 38
Fisher, Antwone 40
Greaves, William 38
Ice Cube 8, 30
Jones, Orlando 30
Martin, Darnell 43
Nissel, Angela 42
Prince-Bythewood, Gina 31
Singleton, John 2, 30

Sculpture
Allen, Tina 22
Bailey, Radcliffe 19
Barthe, Richmond 15
Biggers, John 20, 33
Brown, Donald 19
Burke, Selma 16
Catlett, Elizabeth 2
Chase-Riboud, Barbara 20, 46
Cortor, Eldzier 42
Edwards, Melvin 22
Fuller, Meta Vaux Warrick 27
Guyton, Tyree 9
Hathaway, Isaac Scott 33
Hunt, Richard 6
Lewis, Edmonia 10
Lewis, Samella 25
Manley, Edna 26
McGee, Charles 10
Moody, Ronald 30
Perkins, Marion 38
Prophet, Nancy Elizabeth 42
Puryear, Martin 42
Ringgold, Faith 4
Saar, Alison 16
Savage, Augusta 12
Shabazz, Attallah 6
Washington, James Jr. 38

Sean John clothing line
Combs, Sean "Puffy" 17, 43

Seattle city government
Rice, Norm 8

Seattle Mariners baseball team
Griffey, Ken, Jr. 12

Seattle Supersonics basketball team
Bickerstaff, Bernie 21
Lucas, John 7
Russell, Bill 8
Silas, Paul 24
Wilkens, Lenny 11

Second District Education and Policy Foundation
Burke, Yvonne Braithwaite 42

Second Republic (Nigeria)
Obasanjo, Olusegun 5

Seismology
Person, Waverly 9, 51

Selma, Alabama, city government
Perkins, James, Jr. 55

Cumulative Name Index

Volume numbers appear in **bold**

Washington, Alonzo 1967— **29**
Washington, Booker T(aliaferro) 1856-1915 **4**
Washington, Denzel 1954— **1, 16**
Washington, Dinah 1924-1963 **22**
Washington, Fred(er)i(cka Carolyn) 1903-1994 **10**
Washington, Grover, Jr. 1943-1999 **17, 44**
Washington, Harold 1922-1987 **6**
Washington, James Jr. 1909(?)-2000 **38**
Washington, James Melvin 1948-1997 **50**
Washington, Kenny 1918-1971 **50**
Washington, Kerry 1977— **46**
Washington, Laura S. 1956(?)— **18**
Washington, MaliVai 1969— **8**
Washington, Mary T. 1906-2005 **57**
Washington, Patrice Clarke 1961— **12**
Washington, Regynald G. 1954(?)— **44**
Washington, Tamia Reneé *See Tamia*
Washington, Valores James 1903-1995 **12**
Washington, Walter 1915-2003 **45**
Wasow, Omar 1970— **15**
Waters, Benny 1902-1998 **26**
Waters, Ethel 1895-1977 **7**
Waters, Maxine 1938— **3**
Waters, Muddy 1915-1983 **34**
Watkins, Donald 1948— **35**
Watkins, Frances Ellen *See Harper, Frances Ellen Watkins*
Watkins, Gloria Jean *See hooks, bell*
Watkins, Levi, Jr. 1945— **9**
Watkins, Perry James Henry 1948-1996 **12**
Watkins, Shirley R. 1938— **17**
Watkins, Tionne "T-Boz" 1970— *See TLC*
Watkins, Walter C. 1946— **24**
Watley, Jody 1959— **54**
Watson, Bob 1946— **25**
Watson, Carlos 1970— **50**
Watson, Diane 1933— **41**
Watson, Johnny "Guitar" 1935-1996 **18**
Watt, Melvin 1945— **26**
Wattleton, (Alyce) Faye 1943— **9**
Watts, Andre 1946— **42**
Watts, Julius Caesar, Jr. 1957— **14, 38**
Watts, Reggie 1972(?)— **52**
Watts, Rolonda 1959— **9**
Wayans, Damon 1961— **8, 41**
Wayans, Keenen Ivory 1958— **18**
Wayans, Marlon 1972— **29**
Wayans, Shawn 1971— **29**
Waymon, Eunice Kathleen *See Simone, Nina*
Weathers, Carl 1948— **10**
Weaver, Afaa Michael 1951— **37**
Weaver, Michael S. *See Weaver, Afaa Michael*
Weaver, Robert C. 1907-1997 **8, 46**
Webb, Veronica 1965— **10**
Webb, Wellington, Jr. 1941— **3**
Webber, Chris 1973— **15, 30**
Webster, Katie 1936-1999 **29**
Wedgeworth, Robert W. 1937— **42**

Weems, Renita J. 1954— **44**
Wek, Alek 1977— **18**
Welburn, Edward T. 1950-— **50**
Welch, Elisabeth 1908-2003 **52**
Wells, James Lesesne 1902-1993 **10**
Wells, Mary 1943-1992 **28**
Wells-Barnett, Ida B(ell) 1862-1931 **8**
Welsing, Frances (Luella) Cress 1935— **5**
Wesley, Valerie Wilson 194(?)— **18**
West, Cornel (Ronald) 1953— **5, 33**
West, Dorothy 1907-1998 **12, 54**
West, Kanye 1977— **52**
West, Togo Dennis, Jr. 1942— **16**
Westbrook, Kelvin 1955-— **50**
Westbrook, Peter 1952— **20**
Westbrooks, Bobby 1930(?)-1995 **51**
Whack, Rita Coburn 1958— **36**
Whalum, Kirk 1958— **37**
Wharton, Clifton R(eginald), Jr. 1926— **7**
Wharton, Clifton Reginald, Sr. 1899-1990 **36**
Wheat, Alan Dupree 1951— **14**
Whitaker, "Sweet Pea" *See Whitaker, Pernell*
Whitaker, Forest 1961— **2, 49**
Whitaker, Mark 1957— **21, 47**
Whitaker, Pernell 1964— **10**
White, (Donald) Dondi 1961-1998 **34**
White, Barry 1944-2003 **13, 41**
White, Bill 1933(?)— **1, 48**
White, Charles 1918-1979 **39**
White, Jesse 1934— **22**
White, John H. 1945— **27**
White, Josh, Jr. 1940— **52**
White, Linda M. 1942— **45**
White, Lois Jean 1938— **20**
White, Maurice 1941— **29**
White, Michael R(eed) 1951— **5**
White, Reggie 1961-2004 **6, 50**
White, Reginald Howard *See White, Reggie*
White, Walter F(rancis) 1893-1955 **4**
White, Willard 1946— **53**
White, William DeKova *See White, Bill*
Whitfield, Fred 1967— **23**
Whitfield, Lynn 1954— **18**
Whitfield, Van 1960(?)— **34**
Wideman, John Edgar 1941— **5**
Wiley, Ralph 1952— **8**
Wilder, L. Douglas 1931— **3, 48**
Wilkens, J. Ernest, Jr. 1923— **43**
Wilkens, Lenny 1937— **11**
Wilkens, Leonard Randolph *See Wilkens, Lenny*
Wilkins, Ray 1951— **47**
Wilkins, Roger (Wood) 1932— **2**
Wilkins, Roy 1901-1981 **4**
Williams, Anthony 1951— **21**
Williams, Anthony Charles *See Tonex*
Williams, Armstrong 1959— **29**
Williams, Bert 1874-1922 **18**
Williams, Billy Dee 1937— **8**
Williams, Carl *See Kani, Karl*
Williams, Clarence 1893(?)-1965 **33**

Williams, Clarence, III 1939— **26**
Williams, Daniel Hale (III) 1856-1931 **2**
Williams, David Rudyard 1954-— **50**
Williams, Deniece 1951— **36**
Williams, Denise 1958— **40**
Williams, Doug 1955— **22**
Williams, Eddie N. 1932— **44**
Williams, Evelyn 1922(?)— **10**
Williams, Fannie Barrier 1855-1944 **27**
Williams, George Washington 1849-1891 **18**
Williams, Gregory (Howard) 1943— **11**
Williams, Hosea Lorenzo 1926— **15, 31**
Williams, Joe 1918-1999 **5, 25**
Williams, John A. 1925— **27**
Williams, Juan 1954— **35**
Williams, Maggie 1954— **7**
Williams, Malinda 1975— **57**
Williams, Marco 1956— **53**
Williams, Margaret Ann *See Williams, Maggie*
Williams, Mary Lou 1910-1981 **15**
Williams, Montel 1956— **4, 57**
Williams, Natalie 1970— **31**
Williams, O(swald) S. 1921— **13**
Williams, Patricia 1951— **11, 54**
Williams, Paul R(evere) 1894-1980 **9**
Williams, Paulette Linda *See Shange, Ntozake*
Williams, Pharrell 1973— **47**
Williams, Robert F(ranklin) 1925— **11**
Williams, Robert Peter *See Guillaume, Robert*
Williams, Ronald A. 1949— **57**
Williams, Samuel Arthur 1946— **21**
Williams, Saul 1972— **31**
Williams, Serena 1981— **20, 41**
Williams, Sherley Anne 1944-1999 **25**
Williams, Stanley "Tookie" 1953-2005 **29, 57**
Williams, Terrie M. 1954— **35**
Williams, Vanessa 1969— **32**
Williams, Vanessa L. 1963— **4, 17**
Williams, Venus Ebone Starr 1980— **17, 34**
Williams, Walter E(dward) 1936— **4**
Williams, William December *See Williams, Billy Dee*
Williams, William T(homas) 1942— **11**
Williams, Willie L(awrence) 1943— **4**
Williamson, Lisa *See Sister Souljah*
Williamson, Mykelti 1957— **22**
Willingham, Tyrone 1953— **43**
Willis, Cheryl *See Hudson, Cheryl*
Willis, Dontrelle 1982— **55**
Wilson, August 1945-2005 **7, 33, 55**
Wilson, Cassandra 1955— **16**
Wilson, Chandra 1969— **57**
Wilson, Charlie 1953— **31**
Wilson, Debra 1970(?)— **38**
Wilson, Dorien 1962(?)— **55**
Wilson, Ellis 1899-1977 **39**
Wilson, Flip 1933-1998 **21**
Wilson, Gerald 1918— **49**

Wilson, Jimmy 1946— **45**
Wilson, Mary 1944 **28**
Wilson, Nancy 1937— **10**
Wilson, Natalie 1972(?)— **38**
Wilson, Phill 1956— **9**
Wilson, Sunnie 1908-1999 **7, 55**
Wilson, William Julius 1935— **22**
Wilson, William Nathaniel *See Wilson, Sunnie*
Winans, Angie 1968— **36**
Winans, Benjamin 1962— **14**
Winans, CeCe 1964— **14, 43**
Winans, Debbie 1972— **36**
Winans, Marvin L. 1958— **17**
Winans, Ronald 1956-2005 **54**
Winans, Vickie 1953(?)— **24**
Winfield, Dave 1951— **5**
Winfield, David Mark *See Winfield, Dave*
Winfield, Paul (Edward) 1941-2004 **2, 45**
Winfrey, Oprah (Gail) 1954— **2, 15**
Winkfield, Jimmy 1882-1974 **42**
Wisdom, Dr. Kimberlydawn 1956— **57**
Witherspoon, John 1942— **38**
Witt, Edwin T. 1920— **26**
Wofford, Chloe Anthony *See Morrison, Toni*
Wolfe, George C. 1954— **6, 43**
Wonder, Stevie 1950— **11, 53**
Woodard, Alfre 1953— **9**
Woodruff, Hale (Aspacio) 1900-1980 **9**
Woods , Scott 1971— **55**
Woods, Eldrick *See Woods, Tiger*
Woods, Georgie 1927-2005 **57**
Woods, Granville T. 1856-1910 **5**
Woods, Jacqueline 1962— **52**
Woods, Sylvia 1926— **34**
Woods, Tiger 1975— **14, 31**
Woodson, Carter G(odwin) 1875-1950 **2**
Woodson, Robert L. 1937— **10**
Wooldridge, Anna Marie *See Lincoln, Abbey*
Worrill, Conrad 1941— **12**
Worthy, James 1961— **49**
Wright, Bruce McMarion 1918-2005 **3, 52**
Wright, Charles H. 1918-2002 **35**
Wright, Deborah C. 1958— **25**
Wright, Jeffrey 1966— **54**
Wright, Jeremiah A., Jr. 1941— **45**
Wright, Lewin 1962— **43**
Wright, Louis Tompkins 1891-1952 **4**
Wright, Nathan, Jr. 1923-2005 **56**
Wright, Richard 1908-1960 **5**
Wyatt, Addie L. 1924— **56**
Wynn, Albert R. 1951— **25**
X, Malcolm 1925-1965 **1**
X, Marvin 1944— **45**
Yancy, Dorothy Cowser 1944— **42**
Yarbrough, Camille 1938— **40**
Yarbrough, Cedric 1971— **51**
Yeboah, Emmanuel Ofosu 1977— **53**
Yoba, (Abdul-)Malik (Kashie) 1967— **11**
York, Vincent 1952— **40**
Young, Andre Ramelle *See Dre, Dr.*
Young, Andrew 1932— **3, 48**
Young, Coleman 1918-1997 **1, 20**